With His Head Held High

The Story of Shaheed Mohsen Hojaji

Published by Wilayah Publications

Translated from the Farsi book *Sar-Boland*

Compiled by Mohammad Ali Ja'fari
Translated by Sayyid Haydar Jamaludeen
Edited by a group of sincere lovers of the martyrs

Second Edition in 2023
First Published in 2022

All rights reserved. No part of this publication may be reproduced, stored in a retrieval system, or transmitted in any form or by any means, digital, electronic, mechanical, photocopying, recording, or otherwise, or conveyed via the internet or a website without prior written permission of the publisher, except in the case of brief quotations embodied in critical articles and reviews.

IN THE NAME OF GOD,

THE BENEFICENT, THE MERCIFUL

WITH HIS HEAD HELD HIGH

Compiled by:
Mohammad Ali Ja'fari

Contents

Chapter I
NO MESSING ABOUT!
9

Chapter II
THE ONE THAT CATCHES YOUR EYE!
91

Chapter III
GOD BLESS MARCO POLO!
163

Chapter IV
BUILD YOURSELF IN THE DESERT!
203

Chapter V
LIKE A BOUNCED CHEQUE!
245

Chapter VI
IT WAS HIS OWN FAULT!
277

TIMELINE OF THE MARTYR'S LIFE

- **12 July 1991** – Birth
- **23 September 1998** – Elementary School
- **23 September 2003** – Middle School
- **23 September 2006** – High School
- **8 March 2007** – The Shaheed Kazemi Institute
- **22 September 2008** – University
- **2010** – Military service
- **1 November 2012** – Marriage
- **26 January 2014** – Enrolling in the IRGC and military training
- **1 November 2014** – Enrolling in the Najaf-e Ashraf Division
- **6 January 2015** – Specialised training in Shiraz
- **2015** – First tour of Syria
- **2015** – The walk of Arbaeen
- **12 April 2016** – Ali's birth
- **15 January 2017** – Medic training
- **17 July 2017** – Second tour of Syria
- **7 August 2017** – Captivity
- **9 August 2017** – Martyrdom
- **26 September 2017** – Funeral in Mashhad
- **27 September 2017** – Funeral in Tehran and Isfahan
- **28 September 2017** – Funeral and burial in Najafabad

Chapter I

NO MESSING ABOUT!

Sayyid Yasser Hoseini

The martyr's uncle-in-law

Even though I was married, I still messed around behind my wife's back. I wasn't embarrassed to flirt with other people's wives in front of my wife. My girlfriends thought I was single. I told them, "Sometimes my sister might pick up the phone, don't say a word until I say hello!" so I wouldn't be exposed. If my wife asked who it was, I told her it was a prank caller. Whenever I texted them, I told her I was playing a game. My wife and I were the black sheep of the family. I flaunted around with threaded eyebrows, tight jeans, a tight t-shirt which showed off my arms and a nice hairstyle. My wife accompanied me, wearing a tight and short cardigan, a scarf which showed off the front of her hair and heavy makeup.

One day, I went to my sister's house. I saw a religious-looking youth with a beard hanging around in front of the house. I parked my motorcycle and got off. My sister came out and introduced me to him. We said salaam to each other. His mother and father came out after him, and they left. I was curious and asked, "Who were they?"

"They've come to propose to Zahra," she explained.

"This lad? With Zahra?!" I exclaimed.

It didn't sit right with me. He wasn't muscular nor did he wear nice clothes. I couldn't believe my niece agreed to it. Zahra was very pampered. I thought this union was utter stupidity. Everything proceeded until the night of their wedding. I noticed he wasn't dancing at all and he was just sitting in a corner. I was thinking to myself, "He is such a simple guy, he doesn't know how to socialise," but when I saw him meeting with people, I realised he was very sociable and quite a witty person. However, whenever my wife and I went to my sister's house, he lowered his head and asked how we were very coldly. I was taken aback! What was he trying to say? What kind of behaviour was that?!

These thoughts troubled my mind until one day, my sister called me and said, "I love you so much, my dear brother, but from now on, whenever you want to come to our house, tell your wife to wear a *chador*[1] because it bothers Agha[2] Mohsen!" I told her I would do so and put the phone down. I vowed never to step foot in that house again. A while later, I felt I had to visit my sister's house, so I told my wife, "Put a chador in your bag and wear it when we get there so we don't bother her son-in-law." This time, he didn't lift his head either and he acted very coldly with us, but he didn't leave. He sat down and we spoke with each other for a little bit, but we didn't really make friends. He always had a clay *tasbih*[3] in his hand. I asked him, "Agha Mohsen, what are you reciting with this *tasbih* all the time?" I thought to myself that if it were up to me, I would complete the *tasbih* in two minutes because it only had thirty-three beads, it wasn't one of those with one hundred beads everyone normally uses. He replied, "I'm praying for the ground." When he noticed my extreme surprise, he added, "We sleep on the ground, we walk on it, so we should repay it." I was laughing at him to myself. I said to him, "How did you make up such an act of worship by yourself?!" I didn't understand him.

On Nowruz[4], he came to our house with Zahra. He looked back and saw a statue of a woman in the corner. He said to me,

---

1. A long veil worn by Muslim women generally in Iran and other Muslim countries
2. 'Agha' is a term of respect used for men in Farsi
3. Farsi for 'rosary'
4. The Iranian New Year, coinciding with the 21st of March

"Uncle, if it's not difficult for you, let's put a photo of Shaheed[5] [Ahmad] Kazemi[6] up instead of this statue." I wondered why he asked me to do so, but I thought to myself, "He's probably one of the people he knew from the military." It was as if he read my mind. He smiled bitterly and said, "Insha'Allah, you become like him." For a while, I wondered why he specifically mentioned Shaheed Kazemi. Why the photo of a martyr? Why not the photo of Imam [Khomeini], why not a photo of Mashhad or Karbala? Eventually, I managed to ask him, and he told me, "If you have the photo of a martyr in front of you, you'll feel ashamed to do certain things in front of him."

I asked, "We don't have a frame, what shall I do?"

He replied, "Ok, no worries, I'll bring you one myself."

A few days later, he sent me a small photo frame. I put it in the corner of the room, right in front of my eyes, but it neither made me feel ashamed nor did I feel any change within myself. I went to my sister's house and saw him sitting on the sofa. When I entered, he stood up out of respect. As soon as he sat down, my brother's son came in. He stood up again and shook my nephew's hand. I told him, "You don't need to get up for a child, sit down, be comfortable." He replied, "You are Sayyids[7] and it is *wajib* to respect you!" I was taken aback. My whole existence trembled with these few words. I didn't raise my head for almost half an hour. He asked me, "Uncle, why aren't you talking?" but I dodged the question. I got up to go outside and smoke a cigarette.

---

5. Farsi for 'martyr'
6. Shaheed Ahmad Kazemi was one of the most prominent commanders of the Iran-Iraq War and beyond. He was one of the comrades of Shaheed Haj Qasem Soleimani. He was martyred in a plane crash in 2006.
7. Sayyids are descendants of the Holy Prophet (s)

From that day onwards, I stopped shaving my face. I changed my SIM card and started praying. I changed the way I dressed. I started wearing normal trousers and an untucked shirt. I wore a green scarf around my neck.

He was over the moon. He said to me, "Uncle, you've changed the way you dress!" I replied, "I had to start from somewhere, but it was you who lit the flame inside me." From then on, we started meeting up more regularly. We went to Isfahan together. He asked me, "Shall we go to Takht-e Foolad[8]?" I didn't know what was happening there. I learnt it was the cemetery where the martyrs of Isfahan are buried. He took us to the grave of Shaheed Kazemi. My wife came in the same clothes she normally wore, but I had changed. He talked to us a little about Shaheed Kazemi and then we went to Imam Square. By chance, it was Friday. He asked us if we wanted to pray Friday prayers. I didn't know how to pray Friday prayers or how many units it had, but my wife was wearing makeup and didn't want to remove it to perform *wudu*[9], so she made an excuse to not go. Agha Mohsen didn't insist, and we went back home.

One time, I said to him openly, "I know you know that only my appearance has improved. I want to change myself and my wife." The first step I took was attending congregational prayers. I wasn't a disbeliever, but I prayed in my own way, praying one day, and not praying for the other six days, or if a group of people were praying in congregation, I forced myself to pray with them. I went to pick him up in my car and we went

---

8. A historical cemetery in Isfahan
9. Ritual ablution to be performed before praying or touching the words of the Quran and the names of the Infallibles

to the mosque. He was taking a long time, so I asked him, "Are you praying Salat Ja'far Tayyar?"[10]

He answered, "No, I'm praying someone's *qada* prayers[11]," but later, I learnt he was praying Salat Imam Zaman[12]. I started visiting Gulzar-e Shuhada[13]. I wanted to feel the same as Mohsen did and feel the same passion he got from visiting them. I went all the time, sometimes even at midnight. My mother-in-law was worried about me and said, "If you go to the cemetery, you'll be possessed!" If I wanted to go for a picnic, I chose a park close to Gulzar-e Shuhada so I could visit the martyrs on the way. Sometimes, I saw Mohsen at the grave of Shaheed Alireza Noori. I sat next to him and we had meaningful conversations.

These changes within me took place close to the month of Muharram. I decided to go to Karbala. I went [to Karbala] for the first ten days and came back. Like a true Husayni, I stopped sinning as much as I could. Day by day, my life grew more pleasant. I stopped arguing with my wife as much and most importantly, I felt myself growing spiritually. My wife witnessed everything; I wasn't using my phone all day, I wasn't making suspicious phone calls, I wasn't looking at every girl we passed while riding my motorbike and I was paying more attention to her. All of this made her come to me herself and say, "I want to wear the *chador*." From then on, we noticed that Agha Mohsen now stayed and asked us how we were instead of walking past us

---

10. A long prayer that was taught to Ja'far Tayyar, the brother of Imam Ali (a), by the Holy Prophet (s) through which, many desires and needs of the worshipper are fulfilled

11. *Qada* prayers are prayers which are not performed within the time ascertained for them, and once someone passes away, another person must perform those prayers in place of the deceased

12. A long prayer performed normally on Thursday nights for the fulfilment of needs and desires using the intercession of Imam Mahdi (aj)

13. A graveyard of the martyrs in Najafabad

and greeting us coldly. We grew closer and eventually became best friends.

I asked him one day, "Talk to me about this Sayyid Ali [Khamenei] who's so close to your heart." By the way, when I first got to know Mohsen, I always insulted the Leader (Sayyid Ali Khamenei). He lowered his head and didn't utter a word. That day, he said, "There is nothing to say, you have to walk on his path to know who he really is!" He looked me in the eye and promised me, "I will sit you down in front of the Leader himself or my name isn't Mohsen!"

When he returned from his first tour of duty in Syria, I asked him, "Did you get what you wanted?" He replied, "No, I was lacking in some areas!" He couldn't wait to go again. I also wanted to go because of him. I set out looking for a way to reserve a place for myself amongst the Defenders of the Shrine [of Lady Zaynab (a)[14]]. I put my name down to fight for the Fatihayn Organisation. When he heard, he came and told me to come with him. I don't know why, but one day, they announced the organisation had been disbanded. This itself took a year and a half. My sister then told me he was leaving again. I texted him, saying, "I heard you want to go to Syria. Lucky you! Pray for me." He wrote back, "Pray I return with a clean slate[15]!" I replied, "I was supposed to take you to Syria. How come you left

---

14. (a) stands for *alayhi/alayha as-salaam* (peace be upon him/her), (ra) stands for *Rahmatullah alayh/alayha* (mercy of Allah be upon him/her), (aj) stands for *ajjalallahu farajah* (may Allah hasten his reappearance) and (as) stands for *alayhim as-salaam* (peace be upon them)

15. The original word in Farsi is '*rusefid*' which means to be acquitted, and in this context, he means that he wishes to be acquitted from all sins in the eyes of Allah, which is achievable through martyrdom.

before me?" He said, "She (Lady Zaynab (a)) takes whoever she wishes."

I constantly asked his family if he had called. Was he fine? When was he coming back? Contrary to his last tour in Syria, I was very worried about him. At nine o'clock in the morning, my sister called me. I could only hear crying and wailing on the other end. Our grandmother was elderly and at first, I thought she had passed away. I was asking, "What's happened?" She was crying down the phone, "Come help me, my back is broken!" I asked, fuming, "Just tell me what happened!" She said between the tears, "ISIS has taken my Mohsen!" My knees went weak, and I fell to the floor. I somehow managed to get to their house with great difficulty.

My sister called and said, "Drop whatever you're doing and get over here." I quickly put on my hat and scarf and left. At the door, she told me, "We're going to meet the Leader, so we thought you should come with us too." I thought to myself that we were probably going to see him from behind the fences, so you can imagine my surprise when I prayed behind the Leader, not from behind the fences, but one and a half metres away from him. Is there a greater honour than kissing the wounded hand of the Leader and then he squeezes your hand with his healthy hand and says, "Insha'Allah[16] you have a successful life!" At that moment, I said to Mohsen in my heart, "You made a promise and acted upon it, and I also changed, but take care of me and make sure I never revert back to my old ways!"

---

16. Arabic for 'if Allah wills'

Orinab Hoseini

The martyr's mother-in-law

When he entered, he said salaam warmly. I replied by saying, "My dear, may I be your sacrifice." One day, I was standing next to the dishwasher, deep in thought, and I replied to his salaam without any of the normal formalities. He asked Zahra, "What happened to your mum? Why didn't she say, 'may I be your sacrifice' today?"

If he said goodbye from the hallway and didn't wait for an answer, I knew they had been arguing and he was angry. Zahra sat on the sofa with her phone in her hand and laughed, "He's going to text me any time soon." Two minutes later, you heard his notification on her phone, saying, "Shall I come and pick you up?"

When my daughter became pregnant, we gave them one of the rooms in our home. I wanted to look after them. I woke up for Fajr prayers at the time of *adhan* and went to wake them up for prayers, but he would be sitting on the prayer mat already, for God knows how long. Even after I made breakfast, he would still be praying and supplicating. I was worried for him. I went to see what he was doing a few times. I saw him recite Hadith ul-Kisa[17], Dua Ahd[18] and Ziyarah Ashura[19] every single morning

---

17. A narration which is normally recited at the beginning of a gathering and blessings are showered upon the attendees of the gathering for as long as it continues

18. A supplication which is recited in the mornings and according to the narrations, if one recites this supplication for forty days, he will be among the supporters of Imam Mahdi (aj)

19. A supplication to be recited when visiting Imam Husayn (a)'s shrine. It is highly effective in the fulfilment of needs and requests if one recites it for forty days.

with my own eyes. In the winters, he laid his prayer mat in the room which didn't have a heater. I was worried he would catch a cold, so I told him, "My dear, may I be your sacrifice, it's cold here!" but he replied, "Actually, I like it here." He prayed there so that he wouldn't fall asleep and be deprived of his prayers.

I learnt that he enjoyed performing *mustahab*[20] prayers and fasting the day we went to buy the things for their wedding. At noon, he went missing in the middle of the bazaar and came back with a tray of carrot juice and ice cream. He said he had gone to pray on time. I still wasn't comfortable around him. I asked his mother, "Why didn't Agha Mohsen buy himself some ice cream?" She pulled her *chador* over her face and whispered to me, "He's fasting." When we were choosing the rings, he said, "I won't wear gold because it's *haram*[21] for men." At first, he was insistent that he didn't want a ring, but when Zahra persisted, he agreed to wear a platinum ring. We turned the whole bazaar upside down looking for a set of gold and platinum rings.

When I heard that he wanted to propose, I went to the bookstore he worked in to see who he was under the pretext of buying a Mafatih al-Jinan[22]. He was tall, but quite thin and had a scruffy beard. He didn't look at my face and from that moment, I knew he was the one. The night his mother came to our house to see Zahra, I couldn't wait to say yes, but I was shy. I was wondering what they were thinking about. Are they thinking that we're rushing? After Fajr prayers, I couldn't wait any longer. I picked up my phone and called his mother to say that we had thought about it and the *istikharah*[23] had come out good.

---

20. Arabic for 'recommended'
21. Arabic for 'impermissible'
22. A book of supplications compiled by Shaykh Abbas Qummi
23. A way of seeking guidance from Allah

I was always worried about him because he was very weak. I snuck pistachios and nuts into his pockets. At the dinner table, I specifically found the meat in the food and put it in his plate. He normally came at quarter past two and my husband came home at half-past two. Even though I laid the table for him and put the food down, he wouldn't touch it until Agha Abbasi had come. He didn't eat a lot. He took food out for both himself and Zahra in one plate. I watched him from the corner of my eye. I insisted for him to eat more, but he said, "I have to leave some space to breathe too!" He loved kebab, so every week, we took out the grill and coal to cook some kebab for Agha Mohsen. If we didn't invite them for one week, he said to Zahra, "Call mum and ask her if she can invite us for some kebab." I may have cooked food already, but I still said to my husband, "Agha Mohsen wants kebab, go and buy some meat." I made the skewers myself and took them to the roof for them to grill. I didn't like for him to do any work around the house. I said to my husband, "Grill them yourself. I don't want Agha Mohsen's clothes to start smelling like smoke." Agha Abbasi complained, "But my clothes will start smelling like smoke!"

When Zahra cooked Northern-style chicken[24], we were scared he would eat his fingers because he loved it so much. He loved jelly and side dishes a lot and on the other hand, he hated foods which had *kashk*[25] in it. Whenever he called, he asked, "What's for food?" I teased him and said *kalleh joosh*[26] or kashk and aubergine[27].

---

24. A dish native to the north of Iran, where the chicken is cooked in pomegranate syrup
25. Drained yoghurt or sour milk that is formed and dried, and is eaten in Middle Eastern countries
26. An Iranian soup made with lentils, meat, beets, chickpeas and kashk
27. Pureed aubergine served with a topping of kashk

On the day of the presidential elections, my husband had gone to the polling station. Agha Mohsen had come early in the morning and was saying, "Get up, come, let's go and vote." He added, "Pack the picnic basket and the tea and then come." He insisted that we voted for whoever he voted for. Once we voted, he went and bought some chicken to make *jujeh* kebab[28]. First, he wanted to visit the grave of Shaheed Izadi, and then he took us to Zayanderud. Wherever we said to sit, he made an excuse and said, "They're dancing here," or, "The women aren't wearing hijab here," and so on. He looked around and told us to come with him. He had found a spot out of view from everyone, a place so high that if we didn't hold on to Ali, he would trip and fall into the river. I only said one sentence, "If my husband was here, would he make me suffer so much?" He took this to heart and whenever I said anything, he replied, "If your husband was here, would he let you suffer so much?"

He had told his co-workers that when he goes to his mother-in-law's house, his sister-in-law comes to the door first. He told them that he hugs and kisses her. They said to him, "Have some shame, it's *haram*!" He got everyone together and brought them to our door. He rang the bell and said to us, "Tell Asma to come down." Two minutes later, I heard them all laughing in the courtyard. I don't think any of them expected Asma to be three years old!

When he was working a night shift at the base, I was worried he may be hurt by the morning. I worried so much that Zahra used to complain. I had made a habit that whenever I woke up in the morning, I texted my son Mohsen first and say, "Good morning, my dear."

---

28. Grilled chicken marinated in minced onion, lemon juice and occasionally saffron

Now you can imagine what I went through when he went to Syria. I wasn't too worried when he went on his first tour of duty. I knew ISIS had come and they were a threat, but something in my heart was assuring me that he would go and come back safely. I sent him off from underneath the Quran and I poured water behind him as he walked away. I went to bid him farewell at the top of our road. I filmed every second of it. Zahra was pregnant with Ali, but she hadn't told us so he could go. Agha Mohsen was worried I would prevent him from going. Zahra was struggling a lot. Even though she wasn't supposed to carry the phone too close to her womb, she didn't put it down once. She was waiting for Agha Mohsen to call every minute of the day. When his phone calls were late, she would break down. For these forty-five days, she put her life on hold. She wouldn't even eat. I made sure not to upset Zahra at all, but I would go and cry in secret.

When we heard he was returning from Syria, I suggested to my husband to slaughter a sheep for him when he got back. Zahra told Agha Mohsen that we wanted to put up a celebratory banner and slaughter a sheep for him when he got back, but he said that if we put a banner up, he would leave. We didn't put up a banner for him because of what he said but we did slaughter the sheep.

When we saw him from afar, he was wearing a heavy rucksack. If he was frail before, now he was just skin and bones. When he came to the house, I realised he couldn't hear properly. He answered our questions weirdly. I asked him, "Are you ok, my dear?" and he replied, "I missed you too!" I had to shout at him a few times for him to understand. When I told Zahra, "Something's happened to your husband," she just said, "He's tired and his ears are hurting from the bus," until one night, his commander invited us to his house. We were all surprised when he asked, "Mohsen, do you remember when the missile hit your tank?" We had only just realised why he didn't do *wudu* in front of us or unbutton his cuffs. That night, we saw his hand was burnt, but he didn't mention why his ears weren't working properly.

When Ali was born, we were glad now he would be busy with his children and forget about going to Syria. He was really excited too. Even though he didn't have much money, he bought two bracelets for Zahra. His child was born after eight months and was in the incubator for one or two weeks. He prayed a lot and sought intercession [for the baby's welfare]. When he had a day off, Agha Mohsen said, "Let's take him to Ayatollah Naseri[29] so that he can recite the *adhan* and the *iqamah* in his ears." We searched through all the streets to find his house. Zahra and I stayed in the car. They said he was at the mosque, so he went and prayed behind him and then came back. We saw them from the top of the road. Mohsen was walking beside the Ayatollah and he was carrying Ali. Ayatollah Naseri recited the *adhan* and the *iqamah* in Ali's ears outside of his house. Agha Mohsen said to him, "Haj Agha[30], [please] pray I am martyred, and I can return with a clean slate!" Ayatollah Naseri raised his head, looked at Mohsen and said, "Insha'Allah you have a successful life." At that moment, I realised that no, he was still certain he wanted to return to Syria.

When he went on his second tour of duty, I had no hope of him returning. I had seen a dream. I knew he would go and be martyred. Despite this, I comforted myself, I gave myself hope that Insha'Allah he will return. The day after, when Mohsen

---

29. Ayatollah Naseri is a great scholar, mystic and teacher of *akhlaq*. He studied under great teachers including Ayatollah Khomeini, Ayatollah Khoei and Sayyid Abd al-A'la Sabzawari.

30. The words 'Haj Agha' are normally used for extremely respected members of society or scholars in Iran

came to our house, I told him about my dream. He raised his hands to the air and said, "All praise is to Allah, the Lord of the worlds. Mum, pray I can go to Syria again, pray I reach a successful end!" At noon, he called and asked, "Have you made lunch?"

"I've made something," I replied.

"I wanted to come to your house," he said.

"You're always welcome," I told him.

I was extremely restless. I quickly warmed up the ghormeh sabzi[31]. As we sat for lunch, he said, "Bismillah al-Rahman al-Rahim[32]. By the way, Insha'Allah I'm leaving tonight." I asked, "Where?" He said, "On a mission." I thought he wanted to go to Murchehkhort[33] again. He clarified, "No, mum, Allah has destined that I will visit Lady Zaynab (a) once again!" The spoon fell from my hand. My husband and I were shocked. It was as if this lunch was our poison. We could no longer swallow our food. He left his food half-eaten and went to his mother's house to bid her farewell. He told us that he was coming back at night.

He came at ten at night in a rush. He was leaving at eleven. I asked, "What happened, my dear?" He took a deep breath and said, "My mother's house had become the plains of Karbala." I asked why, and he answered, "My sisters all came, just like when the women came to bid farewell to Hazrat Ali Akbar (a)[34] before he went to the battlefield." I brought a few slices of cantaloupe for him, but he said, "My mouth is sore, it'll sting if I eat it," so I brought him some watermelon from the fridge. He told Zahra, "Go and take photos and videos of your mother and me."

---

31. Ghormeh sabzi is an Iranian stew made with parsley, leeks, coriander, dried fenugreek leaves, kidney beans and occasionally meat
32. Arabic for 'In the name of Allah, the Most Beneficent, the Most Merciful'
33. A town close to Isfahan
34. The son of Imam Husayn (a) who was martyred on the Day of Ashura

He then hugged Ali, played with him for a little and bade him farewell. He said to me in the room, "I know you're worried."

"Yeah, I can't take it," I replied, "You have to come back."

"Mum, if I'm martyred, I'll visit you every day," he said.

"Swear to me," I told him, "Don't say what you don't mean."

"Mum, I'll come," he assured me, "I'll intercede for you in front of Allah, I swear."

We went to the terminal together. On the way back, I sent a *dua*[35] for him to read so Allah would protect him. I then wrote, "I'm already missing you, my son. I swear to God; I can't bear your separation." He replied, "May I be your sacrifice. I feel the same." In the morning, I looked at my phone after praying. He had answered, "Salaam mum! Good morning, how are you? We're in Tehran. Pray there is no problem, and we can leave easily." My eyes welled up with tears as I replied, "Salaam my son, how are you, my dear? You don't know how much I miss you, I miss your views, your blessings, your manliness. You never made me sad, yet you're making me cry so much." He texted back at noon, saying, "Salaam mum. Insha'Allah we're leaving at five. Pray especially for me... Forgive me from the bottom of your heart... I love you...." I wrote back, "Mohsen, go, I am pleased if Allah is pleased, but how can I bear your separation?" He wrote in his last message, "I was very bad to you, with my behaviour and manners... Always remember the calamities that befell Lady Zaynab (a)."

An ugly and ungainly ISIS fighter had come into our house and was standing on the carpet with his shoes on. I was quaking

---

35. Arabic for 'supplication'

in my boots. I thought to myself, " If he comes any closer, I'll die!" Suddenly, I saw that he smashed the head he was holding in his hand on the wall. He went into the room. I looked behind him and saw a few people sitting in a line with their hands tied. He was beheading them with an axe and their heads were falling, but there was no blood flowing.

My husband shook me and asked, "Are you having a nightmare?" My face was sweaty. I told him my dream, the tears flowing from my eyes. He laid back down and said, "Don't worry, it's just a confused dream." I said angrily, "That was Mohsen's head!" My husband replied, "Just as I said, it was a confused dream." I didn't think about the dream until the morning. I gave a lot of money in charity [for his well-being].

When Agha Mohsen called the following night, my heart felt at peace. He told Zahra he was arranging for her and Ali to go to Syria the next week. Zahra was busy packing her bags when the photo of his captivity was released. I was so heartbroken, I contracted an illness of the skin. We couldn't believe it. Everyone was telling each other the photo was photoshopped. I'm not sad due to his martyrdom, I'm proud. His captivity tortured me. I kept saying, "O' Allah, kill me if they don't behead him." The hardest moment was when I saw the photo of his severed head; his lips had turned black from thirst.

We didn't go to see his body. I gave a scarf and a *tasbih* to his comrade and I said to him, "Wipe these on his body as a blessing, not his shroud!" He gave them to me in a plastic bag and said, "I wiped them on Agha Mohsen himself." When we were sitting in Me'raj-e Shuhada[36] opposite his coffin, his last text came to my mind, "Always remember the calamities that befell Lady Zaynab (a)."

---

36. Where the bodies of the martyrs are kept once they are sent back to Iran

Zahra Mokhtarpour

The martyr's mother

My father owned a shop. They made forks and trays from nickel silver. My mother was a believing and religious lady. She sent me to learn Quran every day after Fajr prayers. It was just me and five or six other girls. Later, my father changed his job and learnt how to weave carpets. My aunt also wove carpets and because of this, we visited their house frequently. I saw my aunt's grandson during these visits. On Thursday nights, they held *majalis*[37] at their house. He gave out tea and I saw him there, so when they proposed to me for him, I immediately said yes. His family were known for their piety and God-wariness.

Mohsen was my third child. He was born on the 12th of July 1991 during the *adhan* for Dhuhr prayers. He never bothered me, neither during pregnancy nor after. He was a peaceful child. I finished the Quran two or three times while I was pregnant with him. I was careful not to eat anything from anywhere. I chose his name myself, in the memory of the miscarried Mohsin of Lady Zahra (a).

He had just learnt how to read and write. When I recited the Quran or a *dua*, he came and sat beside me. He loved it. I taught him Hadith ul-Kisa and Ziyarah Ashura myself, but I didn't teach him how to recite the Quran. He slowly learnt over time. From his childhood, he sat in the line at school and recited Quran. On Friday nights when his grandfather held a *majlis* at his house, Mohsen asked, "Shall I read?" His grandfather encouraged him and told him to read. He sat on the chair to

---

37. Gatherings where the calamities which befell the Ahlulbayt (as) are remembered

recite Ziyarah Ashura. His feet didn't even reach the ground. His father was overjoyed and told me, "When they turn off the lights for the *sinehzani*[38], he takes off his shirt and beats his chest hard."

He prayed and fasted since his childhood. When I woke his sisters up for Fajr prayers, he woke up before them. After Fajr prayers, his father recited the Quran loudly. He said, "Let the children all hear the Quran." In the month of Ramadan, I wouldn't wake him up to fast, but when I realised he stayed hungry and thirsty until Maghrib prayers without any breakfast, I had no choice but to wake him up. It wasn't that I didn't want him to fast, but when I saw he was weaker than his brothers and sisters, I felt bad for him. I told him, "Wait until you become *baligh*[39], and then you can fast." When he grew up, he fasted a lot. In the mornings, I put out breakfast, but he left without eating. When he came back, he told me he was fasting. He always prayed on time.

He didn't like some foods, like *aash*[40] or aubergine. I told him, "Wait until you get married and then you can eat whatever you like." He became a man when he went on compulsory military service. One night, he came home, and he was hungry. I had fried some aubergine. I told him, "Mohsen, I've cooked chicken for you," but he said, "No, this is fine."

After his military service, I showed him one or two girls he could get married to, but he told me to wait. I felt he already had someone in mind. He was acting suspiciously. He never used his phone as much as he would at that time. He always

---

38. Beating one's chest in memory of the calamities which befell the Ahlulbayt (as)
39. To become baligh means to attain physical maturity after which it becomes obligatory to pray, fast etc.
40. An Iranian soup made with a variety of herbs, kidney beans and occasionally noodles

went to the book exhibition looking all neat and tidy. He was in a hurry to leave always. He became overly sensitive about how his clothes were ironed. He spent a lot of time in front of the mirror, combing his hair. One day, he was going out when his father was at home. He called me outside. He told me coyly that he'd seen a girl at the exhibition. He really thought she was the one. I spoke to his father and we went to propose. As they knew him from before, they didn't really object to him.

I was always worried about him. When he was a child, I was afraid he would get into a fight and be beaten up. When he grew up and started driving, I always advised him to drive slowly and not to cut anyone off in traffic. I didn't want him to fight with anyone and they end up hurting him badly. I explained to him that some people look for a fight, but he said, "Don't worry, I won't fight with anyone." I never even thought of the possibility that he will go, and ISIS will torture him. From his childhood, he liked to sit and look at the photo albums of his father, especially his photos from the warfront. He said, "I want to grow up and go to war." Sometimes, I imagined that Mohsen had grown up, gone to war and had been martyred. I would shiver and start crying, but I comforted myself, saying, "No! This will never happen." I wasn't content with him going, so the first time he went to Syria, he didn't tell me. I simply believed he had gone to Tehran on a forty-five-day mission. I don't understand how whenever he called me, it was from a Tehran number, and that's why I was at peace the whole time, but he had told his father. When he was returning, his father said, "Your Agha Mohsen is returning from Syria." I was taken aback. I exclaimed, "From where?! Syria?!"

He understood he hadn't been martyred because of me. He said, "A missile landed near me but didn't explode because you weren't happy with me becoming a martyr." At night, I saw the light of his phone when he recited *duas*. I watched him pray Salat ul-Layl[41]. He shed tears at the door of Allah. Before, I thought he had a request from Allah and maybe he wanted to get married, but once he got married, I realised that no, he has another request; he has the love of martyrdom in his heart. Whenever he had a problem and he couldn't solve it, he called and asked me to read the Quran for him. I would be cooking food and he would call, saying, "Mum, recite a Surah Yasin for me." I left whatever I was doing and quickly read it for him. When he wanted to sell the land his father had given him and buy a house elsewhere, I recited Surah Hashr forty times for him. As I recited the Surah the thirty-eighth time for him, the land was sold.

When he came home and saw me reading Quran, he told his wife, "Look, my mum is reciting Quran so that I am not martyred." He became upset and said, "Whenever they're about to sign my name [to go to Syria], they say, 'No, not Hojaji.'" He said, tears in his eyes, "Maybe someone has told them something. Has dad said something?"

In his last Ramadan, he took a ten-day holiday and took his father and me to Mashhad. It was hot. Once we prayed Dhuhr and Asr prayers, he sent me back to the hotel by taxi so I wouldn't be bothered [by the heat], but he wouldn't sleep. He went back to the shrine again. He stood to pray and do *dua*.

On the eve of the twenty-first of Ramadan[42], I was sitting in the Hedayat Courtyard[43]. Mohsen texted me, saying, "Mum, I

---

41. An eleven-unit prayer to be prayed between midnight and Fajr prayers, Imam Sadiq said, "There is no good deed except that its reward has been outlined in the Qur'an, except Salat ul-Layl. Almighty Allah has not specified its reward due to its greatness with Him."

42. One of the Nights of Decree on which the destiny and fate of man is decided for the next year

43. One of the courtyards in Imam Rida (a)'s shrine

beg you, pray I can go to Syria one more time and return with a clean slate." That night, I placed the Quran on my head and prayed from the bottom of my heart that my son is invited by our Lady.

He was shy to hug and kiss me and express his love towards me, but he had made an oath that if he were invited to Syria again, he would kiss mine and his father's feet. On the last night when he was leaving, when he bent down to kiss my feet, I was sure that he would be martyred. I couldn't prevent my tears from flowing. I told him, "I don't want you to be martyred." He laughed and said, "So don't cry, I'm going to be martyred."

When he was in Syria, I recited the Quran and gave charity on his behalf every day. I looked at his photo and said, "O' Lady Zaynab! Give him a clean slate, but I don't want him to be martyred." When he was taken captive, I prayed for his martyrdom. I had gone out. I hadn't cooked yet, so I called Mohsen's dad to tell him to get some food. When he picked up, it sounded like he was laughing, so I asked him what was going on. I then realised that he was crying and eventually, I understood that Mohsen had been taken captive. His photo was circulating on people's phones. The family gathered at our house. We cried until nightfall, praying to Allah. Everything was going through my head; what was he eating? What was he doing? What are they doing to him? I knew they were bothering him, they were torturing him. His words were repeating in my head, "Mum, you won't let me become a martyr." That night, I went to the shrine of the anonymous martyrs[44] and prayed for his martyrdom there. I made an oath to sacrifice a sheep for him. I said, "If he is freed, I will slaughter [the sheep], and if he is martyred, I will still act on my oath."

---

44. Martyrs who were either unidentified or their bodies were lost at war. In Farsi, they are known as *shaheed-e gomnam*.

ISIS uploaded the video of his martyrdom. I was glad he was finally safe from their hands, but I was still very worried. Had they found him? Had they not found him? I wanted to have at least a piece of his bone so that I could sit at his graveside. He returned and what a return! They held magnificent funerals for him in Mashhad, Tehran, and Isfahan. When the Leader came to him and kissed his coffin, I was lost for words. I said, "My son, you're so blessed!"

Mohsen had special love towards Lady Zahra (a). He had a ring with a Durr an-Najaf gemstone on which was engraved, 'Ya[45] Fatimah tuz-Zahra' and went [to Syria] wearing it. We said, "Don't wear this. If you fall into their hands, they'll take their hatred out on you." He said, "Let them." When we saw the video, I realised that they had really taken their hatred out on him. He was like a ferocious lion with his wounded chest. My heart was burning due to his thirsty lips.

---

45. Arabic for 'O'

Mohammadreza Hojaji

The martyr's father

It was the month of Ramadan and the whole family had gathered for *iftar*[46]. Mohsen entered the room amongst all the hustle and bustle. Someone said, "Wow...! Agha Mohsen!" and started laughing. The younger kids were laughing at him because of his new appearance. We locked eyes for a moment. He had shaven his beard and only left a bit of hair underneath his lip. That night, he left early. He said, "I have some work to do in the institute," but he didn't go to the institute. He went home and fixed his beard. My relationship with Mohsen was more indirect. I didn't need to say anything; he understood what I wanted to say through my gaze, my frown, or my smile.

From childhood, he was more inclined to me. When we travelled, he sat close to me. He took advice from me in the most minute of matters. He knew I wouldn't oppose him, and I only guided him. I wouldn't ask him for the details of the matter, but sometimes he told me himself. I was always careful about him. I was the same for all my children. They were more comfortable with their mother and told her all their problems. I had a distant relationship with my children and perhaps I learnt this style of parenthood from my grandfather.

My grandfather, Shaykh Abul Qasim, was the imam of Hakim Mosque in Najafabad. Everyone knew he had studied under Ayatollah Brujerdi (ra), Ayatollah Sadr (ra) and Ayatollah Hojjat (ra). It was custom back in the days that after Fajr

---

46. The time for Maghrib prayers when Muslims generally open their fast

prayers, the businessmen studied Makasib[47] for an hour in the mosque and then open their shops. It brought blessing to their work and stopped them from any *haram* in their business. My grandfather taught Makasib in the mornings and Quran after Maghrib and Isha prayers. I learnt how to recite the Quran in those gatherings, even before I started school.

Shaykh Ahmad Hojaji, my grandfather's brother, was one of the close students of the late Akhund Khorasani (ra). When he came back from Najaf, he thought of opening an Islamic seminary in Najafabad. He established an Islamic seminary with Shaykh Ibrahim Riyazi, and they taught preliminary Islamic studies. They visited the surrounding villages, found the youths who had potential and asked the family to give that youth in the way of Imam Mahdi (aj). They paid for their daily needs and education. He was one of the main opponents of the Bahai faith in Najafabad. It's well-known that he had a donkey which he rode after his lessons and went to do some agricultural work, and this is how he maintained his living expenses.

Contrary to his brother, my grandfather sat at home. He just went to the mosque and managed the people's affairs. After prayers, he took off his *libas*[48] and worked in the kitchens. He had built the mosque with his own hands. Later, they also built Hakim Husayniyyah[49] next to the mosque on the land inherited from their mother. Shortly after that, he took permission from Imam Khomeini (ra), Ayatollah Sadr (ra) and Ayatollah Hojjat (ra) to receive religious dues. The people brought their religious dues to him, but he was so particular that he wouldn't accept

---

47. A two-volume book regarding Islamic commercial law by Ayatollah Murtaza Ansari
48. The gear of an Islamic scholar which includes a turban (*ammamah*), a cloak ('aba) and a long gown-like dress (*qaba*)
49. A building dedicated to the remembrance of the Ahlulbayt (as)

everyone's donation to the mosque. He neither encouraged nor reprimanded. Despite this, we still enjoyed his company. My uncle, Mohammad Ali became a student in the Islamic seminary and his turban was placed on his head by Imam Khomeini (ra). During the era of Holy Defence[50], he left his studies, went to the warfront, and was martyred. After that, all of Shaykh Abul Qasim's children became scholars.

As the inhabitants of Najafabad have a great love for self-sacrifice, jihad, and martyrdom, many of them are very practising. For this reason, the children all pray and fast. They don't start at nine years old or fifteen years old and before that, it's all plain sailing. They start from whenever they can. We don't encourage or reprimand them; we treat it as an obligation. I was the same with my children. If I wanted them to do something, I did it first so they could also learn from me, and if I didn't want them to do something, I simply wouldn't do it. We protect our children's reputations so that they can protect ours. We don't lay down or wear short-sleeved shirts in front of them. We don't like this kind of behaviour.

I dropped out of education during high school. The teachers were female and came to class without hijab in front of the elder students. The atmosphere this behaviour created was intolerable for us and therefore, we were absent every day and eventually dropped out of school. I then left education completely and started working as a construction worker.

When Mohsen was in high school, he went on Rahiyan-e Noor[51] with one of his friends by the name of Hemmatiha from the Shaheed Kazemi Institute. When he came back, he said to me, "I want to join the institute." He had just come back from

---
50. The eight-year war between Iran and Iraq
51. A trip taken to the south-western provinces of Iran where the battles were fought.

the trip and his hands had become dry . As I didn't know [the institute], I said no. I told him, "Look, you've gone on one trip and your hands have dried up. Focus on your studies," until one night, I saw him speaking with a thin youth at the door who was neat, tidy and polite. I told them to come inside and talk. I hated it when people stood at the door. Once I saw Hemmatiha, I gave Mohsen my permission to go to the institute. I went to two or three of their gatherings, I met their headmaster, learnt what they do, and after that, my mind was at rest. For a while, the youth of the institute didn't have a place to do their programmes, so I cleaned the room upstairs, repaired its electrics and gave it to them.

I wanted to make him an active member of society. He was regularly active as it was. He signed up for clubs in elementary school. When they were choosing their courses, their headmaster was insisting that he should go to Sadra College which was linked with the Islamic Development Organisation, but Mohsen was determined to study electrics because his friend Hosein Musa Arab was studying it as well. I wanted him to go to Sadra College. I told him, "It is good for you from a religious point of view, and you'll become a good attorney later on as well," but when I realised he didn't like it, I stopped insisting. He worked with Musa Arab. They printed business cards under the company name 'Saeqeh[52]' and they worked as electricians.

When he graduated, he went for his military service. One of his conditions was he should be allowed to continue his studies. One day, he took me to the grave of my martyred uncle and opened the topic of his marriage . I remembered my youth; I was in military service for six months and had come back on

---

52. Farsi for 'lightning'

leave. I was sitting by a chair and my grandmother asked, "Do you want me to find a girl for you [to marry]?" I replied in the affirmative and she continued, "Thank God! Who? Haj Gholam Ali's Zahra or Dayi Mokhtari's Zahra?" They were both the same person, the one I was looking to marry, the one who I couldn't bear the separation from after our marriage, and I was willing to walk through barbed wire to see; Mohsen's mother.

Two of my children were born in my father's house. Our room was at the end and its door opened to the barn. I did construction work from morning to afternoon and then I took a basket of bread and went to the fields. I was building a house in the middle of the farm fields. When the moonlight illuminated the nights, I worked until one or two in the morning. I dug the basement with my own hands and the local council filled it up with their bulldozers. I struggled a lot to build that house. Mohsen was born there. I then sold it and built the house we live in currently. When my hands became too sensitive to work with cement anymore, I left construction and bought a taxi.

After thinking, I said, "Very well. Do you have anyone in mind?" He answered, "I've seen someone at university." I advised, "Do your military service and come back. Your whole world will change. Maybe you've chosen someone who won't be compatible with you after it." He listened to me. Mine and Mohsen's military service was very alike. Because of our classic Najafabadi stubbornness, we decided to join the AJA[53]. We wanted to experience the strict discipline and rules of the AJA. Mohsen's training was in Ardabil and then he was transferred to Dezful. Despite this, he continued all his previous activities. After his martyrdom, his commander showed me a photo of

---

53. The main army of the Islamic Republic of Iran

Mohsen on his phone. He asked, "Have you ever seen an official keep a photo of one of his soldiers?" and I said no.

When I worked in construction, Mohsen sometimes said, "Dad, don't hire any workers today. I'll come." I always gave my workers their salary before they had changed their clothes. I followed the narration of the Infallibles (as) which says to pay the workers before their sweat dries. I did the same for Mohsen, but I never saw him spend the money. I watched him, and I noticed he wouldn't buy new shoes, no new clothes, nor did he go on trips to Isfahan . I said to his mother, "He keeps all his money, he doesn't spend anything." Later, I learnt he spent it on the trips the institute took to build houses for the misfortunate. He never asked me to buy anything for him. When he wanted to buy a computer, we went to the shop and he chose one. I saw him fumbling around in his pocket and I asked, "Do you not have enough money?" I paid for the rest and he took the computer.

He told his mother that he wanted to get married to someone. I said to her, "May Allah have mercy on us." When he said that the girl was from the institute, he knew her and she was a good person, I agreed. Deep down, I was against it, but because I trusted him, I didn't tell him, and we went to propose. His wife's family only had two daughters. His father-in-law made a condition, saying, "I want a son in this family, I don't want a son-in-law." For that reason, I said to Mohsen myself, "Act like their son. Spend more time with them, fill the space of a son for them."

When Mohsen joined the IRGC [54], his wife's family found out first. I wanted to join the IRGC when I went to the warfront myself. That didn't happen anyway, but I opposed Mohsen's decision to make him steadfast, so no one could object to him

---

54.   The Islamic Revolutionary Guard Corps

later. I said to his father-in-law, "A soldier doesn't have his own will. They can call at midnight and tell him to leave his wife and kids. Don't complain to me later." I also told his mother, "Someone who joins the IRGC doesn't leave it with a clean bill of health. They either get wounded or killed. Don't complain or cry later!"

Once he joined the IRGC, I was constantly worried about him. I was always worried about him, but I didn't think he would be martyred this soon. Sayyid Reza Narimani[55] has a line which reads, "I have a bouquet of flowers, I will give it for the shrine..."[56] I was overly sensitive over this couplet. If I heard it, I fell apart. No one in my house was allowed to listen to or recite that *nowheh*[57].

The night Mohsen wanted to go [to Syria], I realised from his face that he wasn't to return. I had seen this face many times on the warfront the night before the missions, faces which you knew you were looking at for the last time ever. He also had a lot to say for his last words. I didn't hug him a lot. When he kissed my feet, I quickly pulled away. I kept my distance. Everyone went to the terminal to bid him farewell, but I didn't go. When he called, I didn't speak to him much. When he was taken captive, I didn't pray for his return.

I was at the bank when his father-in-law called. I told him I was in the bank, but he couldn't take it, so he came to me and said, "They've taken our son." The IRGC sent some people to our house and they told us, "We may be able to exchange prisoners as they have sent out his photo." I said, "Don't bother. We are

---

55. A famous Iranian reciter who incorporates the martyrs into his sinehzani
56. 'یه دسته گل دارم, برای این حرم میدم'
57. A poem about the calamities that befell the Ahlulbayt (as) to which people generally perform sinehzani to

not willing to." I knew Mohsen wasn't meant to come back. No soldier could force him to come back. You can't force someone who hates this world to stay in it. I prayed for his martyrdom. His mother and sisters were restless. That night, we received the news of his martyrdom. When they told us his body was coming back, his mother, father-in-law and I went to Tehran. It was Thursday and we were waiting. They told us he wasn't coming back that night because they were holding a majlis for him in Syria. I said, "If possible, take us to Syria, even if we have to travel by cargo plane." They agreed. When we went, there was no sign of him. We realised they told us what they did so our hearts wouldn't be broken. They said they had to perform DNA tests [to make sure the body belonged to him]. It was possible the body parts they had returned were not from one body and they could have lied to us.

After that, there were rumours that they had brought him, but [Shaheed] Haj Qasem Soleimani [58] told us not to trust anyone until he called us. Eventually, he called and said, "He has arrived. What do you want to do?" I told him, "If possible, we'd like to take him to Mashhad to bless his body [at the shrine of Imam Rida (a)] because he took his permission for martyrdom from Imam Rida (a)." When we got to Mashhad, somehow people had found out and they held a grand funeral for him. The next day, Ayatollah Khamenei kissed his coffin in the Imam Khomeini Husayniyyah, and they also held a grand funeral for him there. I knew Mohsen would be martyred, but I didn't expect such a reception [from the people]. When I saw the video of his captivity, I didn't expect Mohsen to look like that. He

---

58. Shaheed Haj Qasem Soleimani was a veteran of the Iran-Iraq War and the commander of the Qods Force, a subdivision of the IRGC in charge of foreign affairs. On the 3rd of January 2020, he and five others were martyred when his convoy was targeted in Baghdad by a drone strike at the command of the then U.S. President, Donald Trump.

was being guided from somewhere. He had a goal, and he was hastening toward it. He didn't even look at his surroundings. I never felt sadness for his martyrdom, I only felt sadness that I never recognised him, and I ended up hearing about his virtues from others.

Ashraf Shafee'i

The martyr's grandmother

What shall I say about this child's fate? We didn't expect him to turn out that way. I had many grandchildren, each one I loved more than the other, but from the beginning, Mohsen was one of my favourites and I loved him a lot. He was my third grandchild. He wasn't too mischievous. He fell off his bike and broke his arm. He then said, "Now they're going to bring me some fruit," but this time, we didn't bring him any fruit. Another time, he went to buy a fizzy drink, but he fell, and the glass broke and went into his eyebrow. He needed stitches. He got hurt often and his mother was distressed.

Mohsen's mother is my eldest daughter. My other daughters said she is like Haj Ameneh. Haj Ameneh, my aunt, recited the Quran in the mornings. She ate lunch at noon and sat to recite the Quran again. She didn't have anything to do. She didn't have any children or burdens to worry about. She finished reciting one Quran in a day. Now, my daughter has become just like her. When we set up Quran recitation circles, she will recite six juz'[59] and say she isn't tired. She is also very truthful and open-hearted. If anyone in our family needs anything, they will call her and ask her to recite the Quran for them.

When Mohsen was ten, eleven years old, I was holding ten days of *majalis*. I asked him, "Mohsen, can you recite Hadith ul-Kisa for the ten days when Haj Agha comes to our house?" He said, "Sure, I'll come." When he came, he sat on the chair and his feet wouldn't even reach the floor. Now, my neighbours come and ask me if my grandson who was martyred was the one

---

59. The Quran is divided into thirty parts which are each called a juz'

who came, and his feet wouldn't reach the floor. He also recited Ziyarah Ashura at his father's house every Thursday night. His mother said she didn't understand why Mohsen performs all those prayers, fasts and prays in the middle of the night.

He went to Qom and Jamkaran[60] for forty nights. I said to his mother, "Come, let's go with him at least once," but we never asked, and we never managed to go with him. I said, "It's difficult for him." Whenever I saw him, I asked, "How are you, Mohsen?" He raised his hands and said, "All thanks to Allah." He fixed the ceiling fan in my room and said, "Tell me if you ever need me to do anything for you, grandma." When he was leaving, I was in the garden. He talked to me over the phone. He didn't say he was going to Syria, all he said was, "Khodahafez[61], grandma. Forgive me." I didn't understand what he was trying to say, otherwise, I would've gone to see him off somehow!

---

60. A mosque on the outskirts of Qom which was reportedly built on the order of Imam Mahdi (aj) in a dream
61. Farsi for 'goodbye' which literally means 'may Allah be your protector'

Hosein Hojaji

The martyr's brother

He liked difficulty and enjoyed achieving results by working. This was part of his personality since he was a child; even before he reached puberty, he fasted while playing with his friends on the road. Despite his innocent face, he was very mischievous. When he got into fights with the other children, he ran and called me. As soon as I came to the door, the kids ran away. He laughed and said, "I told them I have a very strong brother, he's coming to hit you now."

When he fasted, mum would get worried and said, "Look at how dry your lips and mouth have become! Either go and drink some water or if you want to fast completely, at least don't go on the road and take some rest," but he didn't listen. I took advantage of the opportunity and brought him a glass of water to open his fast. He begged me with the same innocent and childish look on his face which I will never forget, and I let him go. His eagerness and passion encouraged him to take full enjoyment from it, both from fasting and playing with the children.

When he was about to do something important, he consulted with me, but he took his main guidance from my father. He accepted everything he said and benefitted from my father's experience in all fields.

As his elder brother, whenever I hear the name Mohsen, I remember most of his childhood. I remember the good times we had together. Every now and then, we fought as children do, but we made up immediately.

I remember we were at our father's house during his military service and I said to him, "You have a good degree, you have a record of revolutionary activities and working in the Haj Ahmad Kazemi Institute, you can come and do your service within the city." He replied, "If I try, perhaps I could sort something out, but I personally want to go somewhere far so I can see the world and experience some difficulty. It's a beautiful experience!"

After his military service, he was self-employed for a while until he was accepted in the IRGC. At first, I was opposed to this because being part of the military is a difficult and dangerous job, but he loved this path so much that it was clear he had accepted all the difficulties of this journey and he had elected a great goal in his life.

I didn't know the first time he went to Syria. A week before he came back, my father told me he had gone to Syria. I was taken aback and was frozen stiff. I was worried for him until he came back the next week and removed all our worries. We all went to welcome him. I hugged him tightly; I was proud to have a brother who took steps towards defending the shrine of Lady Zaynab (a) and ensuring the security of Iran.

When he returned from Syria, we went to visit him at night. I said, "If I knew you wanted to go to Syria, I would have stopped you and not let you go. Why did you leave your wife alone during these sensitive times? She needs you right now. Don't you want your child to be born?" He gave me an answer which embarrassed me so badly, I couldn't reply to him. He said, "I love my wife and child, but when the Ahlulbayt and Lady Zaynab (as) are in the picture, I must love them more." Now that I think back to myself, I realise he truly was like this.

When I heard he was leaving again, I talked to him a lot to try and change his mind, but it was clear his mind was set on going to Syria. When he came to our house to say goodbye, I found out he had also gone to our uncle's, aunt's, grandmother's and grandfather's houses. In a way, he had said goodbye to everyone. I was almost certain Mohsen would never come back. He asked forgiveness from everyone and left.

As Mohsen was leaving, I asked him to call mum every day if possible so she wouldn't get worried. He called before noon and talked to mum. These days when I'm at my father's house before noon, I always remember the times when the phone rang and mum went to it joyfully. She knew it was Mohsen. It was as if she knew Mohsen was about to call. During one of the days when Mohsen was in Syria, I was at my father's house. The phone called while mum was cooking. She shouted, "It's Mohsen! Hosein, pick up the phone before he puts it down!" I answered the phone and talked to him a little before mum came. When I realised mum was waiting for the phone, I said goodbye quickly and gave her the phone. Now I wish I talked a little longer to him.

It was the night before Tuesday, the 8th of August. I don't know why my heart was restless and I couldn't sleep. I stayed awake the whole night and I didn't sleep a wink. In the morning, I heard my grandmother crying. My house is close to my grandmother's house. Before I could leave my house, she came to our door and announced with tears pouring from her eyes, "Mohsen has been taken captive by ISIS!" My whole world collapsed on my head! I asked, "How did you find out?" She replied, "While I was in the bank with your father, Mohsen's father-in-law called and told us what happened." I quickly went to my mother. I wasn't in a good state at all. Everyone was there, all my sisters and aunties. There was a large crowd in my father's house. After calling the IRGC a few times, we were certain Mohsen had been taken captive the night before. The next day, the commander of the 8th Najaf Ashraf Division came to my father's house with a few other people and confirmed the news of his martyrdom.

Even thinking about how Mohsen is no longer among us is difficult. His innocent and childish face is always on my mind. The sorrow of losing a brother is so painful and heart-wrenching that even Imam Husayn (a) said over the body of his brother, "My brother! Your sorrow has broken my back!"

All thanks to Allah, we are pleased that Mohsen achieved both a good end in this world and a clean slate and a good fate in the next. He became a source of pride for our family, Iran and all the Muslims of the world.

Fatemeh Hojaji

The martyr's sister

My dyed chick was lying limp on the floor, its bones broken. It was dying, its beak was broken, and it couldn't open its eyes. It was shaking and trembling. I was crying and shouting for Mohsen. We were around seven or eight years old, maybe less. In the summers, we bought chicks and we played with them during the summer. That day, we had taken our chicks out onto the road to play with them. Mohsen's friend had stepped on my chick and it was dying. Mohsen looked at me and then the chick. He went, picked up a brick and hit the chick on the head. I closed my eyes and shrieked. I started shouting and insulting him. He came to calm me down by saying, "It was in pain. I killed it to free it from the pain."

He was three years older than me. We played together. Sometimes, he crawled and acted like a horse and I rode on his back. I shouted, "Onwards, horse!" He never moaned nor would he become upset. We fought a lot, and we threw water at each other. We drew on and ripped each other's books. One time, our fight became quite serious, and Mohsen emptied a whole jug of water on Zohreh's book. We were angry at him. He came forward himself to ask forgiveness and said, "I made a mistake. I went too far this time." We noticed he threw water at us with nothing in his hands. We didn't know how he did this. Later, we realised he used his ring to do it. He collected water behind his ring, threw the water at our faces and ran away. We always chased him. If we didn't argue over the TV remote at least once during the day, it was as if we hadn't even woken up in the morning! In the end, our father came and took the remote from all of us. During one of these arguments, I even knocked the TV over and broke it. When we were children and we bought ice cream, he ate his and looked at me sadly and innocently. I felt sorry for him, so I gave him my ice cream. He wouldn't hold back. He didn't throw it away until he had licked the stick clean. Only then did I realise he'd tricked me.

Despite all of this, when they mention Mohsen, the first thing that comes to my mind is his worship. He prayed his prayers separately. He prayed Maghrib and left Isha for another hour, and the same with his Dhuhr and Asr prayers. He said it was the tradition of the Prophet (s). He was extremely sensitive about our hijab and tell us, "However long and loose an *abaya*[62] is, it still isn't a chador. The inheritance of Lady Zahra (a) is this very chador. Wear your hijab correctly, if a few people see your hijab, maybe they'll correct their hijab too." When I was twelve years old, he went on Rahiyan-e Noor and when he came back, he brought me a photo of [Shaheed] Ibrahim Hemmat with a doll. That photo made me develop a great love for the martyrs. Mohsen said, "Put this photo where you can see it and look at it. Make the martyrs the role models in your life." I wanted to go on Rahiyan-e Noor, but I couldn't until I entered college. He constantly texted me. He was so happy and said, "Remember, this journey you're going on isn't an ordinary journey. Take advantage of it as much as you can!" One time, he texted me saying he felt I was in an incredibly good place. I was next to a martyr whose body had just been discovered. He asked me where I was and I replied, "I'm next to an unknown martyr." He was glad he had text me at such an opportune moment. He told me, "Pray for me a lot!" A few hours later, I texted him to

---

62. A long and loose dress which many Muslim women wear as hijab

tell him I was in Shalamcheh[63]. He answered, "The sunset in Shalamcheh is really beautiful." When he sent these texts, I understood the brilliance of these places more.

When he was serving his compulsory military service, my mother bought fruit rolls, trail mix and kashk and sent it to him. She also wrote letters and sent them with the care packages. We also wrote one or two lines underneath to ask him how he was. We went to Dezful to see him. We were standing outside, waiting for him. Zohreh and I were filming with our phones so we could record the moment he saw us. We were messing around, saying things for the video like, "In a few moments, Mohsen will enter... Myusen[64] is coming... there he is!" When he came out, we went quiet. Our mother went to hug him, but not us, we were too shy. We asked each other how we were, but we were too shy to hug him. The only time I hugged him was to say goodbye when he was leaving for Syria because I was certain I would never see him again. I went and sat beside him. He had lowered his head. He had a green *tasbih* in his hands which he was playing with and his shirt was untucked. It was as if this Mohsen wasn't the same. I showed him a photo of my sister's child who had just been born on my phone. He was happy for them. My mother was worried he'd make bad friends in the army, but his commanding officer praised him; he prayed on time, he went on field trips to Imamzadeh[65] Sabzehqoba and he was overall very organised, and so our hearts were at rest.

After his military service, he was usually busy with the Shaheed Kazemi Institute. He tried to take us to the institute a few times too. He even brought the membership forms for us to

---

63. A city in the south of Iran where many soldiers were martyred defending their country, and it has been known as the 'Karbala of Iran'
64. A pet name they had for Shaheed Mohsen.
65. A son or descendant of an Imam

join the institute, but we didn't because we had to study. Studies were the most important thing in our lives.

When he was working in the bookstore, he told us, "We've set up an exhibition, come and take a look," so we went. Most of the books were about the lives of the martyrs and the Ahlulbayt (as). He often said, "If you read books, your knowledge will increase and only then will your faith increase." He often read the book *The Art of the Ahlulbayt (as)*[66]. He also ran a channel on Telegram by the name of 'Misagh Cultural-Artistic Group'. On that channel, he mostly shared articles regarding the martyrs and the Defenders of the Shrine.

He was extremely sensitive over his things. He liked everything to be organised. He made sure his wardrobe didn't get messy. He emphasised to us not to let any children near it. He mainly wore light colours, like white trousers. He stood in front of the mirror a lot. He always had a round plastic comb with him which he used to comb his beard and hair. He always wore Versace Versus perfume. He took care of himself and he enjoyed it. He made us laugh with these things. When he went to the book exhibition, I said to my mother, "Mum, Mohsen is acting suspicious!" I was too shy to ask him anything. If it were a few years earlier, I would have talked to him about it, but we grew apart over those few years. I said, "Mum, we have to follow him to see where he's going." He went to the exhibition from morning until sunset, but he came home for lunch. He wouldn't even finish his lunch and left quickly. I wanted to snoop on his phone, but I couldn't find a suitable opportunity. He always had it with him, even at night. He listened to *nowhehs* on it. He even took it with him when he went to take a shower; he put in a bag and he played *nowhehs* loudly, and he recited loudly along

---

66. هنر اهل بیت

with it. Sometimes when he recited, I said to him, "You couldn't resist the urge to recite again?!" His voice was beautiful. We loved it; we always listened to him.

Slowly, Mohsen's secret was revealed. He told our mother he had got to know a girl at the book exhibition, and he wanted to marry her. I was surprised; I asked, "Are you sure she's good and you want to share your life with her?" He replied, "As far as I've got to know her, she seems fine. She's good." He had made his decision. His child was also in a hurry just like he was all the time. He was born after eight months and had to be put in the incubator. He took photos and videos of him and showed them to us. He said, "He looks like me. He's slightly tanned and complains a lot!" If we said he looked like someone else, he took it to heart.

When I got married, I bought high-heeled shoes. He saw them, but he didn't say anything. When they went home, he texted me, "Your name is Fatemeh! What were those shoes you bought?!" I replied, "Where do you think I was going to wear them? I bought them for the ladies' gatherings." When I said that, he became happy. He gave me a big Mafatih ul-Jinan as a gift on my wedding day. At the beginning of the book, he wrote a long note in which he said he hopes we start our life with this gift and to keep it as a souvenir from him, and to think of him whenever we read it.

The last moment as he was leaving, he said, "If you feel any sadness in your heart, remember the calamities which befell Lady Zaynab (a) and calm yourselves with the Quran." I couldn't speak over my tears. When he left, I texted him, saying, "Your presence is important for us. When you get there, pray for us a lot. If you are martyred, intercede for us [on the Day of Judgement]." He didn't reply. I don't know if he received the message or not, and I still wonder whether he read the message.

One night, I dreamt I was at a wedding, but I was worried and upset. That morning, I woke up and went to the bank to transfer money to get my driving license. My husband called and said, "Come, let's go to your house." I asked, "At this time? Has something happened?" He replied, "Your aunt called and told us to come." As soon as I left the bank, I started crying. I felt as if something had happened to Mohsen. I sat in the car and asked, "Has something happened to Mohsen?" He replied, "No, nothing happened," but I understood from his tone that something had happened; he was a bad actor. We went home, and everyone was crying. My mother was also crying. I asked, "Has Mohsen been martyred?" I was told he had been taken captive, and I started crying even more. We had seen the photo of him being taken captive. Everyone who saw it on the internet didn't tell anyone else. When they brought lunch at noon, everyone started crying again. Mum said, "Does Mohsen have anything to eat now?!"

The officials came to our house from the military headquarters and told us, "This photo has been photoshopped." It looked as if it had been photoshopped as well, with the smoke, clouds and burnt tents. They said they wanted to swap a few ISIS prisoners [in exchange for him]. We were at peace that Mohsen will be swapped, and he'll return home. Everyone was saying something different. We couldn't do anything; we were completely helpless. It was a terrible Tuesday. That night was so painful, we were just praying for his martyrdom. At 1 am, we went to the graves of the anonymous martyrs. We prayed to Allah there for his martyrdom. We received the dreadful news there, and we didn't know whether to be glad or upset. Mohsen had been freed from the claws of ISIS and we were captured in his grief.

Maryam Hojaji

The martyr's sister

We played with the bricks and coal in the street with our neighbours. We played leapfrog. When dad came, we all ran into the house. We hit each other a lot during these games, and I was often beaten up. Even though I was bigger, they were still stronger than me. I let my nails grow long and scratched them. One day, I went for a shower and he closed the light. When I came out, I threw a shoe at his back. I made sure not to miss; I had to take revenge. He had a bicycle made in China which he really loved. He had put a bell on it and decorated it with green tape.

When he was older, he bought a motorcycle. He took Zohreh, my aunt and I on it, but he crashed into a wall at the end of the street, and we all fell into a gutter. People gathered and we were all embarrassed. We put our heads down and went home, while Mohsen took his motorbike to get it repaired. He was a bad driver, whether he was riding a motorcycle or driving a car. He was always in a rush to get around. My mum was scared to sit in his car. One day, the sun was shining in his eyes while he was driving, and he ended up crashing into the car in front of us. Dad said to him, "Wear sunglasses for God's sake! No one can see in front of themselves when the sun is shining." The night before his *aqd*[67], his mother-in-law and wife came to our house. He took dad's car at night to drop them off. When he came back, the wing mirror was hanging off: he'd crashed into a Nissan.

---

67. The agreement recited between a man and woman to make them a couple

Despite this, he played around a lot. His friends narrate, "We were on the road and someone hit our car. He was driving poorly. Mohsen got out as if he was going to start a fight. He went and said to the person, 'I'm sorry, you were right, Agha!'" His friends mocked him because of that. He couldn't do it. He wasn't that type of person to start a fight. He preferred peaceful solutions.

He had a special affinity for *salawat*[68] and he had it painted on the back of his car. His username on Telegram was *salawat*.

He had kept all his toys from his childhood and when he grew up, he divided them between my son and his son. He had many rings, the gemstones of which were Durr an-Najaf, agate, and turquoise. He often wore light colours. He wanted to win over his wife's heart. When the month of Ramadan came to an end, his wife said, "Mohsen said some of his fasts didn't feel right," so he did them again. He only wore black for the entirety of Muharram and Safar and he was busy helping in the *majalis*. During his childhood and teenage years, he mourned with the people and when he was in university, he played the trumpet as part of the marching band [during the mourning parades]. When he was a child, he hit himself with chains instead of his hand. He had a small chain which he was protective over and made sure no one touched it. When my son was young, he came and stood next to me while I was feeding him water. He told me to give the water to him in three breaths. He then said, "My dear! Say Ya Husayn!"

Dad was against Mohsen joining the IRGC. He and his in-laws tried a lot to dissuade him. They even had his name crossed

---

68. Invoking blessings upon the Holy Prophet (s) and his holy progeny by using the following sentence, '*Allāhumma sallī ala Muhammadin wa āli Muhammad*' (O' Allah, send your salutations upon Muhammad and Muhammad's progeny (as))

off the list. Mohsen wanted to both please our father and join the IRGC. Dad said, "A soldier of the IRGC no longer belongs to himself. He may have to go to war, and something may happen to him," but eventually, he managed to go.

He knew himself. The first time, he didn't say goodbye to us, but the second time, he hugged and bade farewell to us. As he was leaving, he said, "Forgive me. When I was a child, I hit you a lot." I was just crying. The last moment at the terminal, he told us, "Your Ali Akbar is leaving!" He added, "Don't cry, otherwise they're not going to take me!" He was overjoyed, like a child when you give them something.

He sent a message to all of us which read, "Forgive me. Remember the calamities which befell Lady Zaynab (a). Take care of mum and dad. Pray I return with a clean slate." I replied, "You already have a clean slate. Acquiring a clean slate isn't only achievable through martyrdom. Martyrdom is good for you and difficult for us." I picked up my phone again and added, "For the sake of this mother and father who you advised us to look after, come back!"

My husband was asleep. They were continuously ringing his phone, but when I answered, they hung up immediately. I woke him up. He got up to pick up the phone and all he said was, "Alright." The night before, I had also been feeling quite poorly and I hadn't slept at all. I went into the courtyard and sat on the bench. I felt as if my heart had sunk. My husband took me to my mother's house. My mother was crying, and our family had gathered. They were saying Mohsen had been taken captive. I sat and started screaming and crying. We were reciting Quran, praying Salat Imam Zaman (aj) and we were seeking intercession from him. I read in a book that someone was lost in a desert, and he sought intercession from Imam Mahdi (aj). Imam Mahdi (aj) went and put the man on his horse and took him to his destination. After praying Salat Imam Zaman (aj), I said, "Ya Sahib az-Zaman[69], help me... Ya Faris al-Hijaz[70], help me... Save our Mohsen!" We went to the graves of the anonymous martyrs and that was where we received the news of his martyrdom. He had truly attained salvation.

---

69. A title of Imam Mahdi (aj), meaning 'patron of the time'
70. A title of Imam Mahdi (aj), meaning 'the rider of Hijaz'

Zohreh Hojaji

The martyr's sister

He was saying, "What did you say, Zohreh? Say it again! *Patk*?!" and he laughed. I accidentally pronounced *patak*[71] as *patk*. Mohsen heard it and kept teasing me. He wouldn't just bother us, we teased him too, especially when he recited poems or *nowhehs* in front of the mirror. He loved poetry and recitation. They composed poetry and wrote *nowhehs* for them in the Miqdad Club. When he brought his notepad back home, he stood in front of the mirror and started reciting. He beat his chest, walked around, and recited a *nowheh* about the conquest of Khorramshahr. We followed him and teased him. After he left high school, he hid his computer files, but I knew how to find them. I found photos of him with his friends from university. He had styled his hair and left the back of his hair long. There was another photo of them laying down, one of them using the other's stomach as a pillow. There was only one photo of him in a dignified pose, and that was his class photo. We made his life hell with those photos. After that, he made sure to be more careful. The computer was in Mohsen's room. In those days, he went to university and had to use it more often. We only used it to play. We also played on our Nintendo. We connected it to the TV, and we played fighting games. Most of the time, Mohsen won. We argued, cheated, and messed about, and Mohsen also cheated. Us three sisters joined hands and beat him up! When he went for a shower, we turned off the light. One time, I slammed the bathroom door on his face. He chased and scared us, but even though he was stronger than us, he never hit us.

---

71. Farsi for 'counterattack'

Sometimes when he wanted to annoy us, he used a pea shooter to shoot spitballs at us.

He was two years older than me. We were born one after the other. We played with each other as children. When he grew up, he played with the boys in the street, and we played with our dolls with the girls. He was always looking after us. One time, our neighbour's daughter hit Fatemeh. I ran to hit her, but Mohsen didn't let us. I started swearing and shouting. I hit Mohsen and started crying. He took his bicycle, sat me and Fatemeh on the back and took us to our grandmother's house to calm us down. When he was older, he kept his room organised. He ironed his clothes. He really liked eggs. Despite his frail appearance, if you cooked five eggs for him in the morning, he would eat them all. We asked him, "Where do you find space to store the eggs?" He just said, "I know, I ate a lot, so what?!"

If we had a problem, he helped us, regardless of whether it was a math problem or a problem while reciting the Quran. He recited the Quran often, and he also recited poems written by Hafez[72] before sleeping. He listened to different kinds of *nowhehs*. Towards the end, he recited 'Manam Bayad Beram[73]' a lot in our house. He recited Haj Mahmoud Karimi's[74] *nowhehs* the way Haj recited them himself. He had a beautiful voice, but because we wanted to annoy him, we mimicked him. I used to study for my entrance exams in one of the rooms upstairs. He brought his friends from the institute over and they worked on robotic engineering in the adjacent room. Even though there were around seven or eight of them , I never heard a sound from them. He had told them not to make noise. He made sure

---
72. A famous Iranian poet whose poems have great religious meaning
73. A nowheh recited by Sayyid Reza Narimani about going to Syria to fight to protect the shrine of Lady Zaynab (a)
74. One of the most well-known Iranian reciters

I wasn't disturbed while studying. He called me a bookworm during that time. I sat in the room from morning until night and my mother gave me food and water from the window. I stuck a note on the door which said, 'I'm testing myself, don't knock'. When he went to university, he was average, not too religious and not too irreligious. He didn't have a beard and didn't leave his shirt untucked. When he returned from his compulsory military service, he was very religious. He looked more innocent, and our relationship became more distant. We were apart for two years. I noticed he was praying Salat ul-Layl. He performed *wudu,* observing all its rites. He closed the tap after collecting water, washed the part of his body and then opened the tap again for the next stage of *wudu,* all with cold water. We objected to this and asked him why he used ice-cold water. He recited his prayers in a beautiful tone. When I was in high school, I wore my hijab incorrectly just to irk him. He didn't look at me, but he said to mum, "Do you want her to go out like this?!"

He got married when he was around twenty years old. He worked as an electrician. We told him it was too soon [for marriage], but he told us he couldn't wait to get married. He really couldn't wait to just go and propose to her. He had learnt all her favourite things and he knew which kinds of flowers and cakes to take for her. After the engagement, his wife's family came to our house. I had just come back from university and went to pray, still wearing my chador from outside. Every two minutes, he came in and asked, "Why aren't you coming out? They want to see you!" I told him I hadn't prayed, and he replied, "Pray and come out!" When they were talking together, I realised that they were besotted with one another. His choice for marriage was strange for me. I expected him to have a traditional wedding and for my mother to pick someone for him

. The night they were signing the marriage contract and reciting the *'aqd*, music was playing and both floors of their house were filled with people. They were all wearing smart clothes. We were stunned; it wasn't the Najafabadi custom to dress up and invite many guests for the signing of the marriage contract. We normally invite three or four elders and sign the contract. We had worn shirts underneath our *abayas*, not dresses. Mohsen was constantly texting us to turn the music down; he was being tortured. The men signed the contract downstairs and Mohsen and his father-in-law came into the women's side. They recited the *'aqd* and then mum put a bracelet on Zahra's hand as a sign.

Only his wife knew the first time he went to Syria. As he was leaving, he whispered in dad's ear that he was going to Syria. When he returned from Syria, he had changed. It was as if his life could be divided into two; one before going to Syria and one after returning from Syria. It was as if he had left a part of himself in the shrine of Lady Zaynab (a). Every Thursday, he went to Qom. "If your car breaks down, you could die," we told him, "Why do you insist on going every week in this hot weather?!" The second time he wanted to go to Syria, mum called and told us, "All of you have to come. Mohsen wants to go." My sisters and mother were all crying. Maryam was even crying on the way. Mohsen said to us, "Do you think I'm going to be martyred? Do you think something will happen to me? Did anything happen to me last time?" We all knew at the bottom of our hearts that if he goes, he will never come back. We went to the terminal before him, and he brought his in-laws. We took a photo in the darkness of the night amongst the buses as a keepsake. When I hugged him, I asked him, "Where do you want to go?" He replied, "Don't cry, okay? You must be a rock for mum!" When he stepped onto the bus, he looked back and said to us, "Youth of Bani Hashim, your Ali Akbar is leaving!" We all started crying.

He left and the next day, he texted us all to ask us for our forgiveness. I replied, saying, "Pray for me. When you go to the shrine of Lady Zaynab (a), pray for us a lot and take care of yourself." They took their phones from them. He called our mother through their phones. One time, I picked up the phone, and that was the last time I ever heard his voice.

The night before we found out Mohsen had been taken captive, I had a strange dream. Everyone was sitting on a black sheet in a house, gathered around two coffins. I was confused as to where I was and whose coffins they were. Someone lifted the sheet off one of the coffins and told us they had brought the bodies of the Defenders of the Shrine.

My husband called while I was at work and said, "We must go to my dad's house. He called me and told me to come." I asked, worriedly, "Has anything happened? Are you hiding something from me?" He replied, "No! Come, let's go." I told him, "No, something has happened but you're hiding it from me." He came to my workplace to pick me up. I asked, "Am I coming back? Shall I take the day off?" He replied, "No, I don't think we're coming back." I noticed he had been crying. His eyes were swollen and red. I asked him, "What happened?!" but he just answered, "Some dust got into my eyes." I started worrying even more, but I didn't think anything had happened in my own family. I went to their house and sat on the sofa, and my husband started crying. My mother-in-law also seemed agitated. My husband went to bring me a glass of water. "What's wrong with you lot?" I asked them, "Has something happened that you aren't telling me?" Then suddenly, my heart dropped. I turned to look my husband in the eyes. "Mohsen!?" I exclaimed, and he said yes.

I screamed and ran out of the house. My mother- and father-in-law ran after me. I don't know how I managed to go down the stairs and sit in the driver's seat. My husband said, "Get out, I'll drive myself." All the way to my mother's house, I was slapping myself and crying and screaming. I still didn't know what had happened. When we got to my mother's house, I saw everyone had come together. My aunt told me Mohsen had been taken captive. I prayed to Allah for Mohsen to be shot and martyred so he wouldn't fall into the hands of ISIS. We screamed and cried until night. We prayed a lot. I was surprised as to how he could be taken captive. We also saw the photo of him being taken captive. I saw immense courage and innocence in his eyes.

The first night the photo of his severed head was shared, my mother's sister called and told us, but told us not to say anything to our mother. We weren't allowed to cry over his severed head until morning [otherwise our mother would realise]. We were being torn apart on the inside. We noticed our mother was feeling even worse due to Mohsen's captivity, so I told her, "Mum, thank God, Mohsen has been martyred." They had severed Mohsen's head, and later, we were informed they had torn his body into pieces. How did they manage to cut Mohsen into pieces when I could hug him and put my arms around him completely?! He was a *masa'ib*[75] personified. Everything we heard about the events of Karbala, we found personified in our brother and the closest person to us. I still regret the fact that I didn't kiss his neck before he left! Only one thing calmed me down; his courage when they were taking him to the car. I felt this made my heart feel calmer. If I had seen him begging at their feet, I would be in pain, I would cry and feel even more

---

75. Mentioning the calamities which befell the Ahlulbayt (a), generally in a heart-rending tune

distressed, but when I saw him walking with such steadfastness even though he knew they were taking him to torture him, it means [he was saying] I'm fine, deal with it!

Zahra Abbasi

The martyr's wife

When we went shopping for the wedding, he didn't want to wear a suit. He moaned, "Why can't I go without a suit?!" and I frowned at him. He laughed and said, "Anyway, what are these suits and diamonds people wear?" I turned and said to him, "Don't wear a diamond then!" The poor shopkeeper who didn't understand Mohsen brought a whole range of ties for the groom to try on. He said to me, astounded, "What's all this about?" He held the ties up and gave them back to the shopkeeper.

We argued a lot over rings. He looked me in the eyes and said, "Gold? Don't even mention it to me! It's haram!" I replied, "Is it possible for a couple to be without rings?" He laughed and said, "Yeah, of course, it is! Why not?" He tried to make me understand that being besotted with one another isn't due to the rings, it's to do with the heart. I told him, "Whatever we do, we have to get rings! I like it." We made jokes and laugh in the bazaar. Other families looked at us and laughed, "Look at this new couple!" I whispered to him, "I want everyone to know this man is taken . I want them to all know you're mine! " I insisted on buying the rings in a set, so he told us, "I'll be happy if you find one that isn't gold." We turned the whole bazaar upside down until we found a suitable set of rings; my ring was made of white gold and Mohsen's out of platinum.

When I went to try on some dresses , he said to me quietly, "We are still not married! I'll leave you to choose if you don't mind." He went and came back with a tray of carrot juice and ice cream. He had bought one for everyone except himself. He said he didn't have an appetite, but when we insisted, his mother revealed he was fasting. I asked him, "Why today?" and he answered, "So no problems arise, and we can get married easily."

When we sat to recite the *'aqd*, he asked, "What do you see in this mirror in front of us?" I replied, "You and me." He added, "Okay, what does that mean?" I told him, "I don't know." He brought his head closer and said, "In the mirror, there's no one from your family nor anyone from mine. Not my parents nor your parents, there isn't even a child, so remember, now we only have one other." His words calmed my nerves. I asked him, "Will you recite the Quran for me?" He started whispering verses from Surah Nur in my ear in a beautiful tune and I was quietly reading along with him.

He was working at the factory and couldn't come to listen to Dua Arafah[76]. My mother and I went to Gulzar-e Shuhada in Najafabad and by chance, I sat next to one of the graves. When I saw the name, I was shocked; at first, I read 'Shaheed Mohsen Hojaji', but when I looked again, I noticed it actually said 'Shaheed Mohsen Hojjati'. I felt upset that lest one day, I would sit over a grave which said 'Shaheed Mohsen Hojaji'! I started crying and sobbing due to these thoughts.

That night, I took him to Gulzar-e Shuhada to show him the grave of the martyr. I cried the whole way there. Mohsen laughed and said, "It's good, now pray I have a gravestone you can sit beside if I'm martyred!" I felt even worse when he said that. I wasn't calming down in any way. I said to him, "Come, let's go to Haj Ahmad [Kazemi's grave]." We made our way to Golestan-e Shuhada[77] in Isfahan on his motorcycle. His collar was drenched in my tears. I asked, "If I don't have you, what

---

76. A supplication recited on the Day of Arafat (the 9th of Dhul-Hijjah) narrated from Imam Husayn or Imam Sajjad (as).

77. A cemetery in Isfahan for martyrs.

will I do?" and he laughed. "Why are you worrying about martyrdom?" he asked, "Right now, the factory doesn't even let me pray on time, how am I supposed to be martyred?!"

He argued a lot with his manager at the factory over this issue. One day, he came back from work and said, "I don't want to go to the factory anymore." He handed in his letter of resignation, but he didn't have any job to fall back on. One of his friends worked in a bakery, so he talked with his manager and he started working there. During his free time, he went to the bookstore. "Mohsen!" I suggested, "Why don't you join the army?"

We were Islamically married but not living together for a year and eight months. After changing the wedding date several times, we eventually decided to set a date. We rented a house near my father's and bought all our furniture and everything we needed. We argued a lot with Mohsen over buying the furniture. He always argued with my parents over how much money they were spending and that we didn't need these things. He was arguing that he didn't want a sofa. He was worried and said, "Maybe someone who doesn't have one will see it and feel sad he doesn't have one!"

On the night of the wedding, he called me to come outside while I was at the salon. He said, irritated, "What is this woman talking about? She's mocking us!" The camerawoman had told him to pace in front of the salon door and keep making it clear in the video that he was waiting by looking at his watch. He wasn't one for these types of things. He asked me to tell her to stop filming, but I begged him to just leave it this time for me and do everything she says.

When I sat in the car, I saw there were a lot of cars around us even though we hadn't put flowers on our car. They had come to accompany us to the wedding, but Mohsen wasn't happy with this. When he saw they wanted to come and were blowing their horns, he asked me, "Shall we lose them?" I told him, "That's rude!" but he answered, "No, it's fun!" He started weaving through the traffic until he reached a small alleyway. Two cars managed to keep up with us, but he didn't give up. He stepped on the pedal and lost them in the traffic.

When we heard the *adhan* for Maghrib prayers, he parked on the side of the street and said, "Let's pray for one other." He tricked me and told me he would make the *dua* and I can say amen afterwards. The first thing he prayed for was martyrdom and for him to have a clean slate. When the muezzin said, 'I bear witness that Ali is the vicegerent of Allah', he prayed for martyrdom. I started crying, so he took out a handkerchief from his pocket and said jokingly, "I didn't pay so much money at the salon for you to ruin it all!" I said, "Insha'Allah, you get what you want, but there's one condition!" He asked me, "What do you mean?" I answered, "If I pray for your martyrdom, you have to come and visit me, I have to be able to sense you, you have to take my hands and guide me to the straight path ." He looked down, thought a little and said, "Sure, if I can." I asked, "What do you mean if I can?" He replied, "Well, I don't know what it's like on the other side." I told him, "I almost forgot, you have to come back safe and sound after your martyrdom, I have to see your face." I then sat up, looked him in the eyes and said, "No messing about! I shouldn't come to heaven and see you hanging out with the houris and having a good time! Don't come to my dream in white clothes, walking hand in hand with a houri!" He laughed a lot, so I asked, "Why are you laughing? I'm being serious!" He said softly, "I want you to be my bride in heaven too, for you to be mine there as well ." We prayed for Allah to give us a son. I told him, "Look, if our child is a girl, you aren't allowed to be martyred! You have to leave a man behind for me and go." He prayed for our son to be righteous and healthy who could become a martyr himself with the help of Imam Mahdi (aj). We had a lot of fun talking about which parent he looked like. At the end of the night, we walked from my father's house to our own house.

One day, we invited my uncles and aunts over for lunch. As the guests were arriving, he came and told me, "I've been told they're bringing Alireza to the base." Alireza Noori was one of the soldiers of the IRGC. We heard about his martyrdom in Syria about a month and a half ago. I asked him, "What shall we do now?" He started thinking; all he wanted to do was attend his *majlis* to bid him farewell. I said to him, "I'll lay the table quickly so you can get there." The guests arrived one by one. He never put his phone down. He was constantly looking at the time. I quickly laid the table. My aunts came into the kitchen and were asking me, "Agha Mohsen looks upset. Is something wrong?" The men had also sensed something was going on. Once everyone had eaten, he got up and apologised as one of the soldiers in the army had been martyred and he had to attend his *majlis*. He went into the other room, took off his black shirt and put on a dark-blue shirt. I asked him, "Why did you take off your black shirt?" He answered, "I don't want to wear a black shirt to the *majlis* of a martyr!"

Once Mohsen left, we also decided to go. We went to the base. They still hadn't brought the martyr's body. I put myself in the place of the martyr's wife and started crying. What if something like this happened to Mohsen? What if they bring him here one day to bid him farewell? What would I do?! When I saw his wife, I cried. When I saw his child, I cried. I saw Mohsen from far and cried. He texted me, "Look at this honour. Look at his honour. Pray I'm also martyred." I wrote back, "I beg you, don't even talk about it, my heart can't take it. If you aren't here, I'll die." The ambulance came. I didn't text him again; I let him live the experience. The marching band started playing. The men lifted the coffin and took it to the mosque [of the base]. They all came together and started beating their chests. It was the women's turn and I went to the coffin with the martyr's wife. I felt as if Mohsen was laying in there. I felt sick, and nothing could calm me down. They were going to take the martyr to his village, so he texted me, asking, "Can I go with them?" I told him to go, and he wrote, "Are you not coming?" I told him, "No, the home is dirty. I can't come. My mind is occupied." He said to me, "I'm grateful you accompany and support me everywhere." I quickly replied, "Go, don't worry about replying. Benefit from the atmosphere and enjoy it."

He got back at midnight. He said with envy, "You don't know how they treated him! What a crowd!" He sighed and said, "Zahra! If I die, ten people will drag themselves to my coffin after a world of complaints, but the people will kill themselves for the martyrs!" He spoke about martyrdom until morning. He cried and said, "If I am martyred, I will be eternal, but if I die, I'm gone and at that moment, you'll be mournful. You and I can't be separated, but maybe we can remain together through martyrdom." To lighten the mood, I told him, "Fine, just remember the condition I put down in our wedding car, no messing about!" He laughed through the tears and replied, "Fine, I promise there will be no messing about!"

The next morning, we went to his funeral at 9 am. When they came to lay Shaheed Noori's body in the grave, they said, "Let his wife come to see her martyr for the last time!" I followed her. Half of his face had been damaged beyond recognition from the explosion. He was smiling beautifully. When I saw his Shayb al-Khadib[78], I felt weak. I stepped back. I walked amongst the martyrs and cried to my heart's content. He came to comfort me, and he knew what was upsetting me. "How can I get to Syria? Who's going to take me?" he asked. "I haven't even been in the army for two months yet. Right now, it's just complete this course, pass that course. It's not like they just take anyone to Syria. Don't worry, I'm going to be here. I'll grow old and become an old man. Anyway, I want to have five children."

We started visiting Shaheed Alireza Noori's grave every night. They had put an Iranian flag on his grave. He said, "Look at it! Look at how beautiful it is. This is one of the small differences. They put down a black cloth if you die, but if you are a martyr, they lay this blessed flag."

One night, we were walking amongst the graves of the martyrs until we passed them all. We sat beside one of the empty graves. I said, "I want to get in." He told me, "It's nighttime, you'll be frightened." Eventually, I let it be after he insisted I don't. When I was looking at the bottom of the grave, it was as if I was looking into the mouth of an abyss. I cried a lot beside that grave; for myself, for him and our deeds. I looked back and said, "Mohsen, become a martyr! Don't die!" He told me to pray.

One day, he came back from work and as normal, I went to the door to greet him. I realised something was wrong because he kept avoiding eye contact. I followed him and turned him around to look at him in the hallway. I asked him, "Is something wrong? I'm getting worried!" He sat on the carpet and said, his eyes welling up with tears, "They won't take me. My commander didn't permit me, and they closed the list. Zahra!

---

78. A euphemism for Imam Husayn (a) used in Ziyarah Nahiyah al-Muqaddasah, narrated from Imam Mahdi (aj), which means 'the beard drenched in blood'.

I missed my opportunity!" I asked, "Are you sure there is no other way?" He nodded in agreement. "Is there nothing I can do?" I asked. "No, you did your part by praying," he replied, "I don't understand why Allah doesn't accept me." I brought him a pillow so he could sleep a little. His face was drenched in tears. He eventually cried himself to sleep. I went into the other room and cried out to Allah, "Lest it's due to my complaints? Lest it's because of me telling him not to go that you didn't take him?" I picked up the photo of Haj Ahmad [Kazemi] and said to him, "Look at how restless he is! You got him a place in the army, can you let him go to Syria?"

My mother was waiting for us, so I went and woke him up. He was still upset on the way. When we passed by the base, he started crying again. He said to me mournfully, "Zahra! They're leaving and I've been left behind." I comforted him by saying, "Don't feel bad. If it was good for you…" I was interrupted by his ringtone. Someone from the army had called to tell him his name was on the list and he should be on standby. The exact time of his departure wasn't specified; it could've been the day after or in two weeks or three weeks. He turned around at the next roundabout and parked outside of the base. He went inside to make sure. He came back with a spring in his step and said he was going to start packing his bags. Even though I was worried, I didn't say anything to ruin his good mood. When we got back, I read him the following line, "I perceive your love a little more!" I didn't let him see I was distressed. I told him, "If you want to go, go, maybe you won't come back, but just the fact that you are calm makes me calm."

I felt nauseous. Despite this, we went to my mum's house. He took me by the hand and said, "I beg you, don't let anyone find out, not your mum, not my mum. Maybe they'll oppose my decision." I told him not to worry. I couldn't eat properly, and I felt nauseous until nightfall. He took me into the corner and asked light-heartedly, "Are you pregnant?" I forced a smile and replied, "It's not unlikely!" My mum asked while passing by, "Has anything happened?" I tried to look happy, but I couldn't stop vomiting.

The next morning, he took leave, and we went to the doctor's office. We were there until the afternoon waiting for the result. He tried to keep me happy by saying things like, "If there's a baby, please don't tell me not to go!" I kept praising Allah with my *tasbih*. I was praying there wouldn't be a baby involved in this dire situation. I told him to wait at the door of the office and I would go on my own. I was praying the result wouldn't come out positive. When the nurse gave me the results, I asked her, "Ma'am, is it positive or negative?" All she did was say congratulations. I felt as if the ceiling of the building was going to fall on me. I felt as if I couldn't walk. I couldn't go down the stairs. Mohsen leaving was one case, but the baby was a whole new stress on me. He realised from how I was acting that he had become a father. He said, overjoyed, "O' Allah, thank you!" I said quickly, "You should be happy. I'm upset I have to share you with someone else now." He exclaimed, "You mean you are already jealous of a baby?!" He begged me not to tell anyone I was expecting. His departure wasn't specified, and he was worried they would use the baby as an excuse to stop him from going. Keeping my pregnancy hidden was more difficult than the pregnancy itself. I wanted to tell the whole world I was going to become a mother. However, on the other hand, I was worried they would call at any moment and tell him to pack his bags and leave . I told him one or two times, "I should call them myself and tell them to take you so I can be rid of this stress. "

Two weeks later, we went to the shrine of Imamzadeh Shahzadeh Hosein. Mohsen's phone rang, I thought it was one of his friends. "Sure, I'll get ready," he said quietly. I asked him who it is, but he dodged the question. Once I insisted, he admitted, "Tomorrow morning, we're shipping out." I felt as if my legs were weak, and I was going to fall. We quickly returned to Najafabad. He said, "I have to tell my father first, but my mother mustn't know, she'll be upset." He asked me to bear these moments without crying until he's gone. At that moment, I changed my Telegram profile picture to a line composed by Saadi Shirazi which reads, "I see with my own eyes that my soul is leaving..." I couldn't breathe properly. I couldn't catch my breath and I couldn't speak. He spun a whole story for his mother, telling her he's going to the border for military training, and they'll take their phones and it'll take two months. His mother asked him, "Will you be able to call?" He replied, "Only as long as I'm in Tehran." When we were saying *khodahafez*, he quietly whispered in his father's ear, "I'm going to Syria, look after my Zahra." The poor man was stunned. His face went pale, and he was speechless. He followed us to the door as if he were sleepwalking. My mother-in-law started crying that she wasn't going to hear from her son for two months!

When we got in the car, I broke down. I cried so much and started wailing. The thought of Mohsen not being around was killing me. He put my hand on the gear stick, held it tightly and said, "Don't cry, I want to take you to Alireza and Ruhollah." He bought a big bottle of rosewater. We visited the grave of Ruhollah Kafizadeh. He washed his gravestone with teary eyes, and he did the same with Alireza Noori's grave. Eventually, he made his way towards the graves of the anonymous martyrs. I was following him and wailing. He took me by the arm and said, "I beg you, don't cry, I'm dying. I'm not going to go, okay?!" I asked, "What do you mean you're not going to go?" I both wanted him to go and stay. I told him, "I don't understand;

forget all of this 'you're going, not going', what shall I do with this love?" He replied, "Walk with me." We decided to visit Mohsen Haidari, one of the five martyrs from the IRGC. We drove as fast as we could on the Khomeini Shahr Highway. We searched for a whole hour until we found Gulzar-e Shuhada, but to our disappointment, it was closed. He sent his regards from behind the gates and took permission from them [to go to Syria].

As soon as we got home, he went into the other room with a pen and paper. I realised he was writing his will when he told me wanted to be alone. I took out some fruit and ice cream, but I didn't want to disturb his peace, so I waited, watching the door of the room until he came out. He sat beside me, his eyes red and tearful. After eating some ice cream, he quickly went to sleep. He was worried he would oversleep in the morning. He told my mum to call him, he set the alarm on the clock, set alarms on his phone, and told me to wake him up. I had enough. I had tried all I could. I took the alarms off the clock, I put his phone on silent and took the batteries out of all the clocks in the house. I wanted him to stay. I fell asleep at around 3 am in the hope that when I wake up, it would be too late for him.

He jumped from his sleep at prayer time and all my plans fell through. He was joyful and I was miserable. I ironed his clothes, and he wore them, then we went to my mum's house. My mum was sad, and my father kept himself to himself. We were all miserable, but contrary to all of us, Mohsen was happy and enthusiastic. He was making jokes during these dreadful moments of ours. I wanted to beat him up. I quickly bade him farewell and went to my room. I was left alone with my loneliness. I laid down in a corner like someone who was depressed. I was just looking at his photo which was the wallpaper on my phone, and when it went on standby, I switched it on again. We started texting each other, and I was constantly hearing my phone ringing. He still hadn't reached the base, but he said, "I miss you!" I wrote to him, "Why are you playing with my heart now you're leaving? I should be saying this, not you!"

"Pray I am given a clean slate!" he texted.

"Mohsen! I beg you, come back. Don't think about me, think about the child!" I replied.

"Only good will happen. Insha'Allah I'll come back," he answered.

"Promise?"

"Promise."

I thought to myself, "You're right, you'll come back, but you won't say in which state!"

My mum was cooking *aash* and giving it out as a charity for Mohsen's safety. From eight or nine o'clock in the morning, family, friends, and acquaintances were coming and going. I had never seen anything like this. I wasn't feeling well and wasn't leaving my room. I only knew they were coming and going. My father came into my room one or two times to ask, "Are you okay? Has anyone called you? Have you heard anything from Mohsen?" I sensed something wasn't right. Close to Dhuhr prayers, one of Mohsen's friends called me and asked, "Have you heard two people have been martyred?" My heart dropped and I screamed, "Ya Imam Husayn!" He immediately added, "Don't worry! Mohsen is fine." I told him to tell me the truth, and he said Komeyl Ghorbani and Hasan Ahmadi had been martyred and their bodies would be sent back in one or two days. I called my father and told him what had happened. There was a person constantly ringing our bell and came in on a random excuse, and we told him if he is worried about Mohsen, he shouldn't be worried as he is alive.

I heard from somewhere that many soldiers had been wounded, and I was worried lest Mohsen was one of them. I called his friends, but they hadn't heard anything. I took a walk around the block with my phone in my hand. I was hearing conflicting reports. My father even went to the base to find out what had happened, but they didn't even know exactly what was going on, and it was amongst this confusion that they brought Komeyl Ghorbani and Hasan Ahmadi's bodies.

I went to the Hazrat-e Zahra Husayniyyah at 5 am. Their families were coming to bid farewell. They had laid the two coffins in the cemetery for the anonymous martyrs. I wanted to see them up close. The others told me, "Don't go, it'll hurt your child!" but I told them, "They aren't dead, they're martyrs, they're alive!" I went inside and with every step I took, I was telling the child in my womb, "Your dad is a man and he's gone to Syria. Now we're going to see his friends." I first saw Shaheed Ghorbani. His eyes were open, and his neck was slightly disfigured. He looked a lot like Mohsen that you can't tell the difference between them. He had a smile playing on his lips, and his face was shining. His beard had just started growing. I couldn't stop crying. I was thinking about what I would do if it were Mohsen inside the coffin instead of Komeyl. I spoke with him and asked him about Mohsen. I went to see Hasan Ahmadi. Only a part of his face was still intact. I had shivers down my spine, and I held myself tightly. I looked at him for a moment and slowly started retreating. I felt as if I was going to fall. I went outside and I saw Komeyl Ghorbani's wife next to the anonymous martyrs. They were holding her up by her arms. My legs felt weak. I sat on my knees and thought to myself, "What if one day, they hold me by my arms and take me to see my Mohsen?!" I went back to the Husayniyyah and I sat beside Shaheed Ahmadi's wife. She held my hand tightly and I told her, "Our husbands went to Syria together. Now I don't know if my husband is living or dead, safe, or wounded. Please pray he returns safely, I am pregnant."

I wasn't myself until he came back. I asked, "How are you?" and he replied, "I missed you so much too!" It was from that moment I realised something was wrong. I thought maybe he'd misheard because there was a lot of noise. At the dinner table, I had to call him three or four times to get his attention. The others also realised Mohsen was answering their questions strangely. I was worried he had PTSD[79]. Mohsen normally rolled up his sleeves when eating, but this time, he had fastened his cuffs tightly. When he reached over to take a glass of water, I looked under his sleeve; his skin was peeling and the hair on his arm was singed off. I exclaimed, "Mohsen! Your arm!" He shushed me so no one else found out.

I was waiting for our guests to leave so I could see what had happened to him. Before my mother and father even left the building, I ran towards him. I asked him, distressed, "Do you have PTSD?" He looked at me with surprise and said, "No." I asked him many questions. "Why is your arm like that?" He tried to dodge the question by saying, "My body was sensitive to the weather there!" I looked at him seriously and asked, "Are you mocking me?" He knew I wasn't convinced easily, and I

---

79. Post-traumatic stress disorder (PTSD) is an anxiety disorder caused by very frightening, stressful or distressing events, and this can sometimes be a bomb exploding close to oneself. Some of the symptoms include re-living the experience, avoiding contact with others and difficulty concentrating.

wouldn't leave him alone until he answered me. "A bomb struck our tank. When it exploded, I put my hand over my face, and this is what happened!" he explained. I asked him, teary-eyed, "So do you have PTSD or not?" He didn't know himself. He teared up and said, "I could have been martyred, but I was lacking in some places!" He cried out, "What will I do if it's no longer destined for me?! Before I went, I didn't know what goes on over there but now I can't wait to return! Lest I'm not martyred and end up becoming a narrator of the martyrs' stories!" I couldn't take him talking about martyrdom anymore, so I went to the kitchen and stood at the sink. I couldn't take it anymore. He pleaded, "After this great separation, now you're angry and complaining?!" I closed the tap and said with my back turned, "Didn't you say when you called me that you miss my complaining?!" He went and brought his rucksack. I didn't want to keep him waiting, so I went to him. He took out a box full of pearls and shells. He'd made a torch for me with one of the pearls. He put a pen with a light at the end inside the pearl and when you switched the light on, the pearl lit up. He also did some calligraphy on a piece of wood. He'd drawn a heart and candle and written underneath it, 'I love my beautiful wife'.

They were taken to the city of Latakia for training. He was telling me it was one of the coastal cities of Syria. He was talking about how the sound of the waves made him feel homesick and said, "I stood on the rocks. I looked out to sea and talked to you!" He sighed deeply and said, "One time, I even came out of the tank and sat on the gun turret. I started crying because I missed you so much!" He bought a turquoise Arab maxi dress, one of those that looks like an *abaya* and doesn't have buttons on the front .

He began visiting Masjid Jamkaran from then on. My mother, father and I went with him to Qom at the end of February 2016 on the anniversary of the death of Lady Ma'sumah (a)[80]. He asked my father, "Dad, shall we come for *ziyarah*[81] every week on Thursdays?" My father told him, "I'll come with you whenever I can." He told me he had made an oath to do *ziyarah* in Qom and Jamkaran for forty days. "I have to find what I was lacking!" he told me. He said from the depths of his heart, "I want to attain a clean slate!" I don't know why, but he wouldn't stop using the word '*rusefid*'. Whenever he came back from work on Thursdays, he left quickly. I packed his lunch in advance, and he ate his food on the way and sometimes in the car. He hurriedly gathered his things and set out so he could reach Qom for Maghrib prayers. I decorated his food and organised it neatly. I baked cakes the night before and took the shells off some nuts and seeds so he could eat them easily. I was seven months pregnant and really wanted to go with him. I wanted to sit next to him, to speak and laugh until we reach Qom, to pour tea and give it to him, to put sugar cubes in his mouth for him, to wipe his beard when biscuit crumbs fell, to change the clutch when he was speaking on the phone, to change the *nowhehs*, all in all, to share in his spiritual experience.

I cooked him dinner too so he wouldn't have to eat anywhere in a strange city. He was glad and said, "Zahra-cooked dinner hits the spot in Jamkaran!" He only ate outside food for breakfast because on Friday noon, I laid the table for him and prepared lunch for him so he could come back and eat my homecooked food straight away. When a friend or acquaintance

---

80. Lady Fatimah Ma'sumah (a) was the sister of Imam Rida (a) who passed away in the city of Qom after falling ill on the way to meet her brother in the city of Marv. She had been praised by three Imams before her.
81. The word *ziyarah* holds two meanings; the first meaning is pilgrimage of an infallible or a great person, and the second is a specified salutation that is normally recited to greet these infallibles or great people. In this context, it is referring to the first definition.

saw me doing this, they nagged me and said, "You're spoiling him too much! He'll get used to it and in four years, he won't notice these nice things you do for him!" He always texted me on time, saying, "I wish you were here." I asked, "Are you having a good time?" and he replied, "You can't have a bad time next to her shrine!" I then told him, "So take a deep breath and enjoy yourself." He donated money to the shrine of Lady Ma'sumah (a) and texted me, "For your safety and the little one!" If he had money, he wouldn't hesitate and always came back with something, even as little as a pack of candy floss. He knew how obsessed I was with candy floss and that if I were to receive gold as a gift, I wouldn't be as happy as I would be if I had candy floss. He also bought me small things from Pasaj-e Quds[82] like photos of the martyrs. Sometimes, he brought me clothes, perfume, and prayer mats. He even bought souvenirs for Ali who hadn't even been born yet, like toys, rattles, clothes, and shoes. He loved collarless three-button shirts and he bought and wore them often. There wasn't a small size for Ali, but he couldn't take it, so on one of his journeys, he bought the smallest size and said, "Ali has to be four to wear this shirt."

Have you noticed how sometimes when people are happy, they start to sing? When Mohsen was happy, he recited *nowhehs* loudly. Once, he asked jokingly to annoy me, "In your opinion, who will come to recite for me when I'm martyred?" I replied indignantly, "No one, we'll call one of these random reciters." He thought and joked, "You mean Haj Mahmoud Karimi and Sayyid Reza Narimani will come?!" I replied, "In your dreams! Have they got nothing to do for them to recite in your majlis?!" He said sadly, "But that's my only wish!" That year, we went to listen to Dua Arafah recited by Sayyid Reza Narimani. That day

---

82. A mall in Qom where you can get most religious supplies, including books, canvases, etc.

held a great significance in our lives as it was the martyrdom anniversary of Haj Ahmad [Kazemi]. His conscience was being tortured when I was taking care of Ali during the *masa'ib*. When the reciter shouted in the microphone, Ali got scared and started crying. I walked with him outside, far from the speakers. He texted, "Do you want me to take Ali so you can benefit [from the recitation]?" I told him, "No, I'm fine." He wrote back, "You will get so many blessings for what you're doing! I swear to God you're doing such a great thing!" He asked me for my forgiveness. He then added, "Pray for me in the state you're in right now." I prayed for his martyrdom from the bottom of my heart. Something told me that on that day, Allah accepted my prayer in the middle of Dua Arafah.

We really enjoyed Agha Narimani's recitations. During the nights of Muharram, we would tough it out and go to Isfahan. Every night, he recited about the martyrs and put a spell on Mohsen's heart. On one of the nights, Ali started crying, so I picked him up and took him outside. When I came back in, he was reciting the following line, "It was at this same time, this same place, someone's letter of martyrdom was signed..." At that moment, he texted me, "Zahra my dear, pray for my martyrdom also. Pray I am given a clean slate." My heart burnt and I prayed a lot for him. He always did this. He texted in the middle of the *masa'ib* and begged me to pray for his martyrdom. When he came out, I looked at him and said, "You text me when you know I'm feeling a lot of pain [for the Ahlulbayt (as)]! What will happen if Allah accepts your prayer at that moment?" I began to cry again. He was whispering that line and crying all the way back to Najafabad. He was saying, "This *nowheh* reminds me of Komeyl and Dayitaghi, it reminds me of Muharram last year when we did *sinehzani* together in Syria!" He started wailing and said, "Zahra! They were bestowed martyrdom, but I was left behind!"

In the car, he constantly listened to the *nowheh* which read, "We are young and full of passion, we are sensitive over the shrine, o' lady of the two worlds, we are all your Abbas!"[83] Agha Yazdkhasti had recited this. One night, we were going to a *majlis* where he was reciting, and Mohsen was listening to this *nowheh*. At the door, Mohsen said, "I hope he reads that one tonight!" Coincidentally, while reciting, the reciter said, "I don't know why, but I feel like reciting this *nowheh*!" and he started reciting it. Every time he played the *nowheh* by the name of '*The Honour of the Two Worlds*'[84], he told me he wanted to not be disturbed and just weep. Whenever he listened to the *nowheh* by the name of '*These Days, I Yearn for the Trenches*'[85], it drove me crazy because he cried so much. He knew I understood him.

He wore black clothes for the whole two months of Muharram and Safar. He started reciting Ziyarah Ashura every day for forty days before Ashura[86] and he recited it for forty days after Ashura as well. He didn't eat anything he normally ate on good days like seeds, nuts, and good food. From the year our two-person *majalis* became three-person *majalis*, he recited *masa'ib* for Ali separately and [Ali] beat his chest.

At midnight, I heard him reciting something. I went and saw him sitting on the prayer mat, reciting *masa'ib* alone. I couldn't resist, so I sat next to him. When he read with such passion, I found it difficult to breathe, not from tears, but pain. I told

---

83. 'جوونیم و با احساسیم، به روی حرم حساسیم، بی بی دو عالم ماها،همه واسه تو عباسیم'
84. 'آبروی دو عالم'
85. 'هوای این روزهای من هوای سنگره'
86. Ashura is the tenth day of Muharram, the day Imam Husayn (a), his family and companions were martyred, and his remaining family members were taken captive.

him, "Mohsen! Shorten it!" When he recited the *masa'ib* of Lady Zahra (a), I couldn't bear the pain. I didn't let him read a lot. Sometimes, he eventually ended by mentioning the *masa'ib* of Imam Husayn (a) in Karbala, and sometimes he ended by reciting Ziyarah Nahiyah al-Muqaddasah. When he couldn't take the pain anymore, sometimes he took refuge in Munajat Amir al-Mu'mineen (a)[87].

One night, we decided to lay the table in Lady Ruqayyah (a)'s[88] remembrance. We laid a green cloth down. I don't know where he'd found a bunch of thistles, but he put those down too. He wrote Ya Husayn and Ya Ruqayyah on a few small clay pots. We put some clay, lamps, candles, dates, and food down one by one, and throughout this time, he was whispering *masa'ib* and wailing. When we laid the table, we both sat down and cried to our heart's content.

He put up black cloth all over the house and downloaded a whole host of *nowhehs*, and once he had set up the sound system, he told my mum to play them before and after the *majlis*. He took out a bag of headbands he'd bought at Pasaj-e-Quds in Qom and hung them from the ceiling with pins, like a memorial for the martyrs. He suggested getting Ya Husayn written on a piece of Styrofoam with a laser and then to hang it on the black cloth behind the reciter. He went, had it done and came back. We both painted the Styrofoam red together and during this, we were constantly reciting *salawat* for the safety of Ayatollah Khamenei and Imam Mahdi (aj). He had to have a picture of a martyred Defender of the Shrine in the *majlis*. He quickly made a small collage with Photoshop and printed it. When I was bringing the

---

87. The whispered supplication of Imam Ali (a) which he recited in Masjid al-Kufah at midnight.

88. Lady Ruqayyah (a) was the youngest daughter of Imam Husayn (a) who attained martyrdom at the tender age of four in the prisons of Yazid after her father's head was presented to her.

stool for him to hang it up, he looked back at me and said, "My photo is missing. Insha'Allah next year, put mine up too." My heart was shaking because he was continuously talking about martyrdom. My blood came to a boil and I said to him, "Not everyone's blood is worthy of martyrdom!"

I accompanied him on his fortieth visit to Qom and Jamkaran. He put everything in the back seat and laid a blanket over it. He made a small cot for Ali. In those days, Ali was trying to stand up. He enjoyed it when Ali held the chair and stand up. He wanted to have a lot of children so they could misbehave in the back of the car and fight amongst themselves. He dreamt to say, "Ali, sit down, Zaynab, put the window up, Husayn! Am I not speaking to you? Fatemeh, look after your sister." All the way to Qom, we listened to a CD by the name of 'Pure Advice'[89]. He put on a *nowheh* by Sayyid Reza Narimani every now and then in which he recited, "O' Lady Ma'sumah, intercede for us in Paradise." He turned the volume down and started reciting himself when he got excited. Our diet on the way there and back consisted mainly of gummy sweets. Whenever he was coming back, he bought masghati[90] from the shops outside of Jamkaran. He bought it just for the one or two walnuts on top of it.

On Thursday night, we went to the shrine [of Lady Ma'sumah (a)]. We agreed to meet at Shabestan-e Imam Khomeini (ra)[91] after *ziyarah*. I saw from afar that Mohsen was engrossed in a book of *duas*. He was deep in thought, so I didn't go to him so he could have some alone time. I watched him from far. When the

---

89. 'نکته های ناب'
90. An Iranian sweet made from starch, sugar, rosewater, and pistachio. Saffron and cardamom can also be used to make it.
91. The main hall in Lady Ma'sumah (a)'s shrine where congregational prayers and other programmes are held

dua (Dua Kumayl)⁹² started, I went to sit next to him. He became restless during the *dua* and in between his tears, he brought his head close to me and said, "Pray I'm given a clean slate! Zahra, pray Allah forgives me, and I'm martyred!" He wailed like a mother who'd lost her young son, "What if He doesn't accept me?! What if I'm left behind?!" I don't know why, but whenever he opened the discussion of martyrdom at home or in the car, I fell into a bad mood. "Now there aren't any more tours for the Defenders of the Shrine, and you've been left behind as a narrator of the stories of the martyrs! Insha'Allah they've left you for [the war against] Israel!" He replied, "No! I want my name to be written as one of the defenders of the shrine of Lady Zaynab (a)!" After Dua Kumayl, we went to Jamkaran. I was fed up with him because he kept talking about leaving and martyrdom. Mohsen went inside the mosque and I went to a room where they were answering religious questions. I told the scholar there everything inside my heart, "My husband wants to go to Syria. I know that if he goes, he'll be martyred, and I feel restless. I both want him to go and achieve his heart's desire but letting him go is difficult for me!" The scholar advised me with great wisdom, "Well, this path and where it ends is a wish for many of us, but we weren't blessed to follow it. If he can achieve this, help him. Don't feel restless, and on the contrary, support him, your support will definitely not be unrewarded." The scholar's words were very comforting to me. I sat on the carpets laid in the courtyard of the mosque and gazed at the fabulous architecture. I started reviewing the events of the future in my mind; Mohsen will go, he will be martyred, they'll bring his body back and a bullet would have struck his chest. I didn't

---

92. Dua Kumayl is a supplication narrated from Imam Ali (a) who taught it to his companion, Kumayl ibn Ziyad. This supplication is recommended to be recited on Thursday nights and on the 15th of Shaban.

think about the possibility of captivity for even a moment, and as soon as my mind strayed towards it, I refuted it immediately. It was important for me that his head, face, and chest be intact so I could feel him. As I was imagining myself kissing his ice-cold face, I felt as if he was no longer beside me.

The thought that the reason he didn't attain martyrdom was because of his mother was like a thorn in his side. He said he wasn't martyred last time as he hadn't informed his mother. He decided to go to Mashhad altogether in the month of Ramadan and ask her for permission there. At the train station, he bought a lot of snacks. Popcorn, crisps, gummies, mineral water, soda, you name it. Ali was climbing all over the carriage. He wanted to walk again. He was constantly going to the door of the coupe because he wanted to go out. Mohsen took his hand and he waddled with him from one end of the carriage to the other. I heard him saying from outside the coupe, "When my son is around, my heart is happy! When my heart is happy, my son is around!" When he came back to the coupe, he laughed and said, "Zahra, come and take a video of the fruit of our love!"

Before even opening our luggage, he said, "Let's visit the shrine [of Imam Rida (a)]." It was a twenty-minute walk from the hotel. After Maghrib prayers, he said he was going back to the hotel to prepare *iftar*. We got lost on the way back and when we reached the hotel, an hour had passed since *iftar*. He'd laid the table, but he hadn't touched the food. After *iftar*, he wanted to go to the shrine again. We were exhausted and his parents said they had no energy left to go again. I couldn't let him go alone. This time, we took a taxi, and we did *ziyarah* like this every day. We were listening to a speech by Agha Qara'ati[93] in the Jami' Razavi Courtyard[94] but when we looked around, we saw that Ali was nowhere to be found. Mohsen looked for him and found him, and said light-heartedly, "If he's so quick when he can't walk, what are we going to do when he learns how to walk?!"

We went to explore the shrine and we were wandering about the courtyards. He kept talking about Syria and martyrdom, and I was getting fed up as usual. I told him, "I swear to God, I'll pray! I promise!" He kept giving me his phone and telling me to take a photo for them to use after his martyrdom. He was constantly asking me to talk to his mum so she would be willing to let him go and be martyred. We took turns to look after Ali to let the other go in for *ziyarah*. Sometimes he said, "I want to go with my son." He took Ali to the *zareeh*[95] and took selfies with him. As I was coming back from *ziyarah*, I saw a woman doing calligraphy in Dar al-Hujjah[96]. I went back to him and said, "You say something, and I say something, then she'll write it." We decided we were going to frame it above the bookshelf in our bedroom. Mohsen told her to write, "In those days, martyrdom was an open door and now, a narrow opening. There is still an opportunity for martyrdom. One must purify their heart." I then told her to write, "Inform the beloved of my exhausted whispers, no love will remain in my heart apart from yours." He wouldn't take his shoes into the shrine in a plastic bag. He only

---

93. Hojjat ul-Islam Mohsen Qara'ati is a well-known Iranian scholar who specialises in the propagation of Islam in the Western countries
94. The largest courtyard in Imam Rida (a)'s shrine
95. Farsi for 'mausoleum' or 'tomb', generally used for the metal cage put around the grave of a great personality
96. One of the halls in the shrine of Imam Rida (a)

gave it in at the *kafshdari*⁹⁷ and he still queued up when it was busy. He explained that if you are invited somewhere, will you go in with your shoes? It is only respectful to leave them at the door.

I went to talk to his mother one or two times about him leaving and martyrdom, but she thought I was joking and said, "He can go, but he can't be martyred!" While we were sitting by the fountain in Azadi Courtyard⁹⁸, reciting the *ziyarah*, we heard people shouting 'La ilaha illa Allah⁹⁹'. When we looked around, we saw some people bringing a coffin draped in cashmere out from the shrine. As they were passing by, my mother-in-law asked someone who it was, and they answered, "He was a youth who left behind a child." His mother started tearing up, and he took advantage of this opportunity. He said, "You see mum, this is the world! If we aren't martyred, we'll die. If your son is martyred, you'll be happy that at least his Hereafter is sorted, but if he is involved in an accident and dies, what will you do then?"

On the eve of the twenty-first of Ramadan¹⁰⁰, we visited the shrine before Maghrib prayers, and we took our *iftar* inside the courtyard. On the way, he texted his mum to pray for his martyrdom that night. He pleaded from me in the Jami' Razavi Courtyard to ask his mother to pray for him. He pretended as if he was fiddling with the flowers on the carpets as I said to my mother-in-law, "Mum! Mohsen is driving me crazy! Can you just pray for him please?!" Eventually, during the Maghrib *adhan*,

---

97. *Kafshdari*s are tills in mosques and shrines where people give their shoes in for safekeeping before entering
98. A courtyard in the shrine of Imam Rida (a), and it is better to enter from this courtyard as it is at the Imam (a)'s feet
99. Arabic for 'there is no god but Allah'
100. One of the Nights of Decree

his mother couldn't take it any longer, and to his delight, she prayed for him, her eyes welling with tears. During those ten days, he completed the whole Quran once. We stayed in the shrine until morning. We prayed together, we read *duas*, we recited the Quran, we recited Hadith ul-Kisa and eventually, he recited a small *masa'ib* for the two of us at the end of the night. That night, he was constantly saying, "O' Allah, forgive me, my sins, my eyes…"

He really enjoyed this *ziyarah* [to Mashhad]. He said that we should come to Imam Rida (a) for ten days every Ramadan. After eating *suhur*[101], we rested for an hour and then we left for the shrine again. This time, we gathered our belongings and luggage and put them in safekeeping. Our return ticket was booked for ten o'clock. We recited the final *idhn ul-dukhul*[102].

We spent the eve of the twenty-third [of Ramadan][103] on the train. When his mother and father went to sleep, he quietly switched on the flashlight on his phone. He was on the top bunk and I was on the bottom, opposite to him. He was softly reciting *duas* and shedding tears, and they were falling on his pillow.

He was still enchanted by Mashhad, and he didn't feel like going to work. The first day he went, he came back quickly. He had taken the day off. As soon as he stepped foot in the house, his phone rang. He said, "Yeah, yeah, I'm almost at the base." I exclaimed, "How come you're at home?" He said, overjoyed, "They're looking for soldiers for Syria right now!" He ran down the stairs two at a time. He was constantly texting me, "Pray it happens." I was comforting him by saying, "Okay my dear, I have made an oath to recite *Salawat* and Ziyarah Ashura." He

---

101. A meal eaten before Fajr prayers before beginning a fast
102. A small ziyarah recited before entering the shrine to ask for permission from the Imam (a) to enter
103. One of the Nights of Decree

was very restless. He was constantly on alert, waiting for that phone call. He cried all day. He didn't touch any food. His small body was wasting away. "What if they don't take me?! I'll die of grief if they don't take me! What will I do with myself if the war ends and I don't achieve my fate?!" he said. Every day, they ruined his hope by saying, "It's not clear whether we'll take you, the priority is with those who haven't gone before, you also have a small child." I made an oath to recite Dua of Muqatil ibn Suleyman[104] so his duty become clear.

On the 17th of July, he called at nine o'clock and said abruptly, "I have to go tonight." I felt as if someone had poured a bucket of ice-cold water on my head. My whole body trembled. He continued, "Go and leave Ali at your mum's house, let's quickly sort out our business." Tears were pouring from my eyes. I dropped Ali off and waited for him in the car outside of the apartment. When I saw his motorbike from afar, I wiped my tears. I thought to myself, "His heart mustn't tremble for even a moment." His own eyes were completely bloodshot. My heart was burning. "Why are you crying?" I asked.

"From joy. Why are you crying?" he replied.

"Because of your joy!" I told him. My face was drenched [in tears]. I was cleaning my tears from underneath my chador so he wouldn't realise, but he found out eventually. "Are you crying? Isn't my happiness important for you?" he joked.

"I feel as if I can't breathe properly!" I replied. I read him the same verse of poetry again, "I perceive your love a little more!"

"I'm coming back, Zahra!" he said.

"You're going and won't come back!" I answered.

---

104. A supplication narrated from Imam Sajjad (a) by his companion, Muqatil ibn Syleyman. It is recited for an immediate response. Muqatil himself is quoted to have said: "If you read this supplication and your prayer is not answered, you can curse Muqatil."

"I'm coming back, I swear to you!"
"I swear you aren't coming back!"
"How do you know?"
"I can feel it in my heart!"

Chapter II

THE ONE THAT CATCHES YOUR EYE!

HOSEIN MUSA-ARAB

THE MARTYR'S FRIEND

When we were younger, we tried anything we could smoke, as long as it was legal; shisha, tree branches and rolled-up paper. His grandmother, who we all called grandma, held *majalis* every Thursday night and they recited Hadith ul-Kisa, Dua Kumayl and Ziyarah Ashura, so every Thursday afternoon, we went to clean her courtyard and water the plants. An old shisha on the shelf in her room caught our eye. We were always planning to quickly take it without any fear of our families and smoke to our hearts' content. Eventually, on one of these Thursdays, we found our opportunity. Grandma had left the shisha prepared and ready on the bench for her guests. At this time, we decided to make a vital move, according to ourselves of course. When grandma went to check on the tea, we went and attacked the shisha. Despite the pressing conditions, we still wanted to blow the smoke out in circles. We didn't know how to. Mohsen kept blowing his own horn, saying he knew how to smoke from his nose. As he was showing off, he eventually started coughing, and that's how we got caught. Of course, we had to take a good beating as well!

When he was thirteen or fourteen, he started working in a supermarket. I spent most of my time with him. In those days, we couldn't buy cigarette papers, so we were forced to use empty paper. We rolled up the scrunched-up receipts from behind the till, lit them and smoked it. We then put a gherkin in a piece of bread and ate it with a soda.

We really wanted to smoke cigarettes. We trimmed the branches of a tree, lit the end, and smoked it. In our neighbourhood, there were a lot of free lands. We went there or stood behind an old wall so no one could see us. They had built a wall around some land which was about three or four metres high. If someone were to fall from the top, their head would split. We nicknamed this wall 'The Wall of Death'. We always climbed on top of it just for fun.

As we always spent time together, everyone asked us if we were twins. We looked nothing like each other, except the fact that my nose was bent, and the end of Mohsen's nose drooped. We were neighbours; we both lived on Omid Road just off Shuhada Street. At the top of the alleyway, there was a dairy shop which belonged to Agha Abbasiyan, and we called that alleyway the dairy shop alleyway. In the afternoons, Agha Abbasiyan closed the shop but left the small window open so if a customer came, they could call him. His house was connected to the shop and he fell sleep in the afternoons. When we were sure he was sleeping deeply, we popped our heads through the window and start screaming his name. He came to the window sleepily with swollen eyes and we asked, "Can we have a pack of small chewing gum?" At that point, he completely lost it.

The neighbours were fed up with us. One of them was a man who was a bit strange. He really hated eating the fat at the end of an animal's tail, so we went up to him, asked him if he wanted tail fat and ran away. We always hid by the hawthorn tree in our neighbourhood, but one time, he caught us and gave us a good beating!

One time on the eve of Nowruz, we decided to sell goldfish. We named the fish tank Mohsein, which was a combination of our names, Hosein and Mohsen. We put four goldfish in one thirty-by-forty metre fish tank. We also had a challenge. It was common back then to put a bottle cap at the bottom of the fish tank and the children tossed twenty-five Toman coins in the water. If the coin fell inside the cap, they won a goldfish. As we were children and didn't know much, we used a jar lid instead of a bottle cap. Whoever threw a coin won a fish, and that's the story of how we lost all our fish.

In those days, we set up a makeshift stall outside Agha Abbasiyan's shop using a discarded fruit crate. We expected people to buy chewing gum that was normally sold for ten tomans at our price of fifty tomans, but no one was foolish enough to buy from us at this price. At the end of the day, we were forced to just chew them all ourselves, our pockets empty.

We swam in the local river except on Fridays, when we went to the swimming pool. There was a small river in a garden just off Vilashahr Roundabout which was around two metres deep. Even though it flowed quite strongly, we took the risk. Around fifty to sixty metres ahead, there was a hatch where all the water went down, the most dangerous part of the river. All the water had to do was to pull us into the hatch and we'd get stuck and drown. We didn't care though. We dived from a bridge and played in the water.

One day, we decided to have a party. We bought some sheep fat to skewer and grill beside the river. We went and washed it in the river and then grilled it over the fire. As we were getting ready to go back, we saw two dead dogs in the river, merely metres away from where we washed the meat. We were going to vomit.

We went to the park and played tennis. When we were tired, we rested by a tree and told each other our wishes. When someone walked past with a phone in their hands, we said, "It's not fair! We're sixteen, seventeen and still don't have a phone!" We were always miserable about what we didn't have, whether it was a bicycle or a motorcycle.

One time, we decided to go to Isfahan to buy trousers . We got on an intercity bus and we bought two grey Turkish cotton pairs of trousers. A few days later, we decided to check if we could find the same kind of trousers in Najafabad. We found a shop selling them, so we asked the shopkeeper how much he was selling them for. He was selling it ten thousand tomans cheaper than in Isfahan. We were so regretful, and we didn't forget this for a very long time.

One time, we got into a fight at school. Mohsen said in his thick Najafabadi accent, "Where can I hit you, so you don't die?" I replied, "Wherever you want!" We never forgot these two sentences, and we said them to each other and laughed.

For a while, we met up at the Miqdad Centre. We recited together. Mohsen was always the lead reciter of our group. We were reciting in the hall and halfway through the song, the electricity cut out and the music stopped, but Mohsen wasn't fazed and continued reciting. A few seconds later, the music started playing again and we continued. That day, he won a prize for his self-confidence.

We were always together during school, whether it was elementary school, middle school, or high school. Even after our entrance exams in 2008, we chose the same university and major; control technology at the Applied Science University of Alavijeh. Our journeys from Najafabad to Alavijeh were adventures themselves. During our first semester, we left our motorcycle at his grandmother's house and walked for almost three kilometres to reach the highway. Our only hope was the minibus taking the teachers to Alavijeh. There were only seven or eight of us and we eventually convinced them to take us. Mohsen, two others and I sat in the front beside the driver. After about half an hour, the women started asking, "Why did you let these single boys on the bus?!" In this short one-hour journey, we managed to mess everything up. They didn't let us on the bus after that, and the same headache of finding a way to university continued. We left at six in the morning and most of the time, we didn't get there in time for our eight o'clock class. We changed vehicle four or five times from Najafabad on the way to our university. It didn't make a difference to us whether it was a car, lorry, or truck.

After two months, we finally convinced a driver to take only us students in his minibus. At first, he was complaining that we didn't have enough people and it wasn't worth it, but we promised we would find him passengers. We got the girls and boys on and tell him to leave! The minibus didn't have a stereo, so we bought a plug which had a flash drive slot and plugged it in where the cigarette lighter was. Every day, someone put new songs on their flash drive and played it in the minibus. Mohsen didn't like these songs, but if it was a woman singing, he turned it off immediately. Most of the time, he put his earphones in and listened to his *nowhehs*. As soon as he put his flash drive in, everyone knew this was Mohsen Hojaji's flash drive. He loved Mahmoud Karimi's voice. Due to his great people skills, he managed to keep everyone happy. He could have easily been a playboy, but he wasn't into those kinds of things.

To tell the truth, even though Mohsen had a beard and was a lover of the Ahlulbayt (as), from the day he stepped foot in the Shaheed Kazemi Institute and joined the IRGC, his life completely changed. He got married soon after his compulsory military service. One of his wishes during his childhood, while we were resting by the tree, was for us to get married to two twin sisters on the day of Mab'ath[105], but he didn't wait for me. I kept making excuses about my financial condition and so on, but

---

105. The 27th of Rajab, the day the Holy Prophet (s) was chosen by Allah as the Prophet

Mohsen was optimistic. When I finally got married, we started meeting up with our wives, but this Mohsen wasn't the same Mohsen I always knew. He still joked around. We got together and chatted, but he had just changed completely. The first time he wanted to go to Syria, I wasn't opposed to it, but the second time, I told him, "Don't go, think about your wife, your child, your life!" but he replied, "Pray I don't return ashamed, pray I return with my head held high!"

One night, one of my friends called and told me he was waiting outside of my door in the car. His voice was trembling. He knew I wasn't active on social media. I asked, "What's going on?" He replied, "Mohsen has been taken captive!" I couldn't believe it. I was telling myself he's joking because we joked with each other like this. When he showed me the photo of him being taken captive, I slapped my head with my hands. I couldn't control myself. That night, I was praying that the news wasn't true or that the enemy was playing mind games. I remembered the days when we joked with him, "Your face will stay like a martyr's face!"

On the day of his funeral, I didn't go forward. I wanted to speak with Mohsen privately and I couldn't do so as it was too busy. I waited for a time when I could visit his grave peacefully.

Hosein Najafiyan

The martyr's friend

You couldn't say he was a gangster! Us Najafabadis call people like him chivalrous. The first image I remember of him was as a thin boy with a scruffy moustache and long hair that flowed over his ears. He spoke in a very thick Najafabadi accent. He always emphasized the second letter of the word. He said Hassan or Hussein, and he said Reza as Ressa. He was well-mannered and sociable. We went to the park with our friends and played a game to see who would pay. He always lost. He bought the kebab and bread and brought it back. During those days, he worked as an electrician in a building. One time, he made a few mistakes while connecting the wires in one of his friend's houses. He was saying, "When I ring the doorbell, the lights of the toilet switch on, and when I switch the bedroom light on, the corridor lights switch on."

I don't understand why or how, but he started attending the Shaheed Kazemi Institute. Day by day, his appearance started changing. Soon, this Mohsen wasn't the same Mohsen we knew from day one. We understood from his actions and behaviour that he was in love with Haj Ahmad Kazemi. He took me to visit the grave of Shaheed Kazemi several times. It wasn't very appealing to me for the first few times. I don't what he was thinking to himself, but he went every week. We went to Takht-e Foolad on two different motorcycles. He stood back around two or three metres and sent his *salaam*, and then he sat beside the grave. In the end, he walked backwards away from the grave and performed an army salute to bid farewell. Before then, I only knew of one Shaheed Kazemi whose funeral I took part in, but I didn't know him well. Mohsen had got to know Haj Ahmad well through the institute. He was willing to go from Najafabad to Isfahan just to say *salaam*, talk to him and cry a little and come back. He even complained to him, but we just played around. We walked around amongst the graves. We all met up afterwards at the Turkish kebab shops on Feyz Roundabout.

The institute took a trip by bus to help the impoverished. Mohsen, one worker and I stayed behind until the shops opened to buy some equipment. We set off in Agha Khalili's Dacia. The worker sat in the back straight away and fell asleep. As we got to the outskirts of Najafabad, I went and bought five or six cigarettes and put them in my pocket. After we drove a little, I took one of them out of my pocket, but he took it from my hand. I asked him, "What was that for?" He replied, "There's no need for these bad habits!" He started talking about his past and that smoking cigarettes was just a memory for us. I smirked and said, "Well, you stopped, not me!" He started doing my head in, so I promised him I wouldn't smoke for the whole trip just to get him off my back. I then put my foot on the gas and started driving at one hundred and seventy, one hundred and eighty kilometres per hour. The police eventually pulled us over. Mohsen was completely fed up. I felt as if he was about to hit me. He scolded me, saying, "Didn't I tell you to go slower?!" To calm him down, I laughed and remarked, "What's the worst that can happen? All they're going to do is give us a fine, I'll pay it myself!" I took the fine and went back to the car, but I saw him sitting in the driver's seat. He said to me, "You're driving too fast. You're going to get us killed!" I replied, "Go and sit on the other side before we get into a fight!" Eventually, I managed to get him to sit in the passenger seat by promising him I'd drive slower. When I sat in the car, I told him, "I'm fed up! I need to smoke!" He got so annoyed and said, "What's wrong with you!? Why can't you just act like a human?!" We were getting late. I realised he wasn't watching and started driving fast again. Eventually, I got pulled over again. I can't even explain how irate Mohsen was. I told him, "Don't move until I get back! Don't get out, okay?" I went to the police officer and said to him respectfully, "To tell you the truth, we have a commander in the car, and he has a meeting in Fereydoun Shahr." I showed him the fine from last time. He said to me, "Just try to drive a little slower from now on, son!" I quickly got back in the car and when I told him what I did, he got angry about why I lied! I just said to him, "Leave it, man! Stop being a goody-two-shoes!"

I was the photographer on the trip. I don't remember why, but I filmed an interview with Mohsen. I forced him to sit in front of the camera, and I still have the video. He kept trying to make excuses. He kept saying, "That man needs my help, interview someone else who means something, I don't want to." He set up classes for the children of the village and did some building on the side. Half an hour before we were supposed to finish working, he showered and came back neat and tidy with combed hair, while we were all exhausted, sweaty and couldn't do anything let alone take care of ourselves! Needless to say, a few of the guys were bothered by that!

One night, they slaughtered a sheep to cook *abgoosht*[106] for us. A few of the builders took the sheep liver at night and a little later, I heard Mohsen also went with them. I said, "I'll sort them out." I went to the medical room and took a few packs of laxatives. I broke them up and ground them into a powder. I told the chef to put the powder in their bowls when he pours the *abgoosht*. I also said, "Just to be sure, let's mix some washing powder in their food too!" We gave it to them to eat. I

---

106. Abgoosht is a traditional Iranian dish which is a sort of meat stew slow cooked with chickpeas and beans and eaten with bread

don't know what their stomachs were made of, but they were completely fine!

After he enlisted in the army, I saw him on the road a few times. He'd become religious, really religious, but he still called me in the same way, "Hossein! How are you?" I replied, "Have you still not become a human?" He laughed and said, "No, I won't become a human." At one time, he constantly texted me that he was in the shrine of Lady Ma'sumah (a) and was doing *ziyarah* on my behalf. I said to him, "Why are you being silly? Why are you going to Jamkaran? If you say *salaam* from here, Imam Mahdi (aj) will reply to you." On one of these journeys, his child fell over at home and hurt his head badly. I thought to myself sarcastically, "I hope Lady Ma'sumah (a) gives you your reward!" He recited, but I didn't like his voice. I said, "Recitation isn't your forte!" The first time, he recited Dua Kumayl in the couples gathering at the institute and he read it completely wrong. I was sitting behind him and laughing. I was teasing him constantly and asked, "Who told you to read even though you don't know how to read?!" The following week, he said again, "I'll recite!" We didn't have a reciter, so I said, "For God's sake, okay!" He read it all without a mistake. He slowly got better and eventually, he also started reciting *nowhehs*.

The last time I saw him, I said to him, "Why is your child so strange?" He asked what I meant, and I explained, "Look at other children, they talk, they laugh, your child doesn't do anything!" He replied, "Go and do your own thing and don't be nosy, it's none of your business!"

Alireza Mohammadrezaei

The martyr's friend

Mine and Mohsen's friendship reminds me of bang snaps[107]. Our families didn't allow us to make them, so Mohsen and I went looking for them under rocks. We were so excited when they exploded! Mohsen lived in the Kesra Neighbourhood or according to the Najafabadis, at the end of Shuhada Street. Since his childhood, he attended the then newly established mosque in the neighbourhood. His *akhlaq*[108] teacher at the time was an open-minded veteran by the name of Agha Habibollahi. We studied together in the Shaheed Hoseini Elementary School. Until grade three, I was the best student and Mohsen was second-best, but from grade four onwards, Mohsen overtook me. He was skinny and I was broad-chested, and maybe it was for this reason I didn't really get on with him. I hung out with the bigger kids and our relationship was more academic. He became a bit more confident from his regular visits to the mosque. On Thursdays, he recited Ziyarah Ashura with a beautiful tune at school. Sometimes, he even recited the Quran with the rest of us.

Mohsen's father sold their house and moved to Ja'farabad. I slowly drifted apart from him. During high school, he chose to study craft while I studied mathematics and physics. After several years, we bumped into each other in the library. I was taken aback; he looked like a proper man, with slicked-back hair, wearing a white shirt and spinning a large grape-red

---

107. Makeshift firecrackers which are made by putting a small explosive in a cigarette paper.
108. Morals and ethics.

tasbih. He exclaimed, "Oh my God! Alireza!" We hugged tightly and exchanged pleasantries. I asked, "Do you still recite?" He lowered his head and didn't answer. He changed the subject, telling me he'd gone to university and was studying control technology. I was still giving my entrance exams. He said he was stuck on a math problem and needed help. Even though I was busy with my entrance exams, I agreed to help him with his work. We decided to go to his home. His build and face had changed completely. Despite this, his room was still dedicated to the martyrs; there were *chafiyehs*[109], flags, headbands, and photos of the martyrs everywhere. Slowly, we became close again; he was the first person to call me 'dear brother' in a text message. He tried not to dress up too nicely [when going out]. He was scared a non-*mahram*[110] lady would look at him and commit *haram*. One time, he dressed in chic clothes; he was wearing a beret with a special scarf that was tied like a belt. He was also wearing a suit, but he felt as if girls will be attracted to him if he went out like this, so he quickly changed his clothes.

In the summers, he did electrical work for a building and put a lot of effort into improving his skills at the job. One time, he got off at Najafabad Highway late at night. Two men brandishing knives on a motorbike chased him to kill him. He said, "That night, I saw death in front of my eyes." He managed to escape with great difficulty. One day, he said, "That day in the library when you asked me if I still recite eulogies for the Ahlulbayt (as) was truly a wake-up call for me."

We went to visit the martyrs. We tied our 'Ya Zahra' headbands to our motorbike speedometers. Mine was yellow

---

109. A *chafiyeh* is a black and white chequered scarf which is a symbol of the resistance.
110. A non-*mahram* lady is any woman who is not your mother, sister, grandmother, aunt, daughter, niece, granddaughter, etc.

and Mohsen's was green. We were able to express our views to each other with ease. He gathered information about martyrs. He had read that every Thursday night, the martyrs went to Wadi al-Salam, next to Imam Husayn (a). When we went to visit the graves of the martyrs, he told me, "Don't recite Fatihah, because that brings the martyrs back here and cuts their visit to Imam Husayn (a) short."

We slept in graves at night because this is where we will be at the end. In the darkness, we discussed the lectures of Agha Raefipour[111] about Mahdism and freemasonry. Mohsen loved reading books and those we preferred speaking to the non-religious. We didn't care whether the person was ten or fifty years old, and we always brought them to the cemetery of the martyrs. I found them, got to know them, and then found an excuse to bring them to Mohsen in the cemetery.

I got onto the person's motorbike to go for a drive together, then midway I found an excuse or an issue with the motorbike and called my friend Mohsen for help. Mohsen came and during conversation, he brought up the topic. In 2016, there were one or two typical non-believers that I lead to Mohsen and for several nights. they had discussions with Mohsen in the cemetery. I couldn't believe he guided them to the path.

He got to know Shaheed [Ahmad] Kazemi from somewhere and he decided to visit Takht-e Foolad. I hadn't ever been there before. We took refuge in the martyrs of Najafabad and prayed for a chance to make a connection with them. We decided to go via Dorcheh Highway. By chance, Mohsen told me to turn the motorcycle towards Abrisham and we found Takht-e Foolad without asking anyone for directions. We took that as a good

---

111. Ali Akbar Raefipour is an Iranian lecturer who is best known for his lectures on religion, sectarianism, and freemasonry amongst other topics.

omen and made our way there. We visited Takht-e Foolad once every two or three nights or sometimes, even every night. I called it *ziyarah* from one shrine to another: the shrine of the martyrs of Najafabad to the shrine of the martyrs of Takht-e Foolad. We delivered their *salaams* to each other. He showed immense respect to Haj Ahmad Kazemi. One time, I leaned on his grave and Mohsen said irritated, "Please sit respectfully!"

On the way, we listened to *nowhehs*. Mohsen had earphones and he rested his head on my shoulder so he could have one and I could have the other. He played two *nowhehs* more than the rest; '*When Your Shrine Is Paradise, Why Would I Need Heaven*[112]' and '*I Went Crazy from the Tears During Your Masa'ib*[113]'. We were in love with this *ziyarah* from one shrine to the other. Nothing stopped us, not the cold of winter, nor the heat of summer. In the winters, we alternated between using mine and his motorcycle. We left in the afternoon and returned at night, which took around six hours. If one of us cheated and went on their own, they had to pay a fine; they either had to buy ice cream or dinner.

A few martyred children were buried in Takht-e Foolad. He chose one of the martyred girls as his daughter and I chose one of the martyred boys as my son. I said to Mohsen, "Play games with my child until I come back," or, "Today, my son broke the window."

We had special love for the anonymous martyrs and the martyred divers, especially the mothers of the martyrs. When we saw the mothers beside the grave of a martyr, we went and asked for their prayers. Mohsen asked them to especially pray for us. One of the mothers of the martyrs said, "May Allah grant

---

112. 'وقتی حرمت بهشته، چه حاجت به جنته'

113. 'دیوونگی ام رو از اشک پای روضه هات گرفتم'

you wives who are like you." This prayer became our motto. Mohsen said to her, "No, aunty! Ask Him to grant us wives who are better than us!" From then on, we started working on bettering ourselves. We worked hard to build ourselves. Every time we went to Takht-e Foolad, we tried to befriend one of the martyrs and extend this friendship.

Sometimes on the way back from Takht-e Foolad, we went to a *majlis*. The organisation generally suffered from a lack of funds, so Mohsen and I always bought some bread, cheese, and cucumbers for the gathering. Mohsen had learnt wise words from his father, who said, "The giving hand never remains empty."

When I was choosing my major, I only had one university and one subject in mind: control technology at the Applied Science University of Alavijeh, the same major and university as Mohsen. We wanted to spend more time together. By chance, I was accepted, and I was starting my first term whilst Mohsen was beginning his third.

The minibus we took from Najafabad to our university was full of single people, and it was a mixed bus. Whenever I tried to mess about, Mohsen hit me on the head with his *tasbih* and scolded me. He was always protecting me. He had read the book 'The Soft Sands of the Pavilion'[114] and he didn't stop talking about how great it was on the minibus. He then passed it around amongst the students so they could read it one by one. This book completely changed the way some of the girls behaved.

We decided to write a treatise on *akhlaq*, and we swore to remain loyal to it. We made each other sign it. We even swore to Imam Mahdi (aj) that we would remain loyal to it. Whenever we swore, we had to pay a penalty, which could be paid in *Salawat*,

---

114. خاکهای نرم کوشک

prayers, money or fasting. We made a few rules, especially for the minibus. No one could play music unless it was permissible and wasn't arousing. If someone tried to mess around, we scolded them and throw them off the bus. Mohsen enforced all the rules, as I was backing him as his muscles. Mohsen and I sat at the front as like managers. We were in control of the front; we played *nowhehs*, turn them up and recite with them. We included eating healthily and permissibly on our treatise, so any kind of processed meat, baloney and soda was banned. Regarding clothing, we weren't allowed to wear short-sleeved shirts. Because of my height, I couldn't wear some kinds of clothes. I had to double the length of my sleeves to do so, but t-shirts were not allowed. He said to me, "Make a budget and wear nice clothes, but make sure they're appropriate." He also emphasised a lot on perfume, and he sprayed the same perfume they spray at the shrines on his neck.

Five unknown martyrs were buried beside the shrine of Imamzadeh Shamsudeen Muhammad[115] in Alavijeh, about six kilometres away from our university. We walked through the ruins and our shoes tore and became dirty. The other students from the university sat and smoked shisha beside the fountain near the shrine and they looked at us like losers because we didn't join them.

I found out that Mohsen liked one of the girls on the minibus, but not just anyone; it was a girl who wore short clothes, makeup and a scarf which barely covered her hair. After a little while, I found out the girl had told him, "You want to change me, but I don't want to change," and thus, there was no happy ending for them.

---

115. Imamzadeh Shamsuddin Muhammad was the son of Imam Kadhim (a).

The atmosphere of the university was one where men and women could mingle freely. When the boys acted inappropriately, Mohsen fought them. These scuffles happened constantly and every time, I came to back him up and we taught them how to behave properly. I was a wrestler and Mohsen knew karate well. One night, we decided to go to the gym together. While sparring, I put him in a headlock and kept pressing down on his neck. He was in so much pain, he punched me in the face!

For a while, we were in love with doing *ziyarah* of Lady Ma'sumah (a), and despite having no money whatsoever, we worked just so we could pay the expenses for our trip. We walked from the shrine of Imamzadeh Sayyid Jamaluddin[116]. As soon as we reached the shrine with tired and blistered feet, we separated. We sat in separate corners, recited *duas* and established a connection with her. As we considered Lady Zahra (a) our mother, we did *ziyarah* twice in Qom upon the advice of Ayatollah Nokhudaki, once to do *ziyarah* of Lady Ma'sumah (a) and once to do *ziyarah* of Lady Zahra (a). We felt as if Lady Zahra (a) herself was buried there. We especially recited Fatihah[117] for Ayatollah Bahjat (ra)[118]. The Shaykhan Cemetery[119] held a great position in our eyes. We frequented the graves of Shaheed Zayn ad-Din[120] and his brother as well. We then walked to Masjid

---

116. Imamzadeh Sayyid Jamaluddin was the son of Imam Kadhim (a) and his shrine is on the outskirts of the city of Qom.
117. If someone has passed away, it is recommended to recite Surah Fatihah for them.
118. Ayatollah Mohammad Taqi Bahjat Fumani (ra) (d. 2009) was a great scholar, mystic and marja'. He was a student of Ayatollah Mirza Husayn Naini and studied mysticism under Allamah Qadi Tabatabaei.
119. A cemetery close to the shrine of Lady Ma'sumah (a) where many great personalities are buried, including Zakariyyah ibn Adam, the representative of Imam Rida and Imam Jawad (as) in Qom, and Mirza Qummi, the author of *al-Qawanin*.
120. Shaheed Mahdi Zayn ad-Din was one of the youngest and most prominent commanders during the Iran-Iraq War.

Jamkaran and we didn't leave until we had performed all the rites of the mosque.

Sometimes, we didn't have enough time to travel, so we took our school bags with us. We got back to Najafabad at midnight, prayed Fajr at a local mosque and headed off to university straight away.

Mohsen went for his compulsory military service early for two reasons; one was he wanted to get married and the second was he wanted to go to Karbala. He went for military service and I continued studying and that was when everything ended. I couldn't go to Takht-e Foolad on my own. When his service in Dezful ended, he called me and said, "I want to go on a spiritual and fruitful journey." When I asked him where to, he replied, "We'll go to Qom from Dezful, and from there to Mashhad." When I agreed, he said, "Awesome!" Whenever he was excited, he opened his eyes wide and say, "Awesome!"

I went to Dezful and at ten o'clock in the morning, we got on a bus to Qom. We did *ziyarah* for a few hours and then we got on another bus to Mashhad. When we got there, he said, "Let's do *ghusl*[121] for *ziyarah* first," so we went to a public bath. He started walking slowly when we came closer to the shrine. He wasn't thinking about buying things at all; his mind was only on *ziyarah*. Mohsen recited all the *duas* and *ziyarahs* for us. I wanted to sneak away, but he said, "Come, let's sit together and recite the *ziyarah!*" We were carrying our bags with us for the whole journey. All our belongings were in one backpack. We slept wherever we could; in the shrine, in a Husayniyyah, even in the park. I didn't have enough money to make this journey, so

---

121. Major ritual ablution in which one washes their head and neck, their right side and then their left side. It is recommended to do so before visiting the graves of the Imams and Imamzadehs.

he covered all the costs. He was constantly saying, "I want to go on a spiritual journey with you at least once."

He started thinking about work. He told me, "We must work in jobs where we are helping Imam Mahdi (aj) from a cultural perspective." He worked in a bookstore for a while. He got married and I heard he had joined the IRGC. When they were reciting the 'aqd, I started crying, so he pulled me aside and said, "Don't cry otherwise I'll start to cry." We slowly drifted apart, but we always kept in touch via social media.

One day, one of my friends called me and said, "Have you heard Mohsen has been taken captive?!" I couldn't believe it. The Mohsen I knew was always quick and alert. It was impossible for him to fall into the enemy's hands so easily. The Alireza who had always been Mohsen's rock had let him down this time. They beheaded him, and I wasn't there to defend him, and this destroyed me from the inside.

Mohsen Hemmatiha

The martyr's friend

We really wanted to go and eat kebab. During the third break on Wednesdays[122], it was all we could think about, but the cameras were watching us from everywhere. Mohsen went to the headmaster's office and started talking to him, all the while sneaking looks at his monitor to check the blind spots of the cameras and eventually, he managed to find a way out. We sneaked out of school from an angle where the camera couldn't give us up to the headmaster. One week I paid for the kebab, the next week Mohsen paid.

We were both born in '91. We both studied electrical engineering at the Martyrs Culture School. He was one year ahead of me because I was born in the second half of the year. He always said, "I don't know why, but I like you more than the others." He was the assistant leader at a *baseej*[123] group and the year he graduated, he recommended me as his replacement and left. Even though he was held back one year for his entrance exams, I still couldn't catch up to him. He was accepted into the second year. This happened to me too. I was accepted into the second year and by chance, I enrolled in the same university in Alavijeh. Sometimes in the free hour between classes, Mohsen took us to the Imamzadeh near the university. If it was lunchtime, we ate lunch there next to the fountain. We spent our afternoons eating fruit and nuts. It was as if he was the leader of a caravan; he told us what time we were going to leave,

---

122. Contrary to the West, Thursday and Fridays are the weekend in Iran.
123. At every mosque in Iran, there is something called the *baseej* where children come together to learn about religion and the resistance while doing activities.

how long to do *ziyarah* for and when we should be at the minibus after eating lunch. He displayed these leadership qualities on the way from Najafabad to the university as well. We set off before sunrise and he played *nowhehs* or recited Ziyarah Ashura in the bus. He wanted to keep us up for *bayn al-tulu'ayn*[124]. On the days Mohsen didn't have class, the others played music in the minibus.

He didn't mess around when it came to the issue of hijab and he always did *amr bil ma'ruf*[125]. At university, he was like a security guard. At first, he went about enforcing the law and he reported the people doing wrong, but when he saw nothing was being done about it, he took matters into his own hands. In the cafeteria, one of the guys was standing behind a girl with a cup of tea and trying to flirt with her. Mohsen slowly went forward and made sure the guy could see him so he felt embarrassed, but that didn't work, so he went up to him and put his arm around his neck. I was watching what was happening carefully. At first, it looked as if they were talking in a friendly manner and I noticed from Mohsen's face that he wasn't going to let this go easily. Mohsen was slowly bringing him out into the open space behind the building and as soon as they turned, Mohsen took him by the collar and pressed him against the wall. They started hitting each other and according to our prior arrangement, I came quickly, and we gave him a good beating together.

Mathematics and physics were the banes of my existence and I was falling behind quite badly. Even though I was completely broke, I started going to a tutor. I don't know how Mohsen found out, but he said to me, "Why are you taking private classes while I'm here?!" I had heard that sometimes, he

---

124. The time between Fajr prayers and sunrise at which time it is recommended to stay awake.

125. Enjoining good; one of the obligations of the religion.

went and taught the lower classes instead of the teacher. I had also heard that he took brilliant notes and close to exam time, everyone took copies of them, and he gave the notes to everyone except the girls who didn't wear hijab properly. We started studying hard. For a while, he taught me in the Zahraiyyeh Library, and then we moved to his room, a room from which the smell of war and the frontlines emanated; I didn't recognise this smell, but I could sense it. He had hung up *chafiyehs* all around the room alongside photos of Shaheed Ahmad Kazemi. Amongst all the Xs and Ys and differentials and integrals, my attention was often drawn to the handful of soil which he said was from Shalamcheh, my mind wandered to the headbands. My heart wanted to find the answers quickly so I could just smell its perfume. When I said goodbye, I looked at his bookshelf and he introduced me to his books. He talked about a brilliant novel written by Reza Amirkhani.

During his training project, he started making many religious oaths; his professor was an intimidating man, and everyone tried to stay away from him as much as possible. He had no choice. That semester, only he was teaching that class. Amongst the thirty-five students in the class, only five passed including Mohsen. He laughed and said, "I didn't pass myself. It was only the oaths I made!"

He adhered to these oaths strongly. He said to me himself that he only graduated from the university due to those oaths. He asked Allah for something and in return, he recited a specific amount of Ziyarah Ashura or *salawats*. These oaths were quite common in Mohsen's family. Whenever I fell into trouble, I asked Mohsen to ask his mother to do an oath for me.

Alongside his classes, he also worked as an electrician in some buildings. For a while, I became his apprentice. We were happy when we were together. When I was working and wasn't really paying attention to my surroundings, sometimes he poured a cup of water down the back of my shirt or he shook the ladder slightly to frighten me. I also got my own back on him. Sometimes we ended up throwing water at each other in the courtyard of the house and we even used the hoses. Despite all this playing around, he was extremely sensitive over foul language, even for words like 'silly'. He gathered himself quickly and said, "You'll never reach anywhere with that kind of language!" He repeated this sentence often. He taught me morals and quite often, he paid me, or he got the landlord to pay me.

He didn't have enough money to print business cards, so we wrote his name and number on pieces of card. We wandered around and threw the cards into houses under construction which required an electrician. It worked quite well too. They called and booked his services.

He had a small clay pot which stood about half a metre tall in which he put a portion of his earnings. Whenever I asked him what he was saving up for, he told me it was for a rainy day. I never heard of any rainy day. We joked a lot about his little savings pot. He had written the 51st and 52nd verses of Surah Qalam[126] on the pot with a paintbrush. The pot was chipping, and the colour was wearing off, so I said to him, "You could have at least given it to a professional calligrapher to paint it!"

Once he earned his associate degree, he stopped studying and started working. He was busy working as an electrician in different buildings. I continued studying and we slowly grew apart. During this time, we messaged each other once or twice a week just to check up on one another. In 2009, I joined the Shaheed Kazemi Institute. The director of the institute assigned

---

126. Verses of the Quran which are narrated to protect one's belongings from jealousy

me the task of calling a group of people who joined the institute in 2006 but had since stopped attending their programmes. I read the list. The first name that caught my attention was Mohsen Hojaji. I immediately called his number. He told me he was currently busy with work, but I didn't accept this excuse. I called him again and we arranged to meet at Laleh Park. For two or three nights, I insisted for him to come, that he wouldn't regret it and so on. Eventually, he returned after my persistence.

At first, he attended the programmes just as an ordinary crowd member. At nights, we met up with our old friends from university at Kuhestan Park. We normally joked around a bit and then we played two or three games of volleyball. He brought me and took me home on his motorcycle. I had surgery to realign my nose, so he always said during the game, "Come, let me make your nose bent again!" When someone wanted to serve, he shouted, "Be careful of his nose job!"

For a few days, we talked about karate constantly. We trained with the youths at the institute. He really enjoyed this sport. At nights, we practiced our karate kata in Gulzar-e Shuhada under a teacher who had earned his black belt. He tried hard to learn as fast as he could. In addition to karate, we started mountain climbing, but not at a professional level. Eventually, we got bored with karate and we started learning judo. Despite his thin appearance, he had extraordinary bodily strength. We chose to study jujitsu. For a while, Mohsen kept saying this word in his Najafabadi accent and we died of laughter.

As Agha Khalili, the director of the institute, was insisting for us to train a leader from amongst us, we chose Mohsen and I forced him into the spotlight. The first time he showed his real capability was during our study courses. He broke the record for the number of books read. One season a year, Agha Khalili told us about the study courses. He gave us each a notebook which we were meant to use to study certain books and write what we understood from them. Mohsen read a great amount of the books and for this reason, he was chosen as the leader of the study group. These responsibilities made the institute such an integral part of Mohsen's life and slowly, he forgot all about his job as an electrician.

One day, I was busy filling out the names of the youths on the computer when he slapped my shoulder and asked, "Will you come and recite an *'aqd* of brotherhood between us so we become closer friends?" I don't know where he had learnt these narrations. We recited this *'aqd* together arm in arm. This wasn't enough for him though; he wanted to recite it in the shrine of an Infallible with the presence of a Sayyid. He told me to pack my bags and that we were going to Qom. Agha Khalili was living in Qom, so we called him and arranged to visit his house. We bought tickets for midnight, the last bus to Tehran. At around 4 am, we got off at the shrine of Imamzadeh Sayyid Jamaluddin, but he wasn't willing to Agha Khalili's house at that time. I asked, "So what do you want to do until sunrise?" We walked to the shrine [of Lady Ma'sumah (a)] in the unrelenting cold of the winter. We were shivering because we had left our coats. He kept saying that we would feel warm if we ran. We accidentally went the long way around and once we reached the shrine, it was already time for Fajr prayers. We were so exhausted, we were afraid we would fall asleep during prayers. We prayed in turns; one of us stood guard so the one praying didn't fall asleep. Once we had prayed, we fell asleep in a corner next to one of the doors. At around seven in the morning, Agha Khalili called to ask where we were. We went to his house and ate breakfast there. When he went to go about his work, we laid down again.

Mohsen woke me up an hour before Dhuhr prayers and told me to get ready to go to the shrine. We were wandering around the shrine looking for a Sayyid scholar. We found someone and told him we wanted to recite an *'aqd* of brotherhood between ourselves. He thought we were mocking him because Mohsen was laughing so much, so I signalled to him to calm down. Mohsen explained, "Haj Agha, we'll go to the *zareeh*, seek intercession [from Lady Ma'sumah (a)] and then come back." We stood facing the *zareeh* and Mohsen recited Hadith ul-Kisa, but when we looked back, we noticed the Sayyid had left. We quickly made our way back to Shabestan-e Imam Khomeini (ra) and whoever we asked told us it was too close to the time of *adhan* and that we should wait until after prayers. During the *adhan* of Dhuhr prayers, we found a Sayyid standing in a corner. Mohsen and I approached him. He was our final resort. He replied, "I'll be at your service after prayers." We said light-heartedly, "Recite it now please so our prayers will be blessed!" We put our hands together and at that moment, we became brothers. After prayers, we went to the *zareeh* again. We swore to act as a brother for one another and to support one another in times of financial and even spiritual difficulty. From then on, we never called each other by name. Instead, called each other 'brother'.

One of the promises we made was that every Friday, we would visit the grave of Haj Ahmad [Kazemi]. We strengthened our bond by holding hands and saying, "Let's try to become closer to Haj Ahmad." We started searching for footholds, footholds that could establish our connection with Haj Ahmad, the same footholds that established Haj Ahmad's connection with Allah. We found our first foothold in the form of the love of Lady Zahra (a). This was one of our connections with Shaheed Kazemi. After a while, Mohsen revealed one of his wishes,

"I want to be more like Haj Ahmad!" We made an oath. We started looking at different photos of him and reading books which mentioned how he behaved. The first step we took was we promised from then on, we wouldn't clean shave our beards or moustaches, we would wear cotton trousers like Haj Ahmad, and we wouldn't tuck our shirts into our trousers. At first, of course, it was difficult; we had to change our whole appearance!

Mohsen mentioned that we had to increase our spirituality. We read in a book that Haj Ahmad often did *ziyarah* of Lady Ma'sumah (a) and recited the *ziyarah* of Lady Zahra (a) and Hadith ul-Kisa regularly. We visited the grave of Haj Ahmad and Mohsen decided which *dua* to recite that day. One year, we even spent our Laylatul Qadr[127] beside Haj Ahmad's grave. Now imagine us rushing to Takht-e Foolad at midnight on Mohsen's motorcycle!

We always went with something to distribute like dates. Mohsen wrote some sayings of Haj Ahmad on pieces of card and he put them on his grave so whoever wanted could take one; he wrote fourteen for the fourteen Infallibles. From amongst all the sayings of Haj Ahmad, he liked one more than the others, "Try to become closer to Allah and the closer you get to Him, He loves you more than that!" He was always contacting the as-Sabiqun Institute as to whether they had released another clip of Haj Ahmad so he could download it.

Every now and then, we ran out of petrol on the way. Sometimes, we stood on the side of the road for hours, waiting for a kind person to pull over and spare us a few drops of petrol for the sake of Allah. He joked, "We have such strange people [in this country]! Just wait, I'm sure your petrol will run out

---

127. The Layali al-Qadr (s. Laylatul Qadr) or the Nights of Decree are the eves of the 19th, 21st and 23rd of Ramadan on which it is mentioned the Quran was revealed and the fates of all servants of Allah are decreed.

somewhere and no one will come to help you either!" When we were stuck in traffic in Isfahan, he joked, "Shall I break all of their wing mirrors so we can get through? It's not like they're using them right now!" He then thanked Allah that we didn't do those kinds of things, but the thoughts of how we could bother people came to our minds often. He always said, "Satan comes after us more instead of someone who already does these kinds of things."

At Takht-e Foolad, he frequented the section of the anonymous martyrs. He felt close to these martyrs and stayed there for a long time. I insisted to leave before Dhuhr prayers and said, "If we buy lunch from outside, we will have to spend a lot and also, we don't know where the food has come from," but he didn't pay any attention. We stayed until two or three in the afternoon and quite often, we ate biscuits and cakes on the way back to Najafabad.

We slowly started attending the *akhlaq* lectures of Ayatollah Naseri. On Fridays, we planned our trips to Takht-e Foolad in such a way that we could also attend his lectures. He always took notes. From then on, he started watching his every action. He started performing *mustahab* fasts, especially on the virtuous days of the year. The year before he got married, he fasted the entire month of Shaban. On Fridays, we went to Takht-e Foolad in the afternoon, and he opened his fast next to the grave of Haj Ahmad. In addition to these *akhlaq* lectures, Agha Khalili invited Haj Hosein Yekta[128] to the institute during the Holy Defence Week[129]. That night, Haj Hosein talked about cutting off all attachments except your attachment to Allah and he

---

128. Haj Hosein Yekta is a veteran from the Iran-Iraq War and is a well-known narrator of stories from the lives of the martyrs.
129. Every year from the 22nd to the 29th of September, Iranians commemorate the war between Iran and Iraq.

explained, "Once you reach the level where you have cut off all attachments, Allah buys you and when He buys you, you become a martyr!" Mohsen started looking for ways to cut off these attachments. He'd learnt his lesson from that lecture and cried so much over those words. He was so restless to discover the method of cutting off attachments. He read books and surfed the web just to learn something new which could help him achieve this. He found so much material he thought he should share with others, so he started a blog called *Mesbah* which has recently been changed into misagh.ir. I set up the blog for him myself. He concentrated on how the martyrs reached the stage they did.

Agha Khalili established a committee named 'The Noon Wal Qalam Committee of Promoting Books'. This committee was under the supervision of the institute and held largescale book exhibitions. As they were deciding who should lead this committee, Mohsen volunteered for this responsibility. As I was overly attached to Mohsen, we put electrics aside and put all our efforts into this work. We took a commission from the sales of the books and put the rest into the account of the institute. Agha Khalili arranged with the manager of a major bookstore in Najafabad for us to take a load of books from them and then pay them back the night after. He bought a few collapsible bookshelves from Tehran and sent them to us. Our peak hours were from Thursday afternoon to Friday evening: Gulzar-e Shuhada and Friday prayers. We went and spoke with the office of the imam of the Friday prayer so they could let us use the time between the two prayers to introduce certain books. Over the last few weeks when the municipality attended, they gathered our things and confiscated them. We begged the imam of the Friday prayer and told him we aimed to increase the culture of reading books, not profit. This was obvious from the type of books we were selling: memories from the lives of the martyrs, their biographies, and books regarding the Holy Defence. After a few visits, we convinced the imam to permit us so we could get permission from the municipality.

After one or two years of doing this work, Agha Khalili decided to absorb the major bookstore into the institute. One or two people looked after the store while Mohsen and I took charge of the book exhibitions. Many times, we couldn't find a car, so Mohsen sat at the back of his motorbike and carried two boxes of books in front of him. We were forced to go back and forth from the bookstore to Gulzar-e Shuhada or the Friday prayers to bring all the shelves and books. Sometimes, Mohsen brought his father's taxi so we could make more profit for the institute. He preferred to sell books he had already read. We divided the books among ourselves so we could sell them better. We worked a lot to sell the book 'From the Ascension of those who Returned[130]' by Hameed Davudabadi. No one could come to our section of the exhibition and leave without buying the book. He praised the book so much; he practically forced the customer to buy it. Over time, we became professional book salesmen. We took a portable speaker with us and played extracts from different books. We also sold quite a few copies of the books 'Mother[131]' and 'Noureddine, the Son of Iran[132]'. He laughed, "Let's sell more expensive books so we can double the profits of the institute."

We decided to open a shop to print, create and sell cultural products. As we opened officially in Rabi al-Awwal, we named it The Rabi Centre. We rented a basement-level shop on 17 Shahrivar Street. We visited Qom several times together

---

130. از معراج برگشتگان
131. دا
132. نور الدین پسر ایران

and bought a lot of things we could sell. He wanted to set up a *salawati* stall[133] outside of our shop during the special times of the year such as Muharram, Fatimiyyah or the fifteenth of Shaban. He initiated this idea, and we all agreed to buy a crate of juice each. The news spread amongst the members of the institute and they sponsored us until we were able to buy fifteen crates of juice.

The day we went to recite our *'aqd* of brotherhood, we made an arrangement with each other, but there were no promises made; we said we were going to get married to two sisters so we could always be together. We set our standards that they must be Najafabadi, religious and wear the hijab properly, even if they aren't from a well-established family. Time passed until one day, we went to the Ayatollah Khamenei Foundation to set up our bookstall for the exhibition. Mohsen was the photographer that day. The IRGC had brought some military equipment and the people wanted to take photos with them. Mohsen took photos, then we took them for printing and handed them over. He did this alongside selling books at The Rabi Centre. It was then I sensed that Mohsen's mind was elsewhere. He was distracted and always making mistakes. There was a lady who was working in the stall for the sisters' revolutionary programme, and whenever she had a problem, Mohsen was the first one there to help her. After two or three days, he eventually came and asked me, "Brother! Do you remember we agreed on something about marriage? Is it okay if that doesn't happen?" I said sure, and in the space of one or two months, he married Ms Abbasi.

I was the cameraman. It was with the insistence of his in-laws that his engagement was very flashy, and he was deeply

---

133. During the special times of the year such as Muharram or Arbaeen, the people of Iran set up stalls where things such as tea or cakes are given out in exchange for *salawat*. In Iraq, this is known as a *mawkib*.

upset about this. His many efforts to change their mind were to no avail. When he arrived at the engagement, they hugged him and pulled him to the dance floor to dance. He was not that kind of person and suddenly, his eyes fell upon me and he went pale. I left and he followed me. He asked, "Why did you leave?" and I replied, "Because I saw that you were embarrassed." He sighed and said, "This is exactly what I didn't want to happen, I'm so ashamed!"

Once he settled down, he realised the salary he was earning from The Rabi Centre wasn't enough, so he started working at a bakery at the suggestion of a friend. Every now and then, he visited the shop to ask us how we were doing, but he spent most of his time at the bakery.

There were rumours he was going to join the IRGC. I knew him well; I knew he loved cultural work. He said he accepted under his wife's insistence. He had to endure a lot of difficulties to join the IRGC. At first, they rejected him due to his major. They asked, "What do electrics have to do with the IRGC?" After a lot of visits, they accepted his major, but they found another problem in that he required root canal surgery. He was completely broke, but he managed to take a few loans out to go to the dentist. During the surgery, his cheek was cut, and it had to be stitched. He couldn't speak for three weeks.

He said himself, "My problems were solved by seeking intercession from Haj Ahmad [Kazemi]." He joined the armoured branch of the IRGC from the beginning as he enjoyed practical work. He told me, "I want to choose a path which can help me achieve my goal faster." I insisted, asking him what he wanted to do, and he said eventually, "I want to walk a path which ends in martyrdom." That day, I got my answer as to why he joined the IRGC. "I told my wife I'm joining the IRGC, but a branch which will secure my martyrdom. I will go if you don't obstruct me!" he said.

Sometimes, he came to the shop and talked about his work. He also discussed different methods we could employ to sell our products. He often went to kindergartens with his wife and take photos of the children. He then brought the photos back where we enhanced them and put them up on our display board. During these visits, I learnt he wanted to be dispatched to Syria. I joked with him, "Who are you to go to Syria?! You're still in training. By the time you join the IRGC officially, the war in Syria will be over!"

When his friend Alireza Noori was martyred, he wanted to go to Syria even more. He put his name down twice but it wasn't meant to be. He was transferred to Shiraz to continue his training and thus, our visits to Haj Ahmad's grave concluded. Once he joined the Najaf Division, he came and said, "Let's visit Haj Ahmad's grave for forty days so I can go to Syria." During these forty days, I got married and from then on, we went with our wives. His name was drawn [to go to Syria] before our forty days ended. I told him, "So you finally managed to do it!" He laughed, "Yeah, I put all my trust in Haj Ahmad." He whispered to me that only his wife knew. He emphasised I wasn't to tell anyone at all, and the news mustn't be spread among the members of the institute until he returned. It was announced everywhere that he had gone on a mission in Tehran.

His mission took forty-five days. He called me twice from where he was and each time, we spoke for more than half an hour. He quickly mentioned whatever he had witnessed, but of course, he didn't mention any sensitive information. He was crying a lot. He told me how his friends were martyred in front of his eyes. He said mournfully, "I was unworthy!" Once he returned, I went to visit him. Only then had his family realised where he had been. He said, "My mother said I wasn't martyred because she wasn't pleased about it!" He mentioned everything that had happened during the battles in Syria enthusiastically. It was strange to him that he had seen everything he had read about in the books. He said he couldn't believe that one day, he would sit in a tank and fire missiles. I understood from what he was saying that a missile had struck his tank and caught on fire. He immediately covered his face with his hand, and he knew he had survived miraculously. Later, he told me in private he had lost complete hearing in his right ear. He kept this secret from everyone. He only told his wife his hearing had become weak. When we went to Tehran together, the doctor told him bluntly not to try because his hearing would never come back.

A whole year passed until he went to Syria for the second time. It was as if this Mohsen was different from the Mohsen I knew. He had changed completely. I could feel his spirituality and closeness to Allah. I saw him in Qom often as I had moved there for work. He came to complete his transfer because he had heard the division in Qom was dispatching forces to Syria. He was ready to move to Qom just to go to Syria. We called each other every two days. One day, we were talking on the phone for about half an hour, forty minutes. He never missed the lectures of Ayatollah Naseri. I said to him, "You traitor! You're going on your own?!" He replied, "Okay then, I'll go, and I'll send you the recording afterwards." He sent me twenty-five lectures. In one of the lectures of Ayatollah Naseri, he heard if one visits Masjid Jamkaran for forty nights, his problems will be solved. He made an oath for his martyrdom that he would visit Jamkaran for forty Thursday nights, recite Salat Imam Zaman (aj) five times there and then go to do ziyarah of Lady Ma'sumah (a). Whenever he came with his wife, they visited us. The last time they came, I insisted they stay the night, but he didn't accept. The next day was the first of Ramadan and he wanted to fast. Halfway down the road, he stopped, turned back, and said, "I'm not coming to Jamkaran for my thirty-sixth Thursday night. I've packed my bags. I'm leaving for Syria!" My date for serving my compulsory military service was marked for the month after. I joked, "You're still going to have to come back to Qom!" He embraced me. He clasped me to his chest and said, his voice faltering, "If we don't see each other and I leave for Syria, forgive me." We both started crying. I replied, "You could have at least finished the forty nights!" He answered, "I'll compensate for that some other way."

That year, he spoke about martyrdom often. It was as if I was watching scenes from a film. On one of our trips to help the impoverished, my hand got stuck in the elevator. Mohsen joked, "Don't do something which will make them put up your damned photo in the institute!" I replied, "Don't worry, brother! I'm not worthy of martyrdom." He laughed and replied, "I know. If someone out of all of us is going to be martyred, it's me!" When I visited Karbala with the institute, he was serving in the military. He was extremely restless. He begged me before I got on the bus to pray for him to be martyred just like Haj Ahmad. When I prayed under the dome of Imam Husayn (a) and asked for the fulfilment of his requests, I called him, and I could hear the excitement in his voice.

During the second week of my compulsory military service, I called my wife and she told me Mohsen Hojaji had been dispatched to Syria. I started crying and told her, "This Mohsen is gone now!" I even told my wife, "Ring his wife and tell her husband will never return after this!" My wife replied, "What are you talking about?! I can't say those things to his wife!" Around ten or fifteen days later, we were given leave, so I got on a bus. As soon as I left the base, I switched on my phone and called my wife. I felt as if she was upset, so I asked her what was wrong, but she kept dodging the question. I hung up, but I couldn't stop thinking about it. I started checking my messages restlessly and saw Mohsen had sent me a message which read, "Forgive me for anything I've done to you. I'm going to Syria. If you need anything, I will sort it out for you on the other side Insha'Allah." I called him but his phone was off. A few minutes later, one of my friends called and asked if I had heard about Mohsen. I replied, "No, why?" He said, "Okay, so nothing then," and then he quickly hung up. I felt sick to the pit of my stomach. I called my friend and asked, "You're acting suspiciously. If something happened, tell me!" He said with a shaky voice, "Mohsen Hojaji has been taken captive!"

Hameed Khalili

Director of the Shaheed Kazemi Institute

We took around five hundred of the best students to Rahiyan-e Noor for the first anniversary of Haj Ahmad Kazemi's martyrdom. One of the buses was for the naughty kids, and Mohsen was on that bus. At the Mishdagh Base, I caught a glimpse of Hojaji while he was playing a game: he was a sharp and naughty child. After the trip, he occasionally visited the institute. I would love to say he was a very religious child from the beginning, but that would be a lie; he had nothing to do with that, he walked around with very wild hairstyles.

After a while, he stopped attending the institute and we couldn't find him. I got his details from Agha Abedi, one of the members and his middle school headteacher. I learnt he stopped attending our programmes over political issues. I gave Mohsen Hemmatiha the responsibility of bringing him back to us. He came back for Hemmatiha's sake, but it was obvious he didn't enjoy the atmosphere, so I took him aside and asked, "What's wrong?" He replied, "Honestly, everyone is saying the people here are extreme and want to brainwash me." I advised him, "Do this; attend our programmes just as you would any other programme and if you feel you're being brainwashed, don't come anymore." He decided to only come to our *majalis,* and he also took part in one of our organisational camps. We took them to Mashhad and invited well-known teachers such as Haj Hosein Yekta, Ta'eb, Mahdavi Arfa', Biyari, Qambari, Abolqasemi, Vafi, Mo'ammariyan, Agha Tehrani, Anjavinejad, Awhadi and Khorakiyan[134]. He sat in the front row and took notes.

---

134. All great scholars/narrators of the martyrs.

We set up a film club to the best of our capability and our first subject was Shaheed Hojjati[135], a martyr who was a revolutionary guard, a teacher, and a warrior all in one. His three brothers were martyred before him. Shaheed Avini[136] had also filmed a documentary about him by the name of *Halal Sustenance*[137]. Mohsen tagged along with the club to film with them. In addition to this, Haj Hosein Yekta and other comrades of Haj Ahmad including Hameed Khodabandeh, Asghar Habibi, Doctor Jozi (one of the martyrs of Mina), Mohammadreza Omid, Mahdi Rashidzadeh and Mohammadali Nooriyan spoke at the institute and narrated stories from the lives of the martyrs. These speeches converted Mohsen completely. What he was fearing took place; he was brainwashed in a way he didn't even realise!

I found out he was signing up for his military service, so I told him I would speak with my friends in the military so he could serve in Najafabad and in that way, he could attend the institute in the afternoons, but he didn't agree. He replied, "I want to serve in a difficult place." He wanted to serve on the border, but I didn't understand why. He reminded me of the story of Shaheed Hojjati who said at the time of the Shah, "I want to go to the most difficult part of the country," and they sent him to Lamerd, Fars where there was no running water or electricity. He continued, "Shaheed Hojjati had this belief

---

135. Shaheed Ahmad Hojjati was one of the martyrs from Najafabad who died protecting Khorramshahr. He endured a lot of torture during the regime of the Shah for distributing leaflets of Ayatollah Khomeini and eventually, he was martyred on the 24th of April 1982 in the Baytul Muqaddas military operation.

136. Shaheed Sayyid Murtaza Avini was an Iranian documentary filmmaker. One of his most famous works is the Narration of Victory (روایت فتح) series where he filmed on the warfronts of the Iran-Iraq War. He was martyred by a mine while filming in Fakkeh on the 9th of April 1993.

137. رزق حلال

during the time of the Shah. What do you think I should do now that I live in the Islamic Republic?!" He served in the AJA and he came bald to the institute when on leave. He had calmed down and he tried to speak with a more refined accent. His thick Najafabadi accent was clearly bothering him. During this time, we slowly lost contact once he completed his military service. I saw him active in different groups of the institute like robotics, exercise, and literature.

At that time, I was the director of Emad Publications and I was given the honour of visiting Ayatollah Khamenei. I was going to give him a report on how the institute is promoting the culture of reading books. I mentioned to him, "We have around forty-eight bookstalls in different high schools, the Friday prayers and Gulzar-e Shuhada." He was glad to hear this and he even mentioned that the institute should become an example for other publishers a few times during his speech. That Friday, I went to Najafabad and gathered the members of the institute. I told them what I had said and heard during my meeting with Ayatollah Khamenei and at the end of the gathering, Mohsen got up in front of everyone and said, "I'm no longer interested in robotics classes or exercise! I want to start working with books!" From that day onwards, he started promoting and selling books.

We took the youth on a trip to assist the impoverished. I managed to reach the province a few days later than the others. Before the trip, we held a briefing and due to the cultural differences between us and the inhabitants of the province, we wrote up some rules and regulations which we handed out to the members in the form of a booklet. We said people could only come if they were willing to abide by our rules. The first day I got there, I saw a girl who wasn't wearing proper hijab and appropriate clothing amongst the women of our group. She introduced herself as Ms Abbasi. I waited until the end of the trip and I set up a meeting for the ladies of the institute. I then took two or three of the members aside who didn't observe the rules of the trip and the village atmosphere correctly and spoke to them privately. After the meeting, Ms Abbasi said to me, "We come here for Shaheed Kazemi, not you! I am who I am! I dress like this normally!" She was infuriating me. I said firmly, "This institute is for the masses and it has its specific rules. If you don't want to follow them, you can stop attending our programmes!"

I saw her once or twice by chance as she was coming to the *majalis* exclusively for members of the institute. I asked the management on the sisters' side, "Didn't I tell you not to let Ms Abbasi in as long as she dresses like that?" They replied, "We can't stop her!" One night during the *masa'ib*, an unsaved number texted me, saying, "I'm praying for you. I'm asking Haj Ahmad to teach you how to be a human!" I asked, "Who is this?" They replied, "I'm Ms Abbasi, the same person you kicked out of the institute." I felt as if I was going insane. She added in a rude tone, "The *majalis* aren't for you, they are for Shaheed Kazemi!"

In the meanwhile, Mohsen came and told me he wanted to get married and wanted me to introduce a suitable girl to him. I told him about one of the pious and modest girls from the institute and I organised a meeting with the girl's family so they could talk together and see if they are compatible. A few days later, that girl called and started ranting about why I sent a crazy and super-religious guy to their door! A short while later, Mohsen called and told me he had found a suitable girl and he was going to propose. I asked if he knew the family and he told me she was one of the members of the institute. I asked what her surname was and as soon as he told me her surname was Abbasi, I lost it. Everyone knew this girl had driven me crazy with her behaviour and law-breaking attitude! I asked him, "Have you lost your mind?! Are you feeling okay?! You shouldn't let emotion take the reins of your life and pick your partner quickly. You've only known her from one exhibition! Life has accountability. This woman doesn't even fill one of the standards you were looking for in a wife!" I rang two or three of the married members of the institute and told them to speak to Mohsen. Each of them went to talk to him about how this woman wasn't compatible with him and eventually, he called me and told me he wasn't compatible with her and he'd given up on her. When I saw he'd become sane once again, I told him about two sisters who he could go and propose to with Hemmatiha. I had heard they had agreed to marry two sisters, so I felt at rest when he sent his mother to propose to one of them on his behalf.

He rang from the marriage office. I was glad he'd finally recited the 'aqd and said to him, "Congratulations! Good luck!" He replied, "Haji, just don't say no!" I became a little doubtful. He continued timidly, "Haji, allow me to marry her!" I pressed the phone to my ear and asked, "Who are you marrying?" He answered nervously, "The same one you didn't want me to get married to!" I exclaimed, "Abbasi!?" He didn't answer. I yelled down the phone, "Mohsen! Do you know what you are doing right now?!" He replied, "I'll correct her, I promise, don't worry!" I said, "I was worried you wouldn't choose correctly. Now if you are completely sure you're making a good decision, go ahead." An hour later, he told me he had got married. He said excitedly, "Haji, do you know how much we put the dowry as?" I acted indifferently. He broke down the dowry and the conditions for me. He was waiting for me to start congratulating him, but all I said was, "Damn you!" He hung up. I thought to myself, "May Allah bless this marriage whose beginning was led by emotion and whose dowry was paid through emotion, not intelligence!"

Every week, he messaged me, saying, "Do you need anything from Haji?" I asked, "Where are you?" and he replied, "Isfahan, under the rain on my way to Haj Ahmad with my motorcycle." When they reached his grave, they messaged me. I had become their loyal companion; they consulted me before doing anything, whether it was joining the IRGC or the Islamic seminary, if it were to buy a car, if it were to build a house or even if it was whether he should be dispatched to Syria. I asked him many times, "Mohsen, do you have to ask my advice on this?" Sometimes, he did my head in asking for advice.

I appointed him as the cultural director of our trips to aid the impoverished. He was insisting he wanted to visit the village of Vezveh. There was nothing to do in Vezveh; it's where the women normally worked. I told him, "Mohsen! The youth will take it the wrong way. They'll talk about you behind your back," but he insisted, saying, "Don't worry, I'll go and come back quickly." For two days, I thought he had gone for his wife. I decided to visit him, and I found out he had gathered all the youth and he was reciting the *adhan* and praying congregational prayers. I knew he was always smart; he was quietly searching for a place which needed a lot of work. He went around and caused mischief. He delayed routine work and then he went to the next group. He also caused play fights; he started throwing water at someone and as the water fight peaked, he suddenly went missing.

When the book *Mafatih al-Hayat*[138] was first printed, he started visiting different mosques. On the first day of Ramadan, he managed to sell sixty copies. He insisted for the imam of the congregation to allow him to introduce this book to the people between the two prayers. He set off with the other members on a mission to inform the people of these books. In the city of Najafabad, they sold four thousand copies of the book *I Am Alive*[139]. His wife had also come to help him. They even put on a play based on part of the book. The schools enjoyed this very much. They sold so many, they said, "That's enough already! Now the whole city will become *I Am Alive*!" This was to such an extent that we eventually invited Ms Masumehabad, the author, to come and speak at the institute.

He put all his effort into the book-reading competition, but despite this, he didn't take any money from the profits of the books. At the time of the competition, he had joined the IRGC. He said, "I now earn a salary. Put the profits into the trips to help the impoverished." His wife was always searching for a donor who could support our trips to aid the impoverished and I remember she managed to collect around three million tomans by the end of the final year.

It wasn't as if he only sold books; he studied them too. He even lent books to others, especially the books *The Art of the Ahlulbayt (as)* and *I Saw My Soul Leaving*[140].

---

138. A book of ethics written by Ayatollah Jawadi Amoli which in his own words, 'discusses the way man interacts and behaves with the rest of creation'.
139. من زنده ام
140. دیدم که جانم می رود

On Rahiyan-e Noor, I saw him reading the book *Ah*[141] often. He loved the books *Peace be upon Ibrahim*[142], *Shahrokh*[143] and *Teyyeb*[144]. I think he even got the idea of sewing the tag 'Jawn, the Servant of Mahdi[145]' on his military uniform from the book *Who Are the Servants of Our Master?*[146]

Following his first tour of Syria, Mohsen was no longer the Mohsen we all knew. I felt he had grown into a real man and his decisions were no longer based on emotion but rather on deliberation. He wanted nothing more than to serve another tour in Syria. We arranged a meeting in Gulzar-e Shuhada for Nowruz 2017. After greeting everyone, his wife said to me, "Mohsen doesn't feel like living anymore and he wants to go to Syria again." I pulled Mohsen aside and admonished him, "You have a wife and child now! If you want to serve Islam and the Revolution, there's a lot of work left to be done here. Haj Ahmad found martyrdom here!"

Two months later, he came to Qom with his wife and child. He was still insisting for me to find him a way to go to Syria. I asked, "Why do you think you aren't being dispatched?" We spoke a lot until we found the root of the problem: his mother wasn't pleased with him going. On Laylatul Qadr, he sent me a message from Mashhad which read, "She's happy for me to go." It didn't even take a month. He rang me from the airport and

---

141. آه
142. سلام بر ابراهیم, published in English as 'Peace be upon Ibrahim'
143. شاهرخ
144. طیب
145. جون خادم المهدی
146. خادم ارباب کیست؟

said, "You are the last person I'm saying goodbye to. Forgive me." I still remember his last sentence, "Insha'Allah by serving Lady Zaynab (a), I'll show I didn't waste the bread of Haj Ahmad and I was a good soldier for him."

Two weeks later, he rang me from Syria. He was extremely upset and was saying, "They've put me on office work here. There's no fighting. Pray I can go to the frontline." I replied, "Mohsen! Martyrdom came for Shaheed Sayyad [Shirazi][147] in the north of Tehran, I'll pray martyrdom also comes after you."

---

147. Shaheed Ali Sayyad Shirazi was a high-ranking commander during the Iran-Iraq War and on the 10th of April 1999, he was assassinated in front of his house in Tehran.

Hosein Mohammadi

The martyr's friend

I still remember his face from the first time he participated on Rahiyan-e Noor: a skinny boy with a thin moustache and no beard. He looked like a small troublemaker. When I heard his surname, I asked, "Why didn't you become a scholar?" He replied, "I won't be any use as a scholar!" I continued, "Shaykh Hojaji is from your family, how come you turned out like this?" He laughed, "I have the same question."

We went on a field trip to the village of Veshnavah near Qom. After class, we sat down and played together. He wrote on the first page of the books I bought myself, "A gift to my dear friend Hosein Mohammadi, from your friend Mohsen Hojaji." He insisted I read the book *The Bearer of Water and Manners*[148]. He constantly mentioned that he had read it and it was a very enjoyable book to read.

Agha Khalili had given us some homework and one night, he called everyone. I was the first one to get married out of all of them, and I had married a girl from the institute, so they called it an institute marriage. I attended classes with my wife. Agha Khalili asked who hadn't done the homework. I raised my hand naively and that night, Agha Khalili took out all his anger on me and then he told me to get out. I was embarrassed in front of everyone, especially my wife. I went outside and sat on a bench. A few minutes later, I felt someone put their arm around me. I looked back only to see Mohsen standing there. He'd left the class halfway through just to comfort me. Then all the others started coming and saying, "Did you see how he embarrassed

---

148. سقای آب و ادب

you in front of your wife? If I were you, I wouldn't stay here any longer," but Mohsen was constantly stopping them and telling them to leave me alone. He kept assuring me that Agha Khalili was only speaking from exhaustion and it was nothing personal.

We had become close friends during this trip to Qom, but I felt like I couldn't become attached to him. As soon as we returned from Qom, I saw him hanging out with two other new friends. He wasn't one to hang around with just one person. He spent time with many different people. He wouldn't get attached to his friends either. During the trips to aid the impoverished, after finishing his construction work in the afternoon, he socialised with the residents of the village. Sometimes, he even visited their houses. He took erasers, pencils, and different pieces of stationery to hand out as gifts to the children. He was disappointed about their mobiles and he said, "These mobiles have stolen their religion and culture!" He told someone, "Keep my phone for a while, let's see what happens without these photos and stupid videos!" In the night, he walked into a part of the mountains where we didn't even go in the daytime out of fear of snakes and scorpions. He didn't go there to pray Salat ul-Layl or to read *duas*, no, he went there to ponder. Sometimes, he wrote some things in the darkness. At first, he wasn't extremely attached to the Leader, but his views changed slowly after attending the programmes of the institute. I noticed once he acted harshly with one of the students in a class he was teaching. He shouted, "If you want to speak like that, get out!" Later, I learnt the student had said some inappropriate things about the Leader.

Agha Khalili always said, "We're taking the institute to Karbala." I laughed to myself, "Karbala? All of these people?!" I felt as if Agha Khalili wanted to encourage the members to work harder. Time passed and while I was studying at the

University of Tehran, I heard they were taking the members of the institute to Karbala. Nothing was ready for me to go. All the members had gathered by the martyrs of Najafabad. I saw Mohsen wandering around amongst them. I asked him, "Are you going too?" He replied, "No, I'm doing my military service." We both sat sulkily on the railings. The others started coming one by one to say goodbye. Suddenly, Mohsen broke into tears and said, "I wanted to go to Karbala, I worked in the institute so much, why didn't Imam Husayn (a) invite me? Why didn't Haj Ahmad gift this to me?" He was hugging the others whilst crying. I said to him, "Let's go with them to the border and then come back," but he answered, "If I go until there, I won't be able to come back!"

Mohammad Nasehi

The martyr's friend

I knew three or four words of Italian and I acted like a foreigner to entertain the others at the institute. It sounded nice, but I was using made-up words. My accents were perfect. I told them I was speaking Croatian.

During our trip to Veshnavah, Mohsen and I put on a play. I was going to act as an Italian who had just converted to Islam and Mohsen was going to be my translator. Mohsen told me, "Come, teach me some words so I don't look like an idiot!" I sniggered and said to him, "There is nothing to learn. I'm just speaking nonsense!" I changed my appearance; I trimmed down to a goatee and went on the stage wearing a hat and jeans. That night, one of the teachers was sitting with our group and he believed I was from Croatia. No one told him otherwise, so he was completely ready to hear what I had to say. I started speaking and Mohsen didn't hold back. He made up sentences as they came along. He then said, "He says that Imam Khomeini was extremely influential, but after him, the scholars didn't live up to his standards!" That struck a nerve with the teacher and he left the gathering enraged. As soon as the play ended, we only just realised what we had done. Mohsen said, "We spoke so well! I wasn't even thinking about what I was saying!" I stated coldly, "You did it yourself. All I did was speak a 'foreign language'." He fell deep in thought. He sat down and wrote a little speech which he said was a letter of apology. The night after, he took permission from Agha Khalili to apologise in front of everyone. He made everyone cry with his letter.

That wasn't the end of my story with Mohsen. The institute had taken us to Mashhad and Mohsen said to me, "Mammad[149] Nasehi, let's go to Bazaar-e Reza![150]" He always called me Mammad Nasehi because of his thick Najafabadi accent. We stopped outside a cloth store and he told me to start speaking Croatian. I took some cloth in my hand and started speaking my 'foreign language'. Mohsen translated, asking how much the cloth was. The shopkeeper was smarter than us and said in front of his customers, "I've seen him here a few times and he's a regular customer." The shopkeeper turned to Mohsen and said, "Ask him if he was happy with the previous goods I sold to him." Mohsen had fallen into his trap; he didn't know how to speak my foreign language. We turned away from the shopkeeper and he said to me softly, "He's so smart! He's using us for his own good!" We then turned back to the shopkeeper and said, "No, this is the first time he's come to Iran," but he kept insisting he had seen me before so he wouldn't look bad in front of his customers. Once the other customers left, the shopkeeper said, "I don't believe he's foreign!" I quickly started speaking to Mohsen and he told the shopkeeper, "He's worried about his wife. We have to leave," and we made our getaway.

The next time, we swore we wouldn't do this again. We were at Jamkaran, at the Yavaran-e Mahdi campsite and we played around with one of the scholars. I went up to him and started speaking hurriedly. He was looking at me confused when Mohsen arrived and told him, "He's saying he's a new convert to Islam, he's just come to Qom, he doesn't know his way around and his wife has gone missing." The scholar took

---

149. The name Mohammad is shortened to Mammad in informal, friendly settings among Iranians.
150. A very famous bazaar in Mashhad which is close to the shrine of Imam Rida (a)

me by the hand and brought me to security so they could help me. He was extremely concerned. He kept telling those around him that this wasn't good, and they must help the foreigners feel more at home. He was comforting me saying, "Don't worry, this is a safe country!" He didn't even notice he was saying all this in Farsi. I did my best to look upset. Mohsen came with me and was constantly translating. Agha Khalili came and when he saw the scholar was hurrying here and there, he told him I was one of the members of the institute. At first, the scholar didn't believe it and he told Agha Khalili that now wasn't the time to joke about. Agha Khalili turned to me and said, "Nasehi, speak Farsi right now!"

On this same trip, we visited Masjid Jamkaran and prayed Salat Imam Zaman (aj). He felt thirsty and he said we should leave so we could find something to drink. At the entrance of the mosque, there was a man at a stall selling soda and doogh[151]. "Let's buy something from the shop," I said, but he replied, "No, this man is also a businessman, let him earn some money too." He bought two dooghs, and as soon as I was about to open it, he told me to shake it well first so the water and yoghurt could mix properly. At that moment, we saw a poor person. Mohsen put his hands in his pockets and from the way he was moving his fingers, I realised he had nothing on him. He looked at me as if to tell me to give him something. I said to him, "I have less money than you!" When he gave up, he said to the poor person, "All I have is a doogh, do you want that?" The poor person took it and left. Mohsen chuckled and told me to shake the doogh well so we could drink it. A few steps further, we saw another poor person. I told him, "I think you'll have to remain thirsty today!" From that day onwards, whenever something similar

---

151. A salty drink made from yoghurt, water and occasionally mint

happened, we said to each other, "We have to shake the doogh well!"

In a meeting with the municipality, they asked the management of the institute to show them a report of their activities. I was there as the director of literature, and the responsibility of promoting books fell on my shoulders. Mohsen said to me, "Mammad Nasehi! I want you to speak in such a way that they fall in love with books." I talked about the benefits of reading books for around half an hour, and I spoke so well that when the head of education stood to give his input, he spoke in favour of what I had said. Mohsen quickly set up a bookstall with the boxes of books he always kept with him, and once the meeting ended, they all went to him. As we were leaving, I asked him, "How many books did you sell?" He replied, "It's not about selling. I'm glad you spoke so well!" From then on, they took me to different schools to promote books.

Every now and then, he whispered in my ear, "Mammad Nasehi! One has to be well-mannered." He advised me often. During the month of Ramadan, the youth of the institute gathered round to recite the Quran. Mohsen asked me to join in and recite the Quran in front of everyone. I was embarrassed because I didn't know how to read fluently, but he looked me in the eye and said, "You should only be embarrassed when your child asks you to read Quran for him and you can't!" These words gave me such self-confidence that until the end of the month, reciting Quran felt like the easiest task in the world.

On Thursday nights, he recited Ziyarah Ashura in the institute. I wanted to recite too, so I asked him for permission to recite, but he said, "No, I've made an intention for these

Ziyarah Ashuras." I asked what his intention was, and he told me he wanted to attain martyrdom. I raised my right arm and exclaimed, "Oh no! By the time you're martyred, I'll have died!" He laughed and replied, "No, don't worry, I'll be martyred soon!"

For a while, I volunteered at one of the *baseej* groups in my district in Najafabad. I told Mohsen a few times to come and join our *baseej* group, but he acted uninterested. When I insisted, he stood up and said, "Mammad Nasehi, there is no my *baseej* and your *baseej*! Your work and actions must be *baseeji*[152]. If you can promote a book which changes even one person's life, this means you've understood the path of the *baseej* properly." He encouraged me to read the book *The Ambush of the Bats*[153]. The story of the book starts from the beginning of the revolution and ends in the completion and establishment of the government.

I did my military service in the cultural department of the Najaf-e Ashraf Division in Najafabad. We decided to set up a convention. We had a model of the different roles of our division, and I was explaining it to the visitors. During my talk, my eyes suddenly fell upon Mohsen. He was wearing IRGC uniform, he had ranks, his hair was combed over, and his beard was thick. I forgot about my speech and I started looking at him. I had no idea he had joined the IRGC. I hugged him and took him to a room where we could sit and have a cup of tea together. He laughed, "Was I really that bad before?!"

"No, it's just your appearance has changed a lot!"

"Well, a human eventually has to become human."

"Well then, dear human, make me a human too. We've been together for a lifetime."

---

152. A term which refers to the soldiers who volunteered to join the army of the Revolution

153. شبیخون به خفاش

"You have a good nature, you'll become human yourself, just be careful who you listen to." I complained to him that I had to stay in the base until the afternoon because of the convention. He told me, "You have to have the mindset that you're working for Allah. The martyrs were always at war. Don't do something just so the colonels and majors see it. Work for Allah's pleasure so you have an answer for Him." As we were saying goodbye, I patted him on the shoulder and said, "Earn these stars quickly so you can become a colonel." He replied, "Mammad Nasehi! We have to earn our stars for Allah, these stars on our shoulders are perishable."

I saw him at the base every day. I wanted to find out what he was doing; someone who had spent a lot of time causing mischief with me couldn't just suddenly change overnight. He spoke nicely, and he was happy. When we met, I asked him to advise me, even if it was just one point. He said, "Read the Quran every day, even if it is just one page or even a verse. It has a great effect on your soul, but when you read it with the translation, it also leaves an effect on your soul." He loved Surah Qiyamah and spoke about it often, especially the first six verses. He said, "When Allah says He has created your fingerprints, you know that Allah is always with you . We must believe in Him with our whole existence."

I worked mainly in the compilation centre which was separate from the main base in residential areas. Sometimes I visited the main base to follow up on my work. Mohsen walked from the main base to the armoured base, but I used the car which was specifically for use in the bases. One rainy morning, I braked in front of him and told him to jump in, but he told me he wanted to get some exercise. The next day, I pressed the horn and told him to get in, but he told me again that he wanted to get some exercise. The next time I did it, he put his head through the window and said, "Mammad Nasehi! This car isn't for public use, but you can use it because you are on a mission. If they wanted, they could leave a car for me too."

"This car belongs to everyone, it's not like we're going to take it outside."

"This is how people become indebted. Becoming good starts from these things, and if these aren't observed, you'll never become human however much you try!" He pulled his head out of the window and continued, "This is how a man becomes deaf, dumb and blind!"

"What do you mean?"

"I mean that Allah lays a seal on your mouth and ears and you will never be guided to the right path. You'll try, but you'll never reach it."

One day, he got in my car outside the base and we were talking when suddenly, a ball fell in front of us. I couldn't turn in time and it popped under the car. Mohsen told me to pull over and he got out. He walked to the children whose ball popped, stroked the boy's head, and said, "Don't be upset! Go and play something else with your friends until I come back with another ball." We stopped outside a shop and he bought two balls identical to the one we had popped. He was glad there were still children today who could put their phones and video games aside and come out and play with their friends on the street. When he gave them the balls, I applauded him, but he became serious and said to me, "There is no need for applause, learn this and do things like this." I replied, "In this time, I've learnt a lot from you." He laughed, "So you have to give me some blessings from your good deeds!"

We were at the mosque together and as we were leaving, a child came to us with a tray of tea. I told him I didn't want any, but Mohsen stared at me as if to tell me to take one. I took one but I said to him, "I've already had one!" He replied, "Even if they bring ten cups, drink them. Perhaps all this person has is tea and if you don't take it, he might feel ashamed."

Majeed Shokrollahi

The martyr's friend

At the Shaheed Kazemi Institute, they suggested setting up a sports club under the supervision of an experienced teacher. We didn't have a hall nor a teacher nor even enough participants. There was only me, Mohsen and three or four others. We found one of the elder members of the institute who had a national ranking in karate. We asked him to give us lessons and we got the basement of the institute ready for us to begin. We laid a few blankets down and we jogged around on them to warm up. One time during practice, we were under pressure to get ready for the city tournament and one of the boys broke his collarbone. We didn't make a big fuss over it because if someone found out, they would disqualify our team. We just told him, "Don't come to the institute so no one finds out!" Luckily, it was exam time, so we told him, "If someone asks where you are, we'll tell them you have exams!"

We went for practice at a time when no one saw us. No one would think we were doing karate because we wore t-shirts and different colour clothes. We continued in this fashion for five or six months, but the neighbours were getting agitated. We had been looking for a new place for a while and one of the members knew the manager of one of the gyms in the city. After a lot of running around, he finally agreed to let us use a forty-metre warehouse. Once again, we rolled up our sleeves and gave the place a good clean. When our team became strong enough, they took that place away from us too. We didn't have enough money to rent a hall. We decided to go to Gulzar-e Shuhada at ten o'clock at night. At the same time, the institute set up an educational *i'tikaf*[154] at Gulzar-e Shuhada, so during the daytime, we studied and at night, we practiced our karate. We managed to rent some white clothes for a little while. People were afraid of us because we walked past them like ghosts! In this manner, we managed to enter the city tournament and Mohsen won second prize.

In one of the institute meetings, they mentioned we were lacking in the intellectual fields and the Leader had emphasised on the importance of science and the software movement, so we decided to set up a robotics club. Just like when we set up the sports club, we once again felt a sense of duty. We started looking for a teacher and Mohsen brought one of his friends who was experienced in the field of robotics. We began visiting him for classes on foundational mechanics. Just like always, finding a place was a thorn in our side. Mohsen suggested, "My dad has built another floor to our house. It's empty, we can do it there." On Mondays, Wednesdays, and Saturdays, we did karate and on Tuesdays, Thursdays, and Sundays, we did robotics, both at ten o'clock at night. In the meantime, we went to university in the mornings. Neither we nor the institute had enough money for our tools for robotics. We mentioned we didn't have much money and the institute helped us out and bought the necessities for us. We asked the teacher if he could work with what we had for the time being. Slowly, our club grew. From those five-person meetings in Mohsen's father's house, we managed to create a flourishing club with many robots. From robot routers and drones to submarine and firefighting robots, our club was so successful that some of our members even entered international competitions. The institute even

---

154. An Islamic rite where the worshipper dedicates a certain amount of time to remain in a mosque and do nothing but worship.

received an invitation from the USA, inviting us to participate in a robotics competition.

A year after the book *From the Ascension of Those Who Returned* was published, the Leader wrote a commendation on it. It was a large and expensive book. He suggested we put more effort into selling this book. We didn't expect anyone to buy it. It was the month of Ramadan and the Friday prayers were terribly busy, so they didn't give us space to set up our stalls. Instead, we set our stalls up on the main roads. That day, we managed to sell many copies of this book, and this encouraged Mohsen to set up a book-reading competition based on this book.

We set up a few stalls in front of the Friday prayers mosque and we rented a van to move our stuff. Our goal was to promote books and we dedicated the profits to the programmes of the institute. Mohsen spoke with the father of one of our friends and asked if he could help us move our equipment every week. He was very precise when it came to using the money as it was given to us as a trust. He was willing to take less money if he was going to be helping us every week, but when he came and saw we were working out of love, he said he wasn't going to take any money. We told him, "If you won't take money, at least take some books." A while later, we visited his house and we saw he had a whole bookshelf full of our books. At the Friday prayers, people sometimes thought the books were free and took them. In the end, we noticed that the list of books didn't add up with our profits. Mohsen told us that these books were trusts from the institute, so we split the losses and paid out of our own pockets.

We went on Rahiyan-e Noor. Each bus had a cultural director, but we called them supervisors. One of the buses was full of younger children and no one wanted to go on that bus. Mohsen volunteered and throughout the journey, he narrated stories from the lives of the martyrs he had read himself. One of the responsibilities of the supervisors was to promote a culture of book-reading. Mohsen took two backpacks full of books with him on the bus and he talked about them so well that he managed to sell them all. We told the children on the buses to write down the experiences they had on the trip and collect them so we could use them to make a booklet. Mohsen typed all of it up and put a group photo at the top. He kept following up to see when it would be printed as it would act as an encouragement for others.

After the trip, Mohsen became our team leader. He held his meetings in Gulzar-e Shuhada, and he often took us to Takht-e Foolad. He took us to the graves of martyrs who had a book printed about them, including Shaheed Toorajizadeh, Akhundi, Alireza Karimi and Haj Ahmad Kazemi. After reading these books, he fell in love with Haj Ahmad in such a way that he saw him as his commander. He read a novel called *The Line of Contact*[155] which was based on the life of Haj Ahmad a few times and he discussed this a lot during one of our trips to help the impoverished.

When he was doing his military service, he called and checked up on how things were going. They gave him problems with reading books, especially as he talked about them with the others. He told me, "They have searched my closet a few times and taken all my books." He realised he had to quickly distribute the books amongst the soldiers. His favourite books to take

---

155. خط تماس

were *The Soft Sands of the Pavilion* and *Peace be upon Ibrahim*. For a while, he focused entirely on theology books. When he came back on leave, I gave him a few books such as *Then I Was Guided, A Shia-Sunni Dialogue* and *The Principles of Theology*[156]. Eventually, the soldiers started referring to him if they had any theological questions or issues.

That year, we didn't hold any *majalis* at the institute for the first ten days of Muharram. All the members were either working, busy at university or serving in the military. Mohsen called me from the base and asked, "Is Haj Ahmad happy with this?" I replied, "We can't do it, man, they aren't coming." He took some time off and came to Najafabad. We were three people in total. We distributed the work amongst ourselves. Mohsen made a poster for the final five nights of Safar and for a whole week, we texted each of our friends. All the reciters were busy, but Mohsen said he would recite himself. By chance, we managed to find a reciter, but despite this, he still wanted to recite Ziyarah Ashura at the beginning of the *majlis*. He started reciting from then onwards.

I went to Talaeiyeh and after the scholar recited the *masa'ib*, Mohsen lined us up to start the *sinehzani* and he recited a few *nowhehs* by Mahmoud Karimi very well. From then on, he became known as Haj Mohsen Chizari and the boys said, "Do you know Haj Mahmoud? This is his Mohsen!" We asked them where their next programme would be and they replied, "Just come to Chizar!" He became so well-known that some university students asked him, "We don't have a reciter, can you recite for us?"

---

156. اصول عقاید

Mahdi Jahangiri

The martyr's friend

Mohsen always said, "You think you're the only fool? I'm a fool too, pull yourself together!" During work, he said, "That's another blow to the stomach of arrogance!"

We went on Rahiyan-e Noor on Arafah 2009. In Shalamcheh, he was radiating spirituality. As we got on the bus, I started talking to Mohsen. I was worried I would lose this great feeling and was wondering what I could do to retain it. I remember it was raining quite heavily. The road became muddy, and the bus got stuck. In these conditions, Mohsen and I made a promise to always have each other's backs. We agreed that if one of us made a mistake in public, the other would let him know indirectly. Mohsen looked at my little finger and said, "This will be our signal." I had broken my finger playing football and it had been bent, and this became our signal. Whenever either of us was going into dangerous territory, the other would quickly bend their little finger and we would help the other one out.

Eventually, I moved to Qom and my wife started working in the hijab store at Masjid Jamkaran. As her shifts ended at different times of the night, I went to pick her up. On Thursday night, I sometimes bumped into Mohsen at Jamkaran, sometimes alone, sometimes with his wife and sometimes with his father-in-law. I asked what he was doing there, and he told me he had come for *ziyarah*. I thought to myself, "What's his motive to get up every week, regardless of the weather, and come to Jamkaran?" He didn't stay for long either. He recited

Dua Kumayl on Thursday night, Dua Nudbah[157] in the morning and headed back.

---

157. A supplication to be recited on all four major Eids i.e. Eid al-Fitr, Eid al-Adha, Eid al-Ghadeer and Friday.

Sayyid Mojtaba Mousavi

Counsellor at the Shaheed Kazemi Institute

He asked me, "What can I do to become a martyr?" I put a hand on his shoulder and said smiling, "Insha'Allah, you'll be a special martyr!" This made him incredibly happy.

"So, what shall I do?"

"In my opinion, we can't travel on this path on our own. Someone has to take your hand."

I then read the following poem to him,

"If you go, you will achieve nothing,

If you are taken, you will be connected,

Great is the distance between going and being taken!"

I kept telling him to make friends with a martyr. I said this as soon as he stepped foot in the Shaheed Kazemi Institute. In the institute, we set up a programme called 'The Heavenly Companions'. In verse sixty-nine of Surah Nisa, Allah says, "... and excellent are those as companions." He then mentions the reason for this in Surah Al Imran as, "...they are alive with their Lord, receiving provision." For these three reasons, Allah takes pride in His martyrs. We gave lectures on this subject for around forty sessions for the youth that they should make friends with the martyrs, and who better than Haj Ahmad? I told the youth, "This friendship has conditions. You can't betray them, we have to go and see what they want," and I always mentioned memories from the life of Shaheed Kazemi.

Time passed until many of these youths had married. They started sessions with the topic of family life specifically for couples. The sessions were held in different people's houses every month and Mohsen always recited Hadith al-Kisa at the beginning of the meeting. Reciting Hadith al-Kisa had become a tradition for them as they knew Haj Ahmad had a special love for Lady Zahra (a).

He was careful not to make any mistakes. If no one could hold the programme at their house, he volunteered. His house was on the fourth floor and his building didn't have an elevator. The first time I went to his house, I noticed all the stairs had been painted. He told me, "I painted these stairs so when my wife comes up, she won't get as tired as she normally would."

Mahdi Shari'at-Zadeh

The martyr's friend

I joined the institute to make friends, go on trips and socialise. We were put into groups and Agha Mohsen was our group leader. He enchanted me from the very beginning with his good *akhlaq* and ever-smiling face. After reading the book *I Saw My Soul Leaving*, my view towards the martyrs changed. He liked the book *The Art of the Ahlulbayt (as)* a lot and he talked about it with passion. He spoke about how the martyrs sook assistance from the Ahlulbayt (as) during battle on the warfront. He insisted that we choose a martyr and make friends with them and he said, "Go to Golestan-e Shuhada and make friends with the one who catches your eye!" He had established a great friendship with Haj Ahmad himself and he wrote some of his sayings on the board. I remember one of them which said, "O' Allah! I understand with my whole existence that You are true love and martyrdom is the only way to reach this love!"

On Rahiyan-e Noor, we reached Fakkeh and as we got off the bus, Mohsen took off his shoes. He mentioned to us something which Haj Hosein Yekta said, "Here, we are walking on the eyes of the martyrs. When they find the body of a martyr, there are only a few bones, so where is the flesh? Where is his head? Where are his eyes? All of these have been incorporated into the dust."

Every week, he visited Jamkaran, and we went together once. It was Thursday night and the night before Lady Fatimah (a)'s martyrdom. We went to Tehran first to listen to *masa'ib* at the Husayniyyah of the Leader. As we were lining up to go in, he asked, "Do you want to write a letter to Haj Agha [Ayatollah Khamenei]?"

"Why not? What shall I write?"

"Write, Agha, pray we are martyred!"

After the *masa'ib*, they served *gheimeh*[158]. He left half of his food and when I asked him why, he told me, "I want to take some back for my wife so she can take blessing from it." Throughout the journey, he either recited *dhikr*[159] on his clay *tasbih* or listened to Haj Agha Panahian's[160] lectures. He talked to me about how we had given so many martyrs in the path of defending the shrines, yet their names were seldom heard outside of their family and friends' circles. He prayed from the bottom of his heart that his blood could start a revolution.

In his last message to me, he wrote, "Salam dear brother, forgive me if I have done anything to hurt you. Insha'Allah, I'm leaving tomorrow. Pray that I return with a clean slate." I rang him and asked, "When will you be getting back?" but he replied with complete seriousness, "Insha'Allah, I won't be returning."

---

158. An Iranian stew made from meat, split peas, tomatoes and dried lime.
159. Praises of Allah.
160. Hojjat ul-Islam Shaykh Alireza Panahian is a well-known Iranian scholar and lecturer who has studied under the likes of Ayatollah Khamenei, Sayyid Mahmud Hashemi Shahrudi and Ayatollah Jawadi Amoli.

Reza Hojjati

The martyr's friend

When someone mentions the name Mohsen Hojaji, the first thing I see in my mind is his infectious grin. When you met him, his glowing smile made you smile. The first time one of my friends on Gulbahar Street told me Mohsen had gone to Syria, I told them, "Stop being silly! It's not that easy to make a fool out of me." He was never sarcastic, and he didn't gossip. He came to the perfume store I worked in and we joked and laughed a lot.

Our friendship goes back to Rahiyan-e Noor in 2010, bus number six, the Hazrat Salman group. They put all the first- and second-year middle school children on our bus. I got to know Agha Mohsen from there as the assistant leader of our group. I remember the first time I looked at him, I thought to myself, "Why is he so skinny?" When he learnt I was the son of a martyr, he showed me special attention and even though I was seven years younger than him and he was my superior, he showed me a lot of respect out of admiration for my father.

He gathered the youth and took them to Takht-e Foolad. He stood at the front and recited the *ziyarah* for the martyrs. He didn't have a bad voice, but it would be a lie to say he was an extraordinary reciter! He talked a lot about Haj Ahmad Kazemi, and he was careful not to miss the anniversary of his martyrdom. He reminded everyone, even if it was just through a small text message, "O' Allah! One day, I want martyrdom from you. You have given me everything except martyrdom (Shaheed Haj Ahmad Kazemi). Another year has passed since the martyrdom of our dear commander. Recite a Salawat for his noble soul."

After his marriage, we mostly spoke over text and hardly met up in person. I had a dream I had seen his photo being displayed at the Shekarchiyan Junction in Najafabad.

"Salaam, Agha Mohsen. I saw you in my dream. I won't tell you it, but it was particularly good. Pray for me!"

"Salaam dear brother. Insha'Allah it's for the best. For the sake of our friendship, ask your dad to help me go and serve our Lady again. Please pray for me a lot."

After his first tour of Syria, he messaged from Qom every now and then, saying he was praying for us.

"A night will come where sunrise will end the night of separation,

Your shining sun will appear from the shrines,

May the length of your occultation not take from our hope,

So this bitter waiting can become time passed by (Insha'Allah)

Recite a Salawat for the hasty reappearance of the Imam (aj). I am praying for you at the shrine of Karimah Ahlulbayt (a)[161]. Pray for me."

The last time he mentioned he was doing *ziyarah* on my behalf, he said, "Salaam Alaykum. Insha'Allah I am doing *ziyarah* on behalf of you in the shrine of Ali ibn Musa ar-Rida (a). If I did anything to hurt you, please forgive me. Pray for me."

"Salaam. You visited the sister so much that finally, you managed to visit the brother. Please pray for me a lot."

"I need your prayers, my friend. Pray the brother gives me a permit to visit his dear aunt Zaynab."

I wanted to film a documentary regarding Shaheed Jamshidiyan. I managed to get in contact with his friends through Mohsen. He told me he didn't know them personally,

---

161. A title of Lady Ma'sumah (a) which translates to 'the generous one of the Ahlulbayt (as)'

but he could refer me to two people. He then laughed and said, "Insha'Allah, film a documentary about me too!" I replied, "Go and be martyred first, then I'll see what I can do!"

The following are the messages we exchanged the last time we ever met.

"Salaam. Agha Mohsen, are you coming to the mosque for Dhuhr prayers?"

"Salaam dear brother. Yes, I'll be there Insha'Allah. Is there something you need?"

"I wanted to pay you back for all your kindness. I'll see you at Dhuhr prayers. Pray for me."

"Salam. Where are you sitting?"

"Salam dear brother. Opposite the small door in the hall in the sixth row."

"Agha Reza, if it isn't a problem, do you think you could come to the door? I'm in a hurry."

I had a piece of cotton taken from the inside of the shroud of a martyr, and I thought Mohsen should have it. He told me:

"Thank you so much. I'm so happy right now. Your reward is with the martyrs themselves. Insha'Allah you become a martyr. Don't forget to pray for me, the sinner!"

"Who am I to pray for you?! Please pray especially for me."

"Pray, my friend. All that's left is for me to lose my head on the path of Zaynab, my dear."

A few days before he was dispatched to Syria, I was leaving for Mashhad. As soon as I sent a message to him asking for forgiveness, he replied:

"We will sacrifice everything for the head of our master. Don't forget us either. Pray our Lady calls me once more."

"Who am I to pray for you? You pray for us; you are under the care of our Lady regardless."

"I am always praying for my friends, but don't forget us."

Chapter III

GOD BLESS MARCO POLO!

Sayyid Danyal Hoseini

The martyr's friend

He didn't act on his promises and he procrastinated. He always got to work late. When it was time for the *adhan* of Maghrib, he told me, "Sayyid, I'm going to pray on time!"

"Mohsen, wait up! Right now when we're so busy?" I called.

"If you want to cut it from my wage, do it, but I have to go," he replied.

We worked together at the bookstore. At the time for the *adhan*, he ate *iftar*. "Why are you doing this? When do you want to enjoy your youth then?!" I teased, but he said, "Sayyid! We must be dedicated to Allah."

We set up an exhibition at the Ayatollah Khamenei Foundation. Whilst we were unloading our equipment, a woman came and asked why we had not opened the doors of the bookstore yet. Once I had answered her question and she left, Mohsen asked, "Do you know her?" "No," I replied, "but I think she's one of the members of the institute." The next day, Mohsen told me he was going to take some photos. Coincidentally, that woman was also working in the stall for the sisters' revolutionary programme. Agha Mohsen was constantly going and taking photos, God knows what of. Sometime after, he came to me and told me he was going to propose to that woman. I advised him, "You guys aren't a good match!" They had nothing in common, not culturally, not financially and not even in terms of lifestyle. One time, he got angry and left the bookstall unattended. The people thought the books were for free and took them all. A week before Eid al-Ghadeer[162], he came to the bookstore with a woman behind him on his motorcycle. It was Ms Abbasi, the same woman everyone told him not to get married to! I was shocked when he told me they were married.

On Eid al-Ghadeer, we went to his wedding. Halfway through the celebrations, he went to the next room to pray. "What's wrong with you?" I asked. "For once, don't pray or even pray a little later, what's the worst that could happen?!" His extreme religiousness irritated me. We surrounded him to try and make him dance a little. He was sitting in the middle of the carpet. We put him on our shoulders in the hope that he would move even just a little bit, but not even that.

After the wedding, we started spending more time together. I didn't like Mohsen much, but my wife was good friends with Mohsen's wife. Everyone was confused as to why I spent time with Mohsen even though we weren't alike at all . As soon as we got in the car, he started playing *nowhehs* by Sayyid Reza Narimani. He was always mourning for the Ahlulbayt (as). When we were going to pick up his bride, he was still listening to *nowhehs*. I was getting annoyed by this and I told him, "When you sit in my car, we're going to listen to music. You don't even have to pay for petrol." I put on music by Amir Tataloo[163]. He hated it. He didn't let me put on music by women. We went to the Zayanderud River. I told him, "Mohsen! Music, something, please! When I come to the river, I like to smoke shisha," but he was insistent and didn't give in. As soon as we got there, he got up and prayed on time. I objected, "Come on, man, give it a rest!"

---

162. Eid al-Ghadeer is on the 18th of Dhul-Hijjah and is the day the Holy Prophet (s) announced that Imam Ali (a) would be his successor.
163. Amir Tataloo is a famous Iranian rapper

We went to the park and on the way, I wanted to listen to music, but he objected, "No, it's Friday morning. We have to read Dua Nudbah." When we got to the park, he didn't want to come into the swimming pool, but we insisted so much until he jumped in. Halfway through, he said, "It's time for the *adhan*, I'm going to pray." I told him, "We're having fun right now, pray in an hour. You've only just jumped in and you're all wet!" but he didn't give in.

Most of the time, we got together and cooked some *jujeh* kebab. He didn't eat a lot. I told him, "Eat something, you're built like a straw!" He enjoyed falafel a lot. He loved the falafels from a fast-food shop on the highway to Isfahan. We stopped there all the time. He liked ice-cream a lot and he loved sunflower seeds. Sometimes, we all watched a film together. When we watched *Sperm Whale*[164], he hated it and he kept asking why we were wasting our time watching such a stupid movie. I told him, "This movie's been approved by the government. Are you holier than the government now?!" Once, we were laying down and I told him passionately, "My greatest wish is to become rich, have a house in the best part of Isfahan, be able to travel and just have a good time." I turned to him and asked, "What's your greatest wish, Mohsen?" He said without a thought, "Martyrdom!" As the sun rose, he said, "Sayyid, get up, let's go and pray in the central mosque!" I told him, "Are you crazy?! It's freezing outside. Pray here at home!" He prayed Maghrib at the shrine of the anonymous martyr near his house.

We visited my aunt's house in Chadegan. At night, Mohsen and I were laying down on either side of my aunt's husband. On one side, I was listening to music and on the other, Mohsen was listening to Hadith ul-Kisa. My aunt's husband asked us

---

164. نهنگ عنبر

surprised, "What do you two have in common that you spend so much time with each other?!" Whenever I backbit, he got angry and say quickly, "Change the subject, don't talk about others behind their backs!" He was always irritated when he went out and reminded the ladies to correct their hijabs. If they didn't listen, he became upset. Once, we went out to a dessert parlour and the owner was playing music by a female singer. He got up and told him, "Either you turn that off or we'll leave." The owner quickly turned the music off.

He stopped working at the bookstore and took up employment at the gas factory. He loved perfume and for a while, he wanted to open a perfume store. I told him he wouldn't find any business in Najafabad. He always bought the latest perfume.

His wife suggested he join the IRGC. I still don't understand why Ms Abbasi insisted so much for him to join the IRGC. His first training course was in Shiraz.

The first time I went to their house, I was shocked. How could Mohsen allow so much decoration and beauty?! As soon as I sat down, I told him, "Choke on it!"

"On what?" he asked.

"These decorations!" I replied.

"I don't like all of these decorations and adornments," he told me.

"You're so ignorant!" I said to him.

He loved his wife and respected her a lot. One time, I asked him, "Tell me truthfully and like a Husayni, is this all for show?" He replied firmly, "No, I swear!" He continued, "I got my wife from Shaheed Kazemi." I teased him, "No, you got your wife from the book exhibition!"

They had different tastes too. He wanted his wife to wear a black *chador* and hijab, but his wife didn't want to. However, when his wife asked Mohsen to wear lighter colours, he wouldn't. His wife wanted him to wear colourful t-shirts, but he didn't like wearing short-sleeved clothes at all. We came to a loggerhead on this. I insisted he wear short sleeves, but not only did he refuse, but he even told me to change my style too!

Sometimes, I wore sweaters, but he told me, "You should wear shirts with a mandarin collar." He promised he would buy them for me, and I told him, "Be a man and buy them, I'll wear them, I promise."

I didn't want my wife to wear a *chador*. He said to me, "Sayyid! This is really bad!" He gave me a lot of reasons [why she should wear a *chador*], but I told him after, "I'm not convinced!" He said to me, "Even if you have to force her, she should wear it." I told him, "It's just an extra expense. Why should I have to go and pay for a *chador*?" He then suddenly had an idea, and he bought a brand-new *chador* as a gift for my wife.

He actively searched for the programmes where Sayyid Reza Narimani or Salahshour[165] were reciting and when he found one, he called and told me, "Get ready, I'm coming to pick you up," but I said, "Leave me alone, man!" He insisted a lot though. By chance, every time Sayyid Reza Narimani cancelled or when they went to Salahshour, their car broke down. What I mean to say is something always happened for us not to go. On the night before Ashura, there was a football match between Iran and Uzbekistan at the Azadi Stadium. I told him, "I want to watch the football tonight." He replied, "Don't you dare! Tonight, I'm taking you to the programme of Sayyid Reza Narimani himself!"

Whether or not we were together, whenever he went to Isfahan, he first always went to Gulzar-e Shuhada to visit the graves of Alireza Noori and Ruhollah Kafizadeh. On the way, he

---

165. Haj Mahdi Salahshour is a famous Iranian reciter

got off at Karsang to visit the graves of Komeyl Ghorbani and Musa Jamshidiyan. He also visited the graves of Haj Ahmad Kazemi, Moslem Khizab and Hamidreza Dayitaghi at Takht-e Foolad. He visited all his friends at once. It didn't make a difference whether we were going to the cinema or a *majlis*, we always went this way. Sometimes I got fed up and ask, "Mohsen! Why have you brought us to the cemetery?!" When he visited Haj Ahmad's grave, he sat and spoke as if he was talking to his brother.

That night, we reached Sayyid Reza Narimani's programme at Maghrib. The hall was so packed, we only got in after a lot of difficulty. They closed the doors and told us no one could leave until the programme was over. I thought to myself, "Okay, no problem! He'll recite for an hour and then we'll leave." They recited Ziyarah Ashura and then the speaker gave an exceptionally long lecture. Only then did Sayyid Reza Narimani start. As soon as he said *bismillah*, Mohsen started crying. I was staring at him and thought to myself, "He hasn't even recited the *masa'ib* yet, why is he crying?!" They did *sinehzani* for two whole hours. I finally brought myself to words and told him, "Mohsen, what's wrong with you?! Get up, let's go!" He was in his own world. Once the *sinehzani* ended, I said, "Come, let's get some dinner," but he said, "Sayyid, sit down, the reward is given once the work is done!" When Narimani said, "O' Allah, help us all achieve martyrdom!" during the *duas*, he said amen from the bottom of his heart. He was crying and saying amen. That night on the way back, I berated him to my heart's content. He didn't say anything, he just lowered his head. His silence infuriated me even further. Half an hour after we reached home, he texted me, "Forgive me. On the eve of Ashura, forgive me, I didn't mean to bother you." I didn't reply. In the morning, he came to me again so we could go to another *majlis*. He said, "Sayyid! Shall we go to Sayyid Reza Narimani's programme?" I replied, "You've exhausted me!"

One night, he came and took me to a programme arranged by the Rowzeh-ye Rezvan Organisation. There was heavy traffic. I didn't know where he got his stamina from. Where did this love for *majalis* come from? Where had he found this random organisation from the backstreets of Isfahan from? How had he managed to become a volunteer for them? What thoughts, what love took him there? I didn't understand.

Wherever he went for *ziyarah*, he always remembered me, even if it was through one small text. He went for military training for six months in Shiraz and every Thursday night, he messaged me from the shrine of Shah Cheragh[166]. One time, he messaged me, "Sayyid, can you believe not one of my friends reply to me, asking me to pray for them?" but he still remembered and messaged us.

When he went to Syria for the first time, it was just before Muharram. I found out he was about to leave because one of his friends told me accidentally. He messaged me and told me not to tell anyone. When he got back, I joked with him and said, "I guess now you've gone and earned your money, there's no need for all of this love and crying [for martyrdom]!" He got angry and replied, "I didn't even take one *rial*!" I told him, "Yeah, you're right. You won't go if you don't get paid." His friends had been martyred and from then on, he completely changed. He only thought of going to Syria again and becoming a martyr. I couldn't understand for the life of me why this was the case.

---

166. Ahmad ibn Musa (a), known as Shah Cheragh (Farsi for 'the King of Light') was the son of Imam Kadhim (a). He set off for Marv to join his brother, Imam Rida (a), in the court of Ma'mun, but on the way, he was stopped by the ruler of Shiraz who informed him of the martyrdom of Imam Rida (a). Many of his companions left by that time, but this didn't deter him, and he was martyred in battle. His holy body was laid to rest in Shiraz.

I was put in charge of photography for the children's Muharram programme. I was terribly busy, so I told Mohsen, "I need to do something. Can you help me out?" On the day of the programme, he told his wife while taking photos of the wives of the martyred Defenders of the Shrine and their children, "Your space is empty amongst them!"

He was taken captive on a Monday. On the previous Friday morning, I was shocked to get a phone call from him. He said to me, "Sayyid, pray I am martyred!" I told him, "Leave it, for God's sake. Go to Lady Zaynab (a) and pray for us instead! Insha'Allah you come back safely." He replied, "No, don't say that Sayyid, pray I am martyred." I got annoyed and said, "O' Allah, by the right of Lady Zaynab (a), you will be martyred."

At 9:30 am on Monday, I saw the video of him being taken captive. I was falling apart. It was as if I was going crazy. I was seeing Mohsen everywhere I looked, in every corner of the house, inside the car. He was praying here, eating there, playing *nowhehs* here. The next day at half-past three in the morning, my wife woke me up and exclaimed, "Mohsen has been martyred!" I couldn't bear being inside the house. It was as if the walls were closing in on me. I went out into the road. I was walking and saying, "Mohsen! Were you martyred?! Did you get what you wished for?!"

The members of the institute had gathered at Gulzar-e Shuhada. They were all crying. They asked me, "How come you're so calm?" I replied, "You should be glad, Mohsen finally got what he wished for!"

I miss him all the time, I miss our crazy times, even just when we went out together. I don't have him anymore. I never went to that falafel store again or even that ice-cream shop. I haven't even been to my aunt's house in Chadegan. Amongst all the programmes, my heart only broke once, and I cried my eyes out, and that was when Sayyid Reza Narimani recited about him in the central mosque of Najafabad, and he recited, "I must also go, yes, I must go and my head too...[167]"

Majeed Salehi

The martyr's friend

He got into an accident on his motorcycle and fractured his leg. His leg was in a cast and he was laying down in a corner of the room. His friends and I arranged to visit him. They said we shouldn't go empty-handed, so I took responsibility for this. I didn't do things by half; I bought a ten-kilo watermelon and tied a black ribbon on it. Us four decided to have some fun with him. As soon as we came in, I threw the watermelon to Mohsen. He made a whooping sound and shook as if I'd thrown it into a pool. I said, "Tell them we don't want any cakes or tea, just bring a tray so we can tear this watermelon apart!" We fed him half the watermelon whilst joking and messing around. We got him good; in the middle of the night, he called and said, "You traitors! I'm dying. I have to keep dragging myself to the toilet with this broken leg!"

We arranged to play volleyball in the park every Friday morning and whoever came late had to buy ice-cream for the others as a fine. One day, it was raining very heavily, as if the sky had been torn apart. We were waiting for Mohsen in the car, and he eventually turned up on his motorcycle. He looked like

167. منم باید برم، آره برم سرم بره

a drenched mouse due to the downpour. The rain was so heavy, he couldn't come to the park, so he stood under a bridge. We just sat there looking at him. He texted, saying, "You cowards! I'm going to fall sick!" I showed him the time and that he had to buy us ice-cream. He didn't have a choice. He turned around in the rain and we followed him whilst blowing the horn.

I always had a shisha with me. One time, we went to the riverside together and I got the shisha bag out. He said, "For God's sake, do something I can enjoy too!" I replied, "Cool, that's what I'm doing right now, can't you see? I'm getting the shisha ready." He frowned and said, "I hate these things." He ran and brought Ludo out of the car. We could never enjoy shisha as much as we did snakes and ladders. We laughed so much. Even the El Clasico[168] wasn't as exciting as this. Despite this, we were still not allowed to talk. As soon as we started talking about someone, he became serious and say, "Hey, don't backbite!"

At midnight, we went out with our wives on our motorcycles just to drive around a bit and get some fresh air. I said, "Why don't you buy us some ice-cream?" It had snowed the night before, and it was freezing.

"If you want ice-cream, we have to go to Isfahan," he said.
"Fine, let's go. Do you think I won't go?!" I replied.
"On motorcycles?" he asked.
"I'll get the car, don't worry," I replied.

---

168. A football match between Barcelona and Real Madrid

He didn't expect me to pull my brother out of bed at that time of night just to get the keys. On the way, he said, "For God's sake, do you have nothing to do? I have to go to work in the morning." I replied, "We have to get ice-cream tonight, whatever happens." All the ice-cream shops around the Khaju Bridge were closed. We turned back towards the Si-o-Se Bridge and from afar, we saw a shop's light close, and the owner was pushing the ice-cream machine into the shop. I pulled up and started shouting out to him to not close. The shopkeeper started laughing and said, "Are you crazy?! You want ice-cream in this cold at this time of night especially?!" When he poured the first ice-cream, I told him to pour as much as he could. We took two normal ones for the ladies. He poured almost twenty-five centimetres worth of ice-cream into a cone. I asked, "Is that all?" He replied, "Give this one to your friend," and I gave it to Mohsen. The shopkeeper didn't hold back; I wouldn't be lying if I said he poured forty centimetres worth of ice-cream onto my cone. It looked like a minaret. We sat in the car and started laughing. I got brain freeze but Mohsen told me, "I've already paid for it, you're going to have to eat it!" From that night onwards, he told our friends, "Don't joke around with Majeed, he doesn't understand them!"

One snowy night, I rang Mohsen and told him the weather was perfect for two people and we should go out. He replied sleepily, "You fool! It's dangerous to go out on a motorcycle in this weather." I had just bought a car, so I replied, "We'll go in the car and if anything happens, it's my car, so don't worry." He kept refusing but I was insistent. On the other hand, the ladies also wanted to come along. As soon as we left, it looked as if someone had thrown the cars into a slide. They were slipping themselves. As we were laughing at the cars that had slipped into the gutters, Mohsen said, "Majeed! Go that way!" Boom, we crashed straight into the trunk of the car in front of us. If someone saw us, they would have thought we had smoked something because of how much we were laughing. He said, "Stop being silly!" I replied, "The fun doesn't start until 3 am!" He said, "I'm an idiot if I ever pick up your phone call after 10 pm!"

He normally contacted me once every two to three days latest, but I hadn't heard anything from him for the past week. His phone was always off. My wife suspected something was up after she saw his wife's Telegram profile picture. I asked one of his friends from the institute about him and they told me, "He's gone to Syria!" He hadn't let anyone know.

When he got back, I went to see him. He painfully told me how Pooya Izadi and Komeyl Ghorbani were both martyred in front of his eyes. He was struggling to speak through the tears. He said ruefully, "But I wasn't worthy!" I slapped his leg and said, "Hey! If you are martyred, do you expect me to fight ISIS?! There's no need, you have to be here to kill them!" He was confused. He said in his thick Najafabadi accent, "Stupid! If we aren't martyred, we will die [normally]!" I didn't understand what he truly meant. I asked him, "So, as you love martyrdom so much, how do you want to be martyred?" He said, fighting back the tears, "It isn't important how I'm martyred, but I want to have no name or grave like Lady Fatimah Zahra (a)!"

There were ten days left until Nowruz 2017. He came to me and asked if I knew anywhere that was employing during the holidays. I told him, "Actually, the bakery I work at is." If it were me asking, I would ask how much they were paying, if they provide insurance or not and what their working hours are like, but his first question was, "Will they let me pray my Dhuhr prayers on time?" He started working with us on the 2nd of April.

Whilst working, all he talked about was Syria, martyrdom, and his martyred friends. To lighten the mood, I said, "Come on, man! Even I'll be martyred if I go." The shop owner said, "Mohsen! There's no point going on like this. Go and bring a big bag so Majeed can walk around with it on his head." Whilst putting cakes into the box, he said, "He's becoming bold, but even in our war [the Iran-Iraq War], there were hypocrites who hit their heads on rocks and were martyred. One day, you'll see Majeed has been martyred and we will still be here, searching for martyrdom!"

A few days before he left on his second tour of Syria, we arranged a trip to the waterpark with our friends. Our allotted time to go was from 8 pm to 12 am. Mohsen messaged in the group, "What will we do about our prayers? *Adhan* is at half-past eight." I replied, "I swear we are also Muslims, we'll sort it out together." He wrote back, "Don't take this the wrong way, but I'm going to pray and then come." I warned him that if he came late, he had to treat us all to ice-cream, but he was willing to do so.

We arranged to meet up in front of the park at half-past seven. We went inside and at around nine, I came out to see if he had come. I couldn't find him even after searching the dressing rooms and showers. I went back to the pool and saw him there.

"They let me pray in the lifeguard room after I begged them," he told me. There was a small prayer room in the pool where everyone prayed in their swimming costumes. At the door, they told him to go there and pray, but Mohsen said he didn't want to pray in his swimming costume.

We got hungry but because he came late, he hadn't put any money on his wristband[169], so I paid for his dinner. When we came out, he said in the car, "Send me your card details." I replied, "You don't have to do it right now." As normal, he started talking about leaving and he mentioned that once he's in Syria, he would still be indebted to me. I told him, "I want you to be indebted to me so I can use you in the next world!" He said eagerly, "If you pray for my martyrdom, I promise to put twice the amount into your account." He didn't even wait until sunrise; at half-past one in the morning, I got a message from my bank saying money had been transferred.

As soon as his message arrived that said he was going to serve Lady Zaynab (a) and to forgive him, I felt empty. I replied, "Please pray for me," but I didn't feel at rest. I called him and said, "Mohsen! I didn't like your message, there was something about it." He replied, "Pray I return with my head held high." I felt bothered and asked, "What else do you want?" He repeated, "Pray I get what I want. I'm thinking of you wherever I go." I fought back the lump in my throat to say, "Both on this side and that side, huh?"

---

169. In Iran, there are electronic wristbands which you can top up with money and use it to buy things in the stores inside the waterpark

While I was working at the bakery, one of my friends called to tell me Mohsen had been taken captive. I had to sit down; my hands were shaking. My knees felt weak, and I felt as if I couldn't speak. They thought I had suffered a heart attack. I sat like that in the corner of the shop for half an hour. I couldn't bring my hands to unlock my phone. The others weren't in any better state than me. Everyone was in shock. The shop owner called a taxi and sent me home.

When I saw his coffin from afar, I thought to myself, "Mohsen! Well done! Don't forget to intercede for me!" I couldn't bring myself to go forward through the crowd of the funeral. I waited until it calmed down to talk with him to my heart's content.

Milad Haidari

The martyr's friend

As soon as I walk up to the diving board, I think of him. We went to the swimming pool together and I just jumped in like an amateur. He came and asked, "What kind of diving is that? Come, let me teach you." I asked, "Do you know how to dive?" He replied, "You haven't seen anything. I've done a whole course!"

He was a natural teacher, ever since we were in university. In my second semester, I found electronics quite difficult. We had a strict teacher, and I was failing the class. I hadn't understood anything from this damn class since the beginning of the semester. I was on the verge of giving up. In the best-case scenario, I was hoping to get three or four[170]. I begged Mohsen to come and just help me a bit. He told me, "I'll go and read these notes and see if I can understand anything from them or not. If I can, I'll tell you to come around so we can put our heads together." He called and was shouting "Eureka! Eureka!" like Archimedes. From night until morning, he had looked at a few books, read notes from different teachers and he had reached a completely new solution. Just to make sure, I used his formula for two or three different problems and the answers came out the same. The next day, I went to my exams and the questions were as easy as pie. When the teacher put the results on the board, Mohsen was annoyed. I got twenty and he got eighteen. He said, "I had all those sleepless nights, and you got the twenty!"

---

170. In Iran, the best one can get in an exam is 20.

He didn't have a great physique; he was just a bunch of skin and bones. In the beginning, the security stopped him as he was going in and asked to see his student card. They thought he was a high school student who wanted to see what university was like. He eventually got annoyed with them and told them, "Come on, I'm the same guy you stopped yesterday!"

We met up with our friends in the park. We laid down on the grass and we started eating sunflower seeds. Mohsen revealed his true environmentalist self and told us not to throw the shell on the ground. He suggested someone put their shoe in the middle. Everyone looked at me; after all, I was the only one who wore size ten shoes.

We made a Telegram group and we named it 'Old Friends'. There were four members, just us friends from university. Mohsen was the admin of the group. Since he went to Syria, there are only three active members.

I was always looking at news from Syria because I was waiting for him. At around nine in the morning, a news channel announced that ISIS had taken an Iranian soldier captive, but there was no name. I downloaded the picture quickly. I don't know why it took so long. My internet wasn't lagging. I was worried it may be Mohsen. O' Allah, have mercy! It was him. The hairs on the back of my neck stood up. I couldn't believe it. I kept zooming into his face. I couldn't control myself; it was as if I had gone insane. I quickly forwarded it to the 'Old Friends' group. I wrote beneath it, "Ya Abul-Fazl[171], what do we do?!" Less than two minutes later, his wife rang me. I didn't know what to say. I gathered myself and picked up. I could only hear screaming and crying. I only then realised what had happened; Mohsen's Telegram account was open on his wife's phone. She asked, "Is it true?!" I was lost for words. I replied, "Insha'Allah, it's nonsense." Her voice kept cracking up.

---

171. A title of Hazrat Abbas, meaning 'father of virtue'.

Yousuf Sheydaei

The martyr's friend

Mohsen was the clerk of the commando company of the Dezful Armoured Brigade, and he wrote most of their letters. He was the senior clerk. When we were being assigned, he came and said, "We need a few clerks in the command office, come and be my assistant." I went and gave the handwriting test. I had to be able to write quickly but legibly. They liked my handwriting and told me to work there. He explained to me that he owed his letter-writing abilities to an institute in Najafabad. He didn't need a commander to write it for him so he could organise it. He wrote it himself in pen and sent it to be signed.

If a soldier started missing their family and stopped doing any work because of this, we said they had gone into a coma. Whenever Mohsen came back from leave, he was always eager to start working again. One of the soldiers said to him, "When we come back from leave, we are in a coma for two days. Don't you miss home?" He replied, "These are mental constructs we create for ourselves. You can think about both your family and military service at the same time, there's no need to go into a coma!"

One of the soldiers lost his mother and he became quite depressed. He was never calm, and no one could calm him down either. I went and told Mohsen to go and speak to him. I don't know what he told the poor soldier, but afterwards, he was completely calm. He then went to talk to the commander of the company to give him a few days of leave. The next morning, that soldier went home.

As we were in a commando company, they took us to the obstacle courses every morning after Fajr prayers. One day, the commander of the battalion announced, "Soldiers to the side. I want to see how ready the clerks are!" We said to Mohsen, "The senior has to go first, we are right behind you!" Mohsen and I were paired up together and they put us on a height of two and a half metres. The commander said, "Jump down and do a roll!" I told Mohsen, "If I jump from this height, I'll break every bone in my body!" He thought a little and replied, "It's nothing, just jump! You can do it!" I said, "Don't flatter me!" He jumped down and rolled. I wouldn't jump, however much they insisted. Eventually, the commander came and pushed me down. Mohsen laughed, "I told you to jump, are you happy now?"

One day, he suggested, "Guys, let's go and take photos together. In four days when we've left this place , at least we will be able to keep some souvenirs from it." We called the photographer over and we found a log from a eucalyptus tree. We all sat on it in a row, and we took photos. Mohsen looked at them and said, "There's nothing different about these photos!" He pointed at the eucalyptus tree which stood more than two metres tall and suggested the photographer stays on the ground while we climb up. We told him, "We don't want to die !" but it wasn't easy to dissuade him. "A soldier in a commando battalion of the AJA should never be scared of heights!" he taunted. Eventually, he couldn't force us up the tree. He went up himself and took a photo.

I wrote 'Command Office Janitor, Mohsen Hojaji' on a piece of paper, stuck it to his door and took a selfie with it. I went back on leave and somehow, the others managed to get a hold of the photo. When I got back, I told him, "One day, I want to show this photo to your wife and tell her not to think her husband had any kind of special position!" He chuckled and replied, "I've got one for you too!" He used this opportunity to get back at me. He had stuck a piece of paper to my door which read 'Command Office Janitor, Sergeant on Duty, Yousuf Sheydaei' and taken a selfie pointing at it.

Sometimes when we sat down to chat, he gathered us around himself and suggested, "Let's read some Quran." Once we had finished our Quran, I said, "Guys, now we can joke around!" He got annoyed and reply, "I won't sit with you guys, you always backbite!" Because of these jokes, he called me 'the bad Shirazi'. However, he played chess with us, and he was exceptionally good too.

When he had nothing to do in the afternoons, he recited the Quran. After Dhuhr prayers, one clerk had to remain in the office. He never missed congregational prayers once and he was given an 'exemplary soldier' award for this. For a while, I saw him get up at midnight and pray at the end of the hall. I was curious so one night at half-past one, I went to him and I noticed he was praying Salat ul-Layl.

I went for my interview to join the IRGC and I passed. I wanted to work with him. The battalion's second-in-command wasn't allowing me to go back on leave, so Mohsen went and spoke with him. However, his mediation didn't bear any fruit either. Mohsen told me to call the commander of the company. He came into the telephone kiosk and he spoke himself. He explained the situation to the commander. The company commander replied, "I'm coming to the base right now, stay there, I'll come and approve his leave." Once my work issues were sorted, I asked Mohsen, "What do you have planned for your future?" He replied, "Many of my family members are scholars, so I want to attend the Islamic seminary."

When I woke up in the morning, he was gone. I asked where he was, and one of the soldiers told me, "He's gone to the post in my place." When I went back to the room, he was there. I asked him, "Why did you go to the post?" He replied, "The soldier was tired and mentally fatigued. I was afraid he may hurt himself with his weapon." Do you know what his post was? Patrolling the borders of our base in the freezing cold.

There was a soldier who self-harmed so much that when he pulled up his shirt, all you could see were razor and knife wounds. One night, one of the soldiers went to wake him up to go to his post, but he told him, "I'll beat the hell out of you, this is the last time you ever wake me up!" The soldier came back and said he wasn't waking up. I told him, "Go and wake Mohsen up and tell him to speak with him." He went and spoke with him and the soldier yelled, "I'm not okay, I want to go back on leave!" Mohsen told him, "Go and stand on patrol tonight, I promise I'll try to persuade the commander in the morning to let you go back on leave." The soldier replied, "You have to stand by your word!" In the morning, he went to take leave for the soldier and eventually, he got the approval.

One of the soldiers gathered the others around himself and propagate Baha'ism. Mohsen pulled him aside and told him, "This is the last time I see you gathering the soldiers around yourself!" It was to no avail as he continued the same path. Whenever Mohsen saw the soldier gathering others, he ambitiously got ready to rush towards him, saying, "Let me go mess his gathering up."

Hadi Afshari

The martyr's friend

I called and told him, "Don't take too long! Come down quickly." We had to pick up two others, one of them from Isfahan and one from Zarinshahr. When we got to Isfahan, we couldn't find the address. We drove around a roundabout a few times and he laughed, "I didn't drive around this much even on my wedding night!" He kept changing the *nowheh* that was playing, so I asked, "What are you looking for?" He replied, "Sayyid Reza Narimani." I told him, "There are only *nowhehs* by Meysam Moti'ei[172] on this flash drive." He had forgotten to bring his flash drive. He asked, "I have some on my phone, do you have an aux cable?" I replied, "My stereo doesn't have an aux slot." When the others got in, he gave them the *ziyarah* of Lady Fatimah (a) so they could read it on the way.

When we reached Boroujen, he said, "Wait here, I want to buy a flag." He chose a small flag he could put on his backpack and he also bought a small notebook so he could write down the memories of the trip. After travelling thirty, forty kilometres, he remembered he left his *tasbih* in the shop. He implored me to turn around so we could get it. I told him, "Leave it, man, the *tasbih* isn't that valuable." He sighed and told me the beads were collected from the places where his friends had been martyred. I turned around and headed back immediately. He was praying that would find it. When we got there, we found it exactly on the shopkeeper's till.

---

172. Meysam Moti'ei is a famous Iranian reciter who is known for incorporating the revolutionary spirit into his recitations and for the deeper meanings in his poetry.

While we were going through the war zones, he told us all about the Kumayl Trench[173] and he insisted we visit it on our way back. We reached the Chazabe Border[174] before the *adhan* of Fajr, so we parked on the side and did *wudu*. After passing through security, he found a small corner to pray in, and we all prayed behind him.

We couldn't find a vehicle to take us at that time of morning amongst the crowds, and we were forced to get on the back of an open-roof lorry which had come to transport the pilgrims. The cold weather coupled with the dust was blinding. We huddled together and we were all shivering. Mohsen was constantly holding his *tasbih* and reciting *duas*. After half an hour, he brought himself close to my ear and whispered, "Why is everyone so quiet?" I told him, "Well, recite something then!" He replied as hopelessness flashed in his eyes, "Watch how they won't join me!" I said, "There's no harm in trying." It was as if he had predicted this situation; he pulled a notebook out of his pocket and he started reciting *nowhehs* from it. Slowly, the others started gathering around at the back of the lorry and recited the *nowheh* along with him.

When we got off the lorry, we got on a bus to take us to Najaf. He quickly sat next to the driver and he sorted out the cost of the bus in his broken Arabic. He made friends with the driver quickly and he connected his phone to the bus's stereo. His greatest wish was to listen to Narimani's *nowhehs* all the way to Najaf. Due to the passion in the *nowhehs*, the driver unconsciously started speeding up, so I told Mohsen, "Turn it off before he kills us all!" When we got off, he gave ten thousand

---

173. The trench where Shaheed Ibrahim Hadi and many other Iranian soldiers were besieged for more than five days without any access to food or water and were slaughtered mercilessly by the Baathist forces.
174. A southern border between Iran and Iraq.

tomans extra to the driver so he wouldn't feel indebted to him. "Maybe I didn't understand what he was trying to tell me," he said.

We reached the shrine at 10 pm. This was the first time going for *ziyarah* on Arbaeen[175] and we didn't know the way . We went straight to the shrine. The others said, "We haven't eaten dinner, what shall we do?" Mohsen stroked his beard and replied, "God is great, He'll sort it out Himself." When we reached the entrance of the shrine, he said, "I'll sit here with the bags and shoes, you go and do *ziyarah* and come back and then I'll go." He waited with our things all on his own. When we came out from *ziyarah*, we could smell ghormeh sabzi. Someone came to us with a bag full of food and Mohsen came to me and said with a beaming smile, "Here's your food! What else do you want?"

We couldn't find anywhere to sleep so we went to the Lady Zahra (a) Courtyard[176] and each of us found a small spot for ourselves amongst the pilgrims. When they woke me up in the morning, I noticed Mohsen had put his blanket on me.

He started reciting Dua Ahd as soon as we set off on our walk towards Karbala. He recited it line by line so we could also read along with him. He constantly made sure his flag was still clipped to his bag. Every now and then, he pulled out his *nowheh* notebook and recited. We all beat our chests and recited along with him, us four, as we walked on. Whenever we sat down to take a rest, he quickly jotted down the memories of the trip in his yellow notebook. At nights, he gathered us all together and we recited Surah Waqiah. Even though he didn't eat a lot,

---

175. The fortieth day after Ashura, the day it is highly recommended to visit Imam Husayn (a). The believers walk from Najaf, where Imam Ali (a) is buried, to Karbala, the place of burial of Imam Husayn (a), in an act of allegiance to their Imams (as).

176. The largest courtyard in the shrine of Imam Ali (a).

he always made sure to visit the *mawkibs*[177] which were serving falafels.

We reached Karbala as the sun was setting on our third day of walking. As soon as we saw the dome of the shrine of Hazrat Abul-Fazl, tears started flowing from our eyes. Mohsen started reciteing the *ziyarah* of Hazrat Abul-Fazl. We decided to find a *mawkib* and then go for *ziyarah*. An Iranian youth asked when he saw us wandering around, "Are you looking for a *mawkib*?" We said yes eagerly, and he showed us on a card how to get to Mawkib Sahib az-Zaman (aj), established by the good people of Jahrom. Mohsen took a photo of it with his phone. We managed to find our way after asking for directions many times. The *mawkib* was completely full, but they let us in. After dinner, the others wanted to take a shower, but Mohsen said, "No, it's better to go with these dusty clothes." The next day, he fell ill with a cold and fever, and he was shivering a lot. He didn't come out from under the covers in the *mawkib* for one whole day. We brought him soup and eventually, he managed to stand that night. He went to the shrine all on his own and came back.

When we were organising how we would get back, Mohsen suggested we stay until Thursday night and he said, "We've come all this way to Karbala, it would be a shame if we miss the special night to do *ziyarah* of Imam Husayn!" He managed to convince everyone by saying this. We wanted to go for *ziyarah* altogether that night, but he betrayed us. He went alone and found a quiet corner where he could do his own *ziyarah*. We couldn't find him wherever we looked in the shrine. When we got back to the *mawkib* in the morning, he got back at exactly

---

177. Stalls which provide food, shelter or both to the pilgrims of Imam Husayn (a).

the time we agreed with a whole variety of *turbahs*[178] and *tasbihs* as souvenirs.

---

178. Clay tablets made from the soil of Karbala upon which prostration is recommended.

Ali Sadeghiyan

The martyr's friend

God bless Marco Polo! Whenever I called him, he was always travelling. "I am doing *ziyarah* on your behalf in the shrine of Lady Ma'sumah (a)," he said one day, "I'm at the grave of Haj Ahmad," the next. Sometimes he was in Jamkaran, sometimes in Mashhad. I wouldn't care so much if he had a safe car. He thought he had a Peugeot ROA[179], but it was really a bunch of scrap metal on four tires. In the mornings, I had to push it so he could finally switch it on and get it into first gear with great effort. I can't count how many times I told Mohsen to sell that heap of garbage and buy a suitable car, but he laughed, "It's one of my plans for the future." I joked that if he didn't have enough time to change the car's oil, he could give me the key and I'd get it serviced in the morning, but he laughed, "No, dear brother! I took it to the mechanic yesterday." I replied, "Yeah, of course you did! You were with so-and-so yesterday!"

I expected that once his child was born, he always would always stay at home and never come out with us, but far from it! He picked Ali up and left. He said the custom of not taking children outside the house until they are forty days old is an old housewives' tale. A few days after his child's birth, he wrapped him up in a hat and scarf and we visited Golestan-e Shuhada in Isfahan together. As soon as we reached Haj Ahmad, he took Ali from his wife's hands and laid him down on his stomach on top of the grave and told him to hug Haj Ahmad. His wife ran towards the child so his clothes wouldn't get dirty, but Mohsen

---

179. An Iranian-made car which is a hybrid between a Paykan and a Peugeot 405.

stopped her and said, "No, let him sit in Haj Ahmad's lap." He then quietly asked Haj Ahmad to look after his little Ali Agha.

We visited Golestan-e Shuhada once or twice a month and sometimes, we brought a mat, tea and some snacks and had a small picnic by Haj Ahmad's grave, but of course, Mohsen didn't drink any tea or soda. He preferred herbal teas and medicine, but they never failed to bring the Najafabadi bag; the one filled with dried chickpeas, raisins, and dried berries. As soon as we reached Golestan-e Shuhada, he looked for a martyr who was Sayyid, greeted him and then we visited Haj Ahmad.

He didn't play around; he paid attention to every little action of his so he could reach his goal of martyrdom. One day, I saw him running down the stairs two at a time. As soon as he reached the door, I asked, "Is a thief chasing you or something?! Try not to kill yourself! The worst that will happen is you'll reach work one minute later." He quickly switched the car on and replied, "These one minutes push our martyrdom back a whole day!"

One time, we decided to visit Chamgordan. We went to a park by the waterside and a couple came and laid their things on the platform beside ours. Mohsen was getting annoyed because the woman didn't have proper hijab on. A vendor came by selling plastic bags and he asked, "Agha, do you want some bags?" Mohsen replied loudly, "Give your bags to this woman so she can fix her hijab!" The vendor paid no attention to him and came over to me, but Mohsen repeated, "Aren't you looking for customers? I'm telling you to go and give them to that man so he can tell his wife to wear her hijab properly!" His wife stepped in and told him, "Leave it! Are you looking for trouble?" At that moment, I noticed the woman pulled her scarf forward and left with her husband.

We went to pray Maghrib in the prayer room and he kept trying to send me forward so I could lead the prayers. When I saw he wasn't going to give up, I told him, "Only on the condition that you lead the second prayer." I led the first prayer on this condition and after we finished, I turned back and asked him, "Do you want to pray Fajr at the mosque tomorrow morning?" Excitement flashed in his eyes and he replied, "Actually, I've been going on my own for a while, but I've been looking for a companion."

From then on, it began. We put our phones beside our heads and whichever one of us woke up first called the other. We prayed at the central mosque of Najafabad. It took us fifteen minutes to get there and around half an hour, forty-five minutes or sometimes even an hour to get back. Sometimes our conversations in the parking lot went on for so long that we had to go to work from there. We talked about all sorts of things, but all Mohsen talked about was the martyrs and martyrdom. "Don't you say you are so attached to Shaheed Kazemi?" I asked him once. "Why are you rushing for martyrdom so much then? He stayed until the end of the Holy Defence, he became a trustworthy asset for the Leader and then he reached his goal after all his service."

"No, look at it this way; I want to go to Syria and be martyred and when Imam Mahdi (aj) reappears, I'll ask him to bring me back so I can be martyred in his army again!" he replied.

"You're so spoilt! So, you want to have your cake and eat it?" I asked.

"Yes, exactly!" he told me.

After his first tour of Syria, he was confused as to why he didn't achieve the status of martyrdom. He was questioning everything. I went to visit him three or four nights after he returned. I poured salt in the wounds of his heart by asking, "So what happened? You said you're going to leave, and I won't see you again! I thought you were going to go standing and come back laying down." He fell deep in thought for a few minutes. He brought quince tea and offered me some. He then sat on the three-person sofa, patted me on my leg and replied regretfully, "Maybe I wasn't martyred because the uniform I fought in didn't belong to me." I said happily to calm him down, "Weren't Pooya Izadi and Komeyl Ghorbani both martyred in uniform? You're no greater than them!" He insisted, saying, "From the moment I flew over there to this moment right now, I've been wondering why I wasn't martyred. Everything was in order except for these clothes."

That night, he didn't mention any stories from his time in Syria no matter how much I insisted, but he briefly mentioned a little bit about going to Latakia and how they were trained to use T-90 tanks on our way back from Fajr prayers, and that was only to tell me that the Russians didn't want the Iranians to learn the intricacies of operating their tanks. He mentioned, "I kept asking one of the Russian officers why they didn't want us to fully learn how to use the tank, and he eventually told me their commanding officers told them the Iranians can learn ten different things just from knowing how to use a valve stem properly."

Some days, we wouldn't reach in time for congregational prayers, so we prayed individually and then went back. We stayed long enough to read the post-Fajr prayer *duas*, but we didn't stay for Ziyarah Ashura. One day, I called many times to wake him up and when he came down, he said with bags under his eyes, "I was kept up until three last night!" He had set up a website with a few of his friends to answer religious queries.

"We go and read up about every query," he told me, "and we answer it to the best of our capabilities." On our way back to our neighbourhood, I asked him as we were passing by the cemetery of the anonymous martyrs, "Now, imagine if you go to Syria and you are martyred, how would you like to be martyred?" He patted me on the shoulder and said, "It's not important to me, I just want my martyrdom to serve a gain."

One day when he didn't wake up for congregational prayers, I saw him in the parking lot at nine o'clock. I started complaining as to why he didn't come, and he admitted he didn't wake up at all and he missed his Fajr prayers. Two or three days later, I reprimanded him when I saw his dried-up lips, asking, "Why are you fasting again?" He said truthfully that he was paying the penalty for missing his prayers. If he wasn't fasting on Fridays, we ate breakfast with his wife after prayers and then we went back to the central mosque to listen to Dua Nudbah.

Towards the end of 2016, we started slacking on our visits to the mosque and then as we were getting back into our rhythm, Nowruz holidays began. I started seeing him less until one day, I bumped into him as he was speeding down the stairs. I exclaimed, "What's got you so excited?!" He told me as he was jumping for joy, "My next tour of Syria has been arranged!" He left and I saw him again the next day, but this time, he seemed dejected. I asked him, "What's wrong with you then? Have you been cancelled?" He lowered his head and said yes. In the middle of the night, he called and told me to come down. From afar, I could see he could barely hide his joy. I realised he was about to go. I instantly embraced him and whispered in his ear, "I feel like this time, you're going to go, and you won't come back!" He answered, "Insha'Allah. Pray for me by the right of Lady Zaynab (a)." I grasped him tight to my chest again and said, "I'll make you a coffin so beautiful, you'll be delighted to see it!"

Sayyid Asghar Azeemi

The martyr's friend

Whenever he received a wedding invite, he laughed, "Another night with the martyrs again!" He hated the dancing and music at weddings, so he showed his face outside the hall and met the bride and groom's family, then he went to Gulzar-e Shuhada. All he thought and talked about were the martyrs. One time, we went to a neighbouring village for a programme and while we were having fun, he was asking around as if he had lost someone, "Haj Agha Sayyid, is there any martyr around here I can visit?"

We set off for Isfahan to visit Haj Ahmad Kazemi's grave and my wife said to him, "You don't take care of your car just like Sayyid." He replied, "We'll have to leave these and go one day. We have to take care of our hearts first and then our cars." Whenever I asked after him, I always heard similar answers; where is Agha Mohsen? He's gone for Friday prayers. Where is Agha Mohsen? He's gone to Gulzar-e Shuhada. Where is Agha Mohsen? He's gone to Isfahan to visit Shaheed Kazemi's grave.

I said to his father-in-law, "It's good he's busy with these things, but he shouldn't end up being talked about behind his back by the family." He held the same view as me. He replied, "Nothing will change if I talk to him, but you talk to him as his co-worker and friend." The first time he came to my house with his in-laws, he asked me whether he should join the IRGC. I realised he didn't want to join, but his wife was insisting. This visit was part of his wife's plan so I can encourage him to join them. I tried to deter Mohsen from joining them and change his view about them. I had fifteen years of experience in this career.

I told him, "If you want a career in the IRGC, you're looking at no life in this world or the next! Aside from all the distance, danger, wounds, and martyrdom, what are you going to do about all the abuse from the people?! You have to ride with them until the end of the line." I don't understand why, but he immediately went and started sorting out his paperwork to join the IRGC! From then on, we started meeting more regularly.

On Sizdah-be Dar[180], we visited his wife's grandfather's garden. There were many of us and not enough space to sit, so they laid a carpet on the adjacent land. Mohsen asked, "Whose land is this?" One of them told him, "The land belongs to our family," but another interrupted and said, "No, the land belongs to a stranger." He wasn't willing to sit on that land and was insisting they call and take permission from its owner.

His training in Shiraz ended and he joined the army at the same time I went to Syria. He was insisting he wanted to come with us, but I told him, "You've just joined, wait a little. First, gain some experience and then come," but he replied, "I'll learn, I'm a genius in electrics!" When I got back from Syria, he made a scene at our house. He was saying, "You have connections, go to the base, go to the command centre and tell them to take me." I asked his wife, "Are you happy with this?" She said yes firmly and steadfast and I asked again, "What if he goes and is martyred?" She replied, "The grace of martyrdom comes from my God!" I didn't know what to do with the both of them. I said to his wife, "You're not thinking straight right now. Come and tell me the same thing once you've been apart for two, three weeks and you've overheard from here and there that he's gone for the money!"

---

180. (Farsi: سیزده به در) Sizdah-be Dar or Nature Day is celebrated on the 2nd of April and is usually celebrated by families going out for picnics.

The commander of his battalion told me he managed to do his work himself. He'd gone here and there and persisted so much that they added his name to the list [of soldiers on their way to Syria]. When he found out I had heard, he begged me not to say anything to his father-in-law and said, "Wait until I see what's going to happen, and if it is definite, I'll tell him myself." He told his family right at the last moment. He left but he came back later than the others because he'd gone to take a course on how to operate a T-90 tank in Latakia. When I went to see him, he told me how a missile had struck his tank, but he didn't mention he had lost hearing in one of his ears from the shock of the explosion. Only his wife knew. He said that night, "If my father-in-law says something to me, repeat it loud so I can hear it." He was worried that if they found out, they could prevent him from going again. He didn't even inform the headquarters and was even willing to pay for his medication and treatment himself.

I joined him on one of his trips to Jamkaran and I asked, "Have you made an oath?" He replied, "No, but I want to go for forty nights if possible." For the whole way, he either listened to *nowhehs* or lectures. I was tired of it, so I told him, "Can't you put another CD in? If not, just turn it off." Once we reached Qom, he got out before *ziyarah* and went to meet Agha Khalili. We met up later at night in Jamkaran.

I understood from what he was saying that he was annoyed with his family. Because he was so simple and straightforward, they mocked and teased him about everything, about his beard, his job, his appearance, his visiting the graves of the martyrs, even his love for the Leader. I even saw sometimes that when he walked in, they all recited *salawat* and changed the subject while making snide comments towards him. Regardless, he didn't get annoyed or show his anger. He never cut off relations, but he stopped attending family gatherings as often.

The last time I saw him was at the wedding of a family member or in his own words, a night with the martyrs. He arrived before the *adhan* of Maghrib. Everyone was singing and dancing inside, so we sat outside. He was waiting for the groom to come out so he could congratulate him and then escape. When it became prayer time, we went inside to pray. Mohsen led prayers and took so long, I felt as if I was praying Salat Ja'far Tayyar! I knew he was being deployed one of those days, so I called his commander and told him not to take him because he has a little child. "What can I do about him?!" asked his commander. "If I reject him at the door, he'll come in through the window, and if I reject him at the window, he'll come in through the wall!" I told Mohsen, "If you go this time, you'll be martyred!" He said excitedly, "I didn't come to stay, I came to leave!" However long we waited, there was no sign of the groom, so he said, "Send my regards to the groom and tell him Mohsen waited for you, but you didn't come!" He then left his family and went to Gulzar-e Shuhada.

Two or three days later, I went out on an operation. I called from there to find out what was going on about his deployment and his commander told me, "One person has to be struck off our three-person shortlist for Syria." I insisted that in that case, they shouldn't take Mohsen. I quickly put the phone down and called Mohsen. He told me, "I've got three tickets to Tehran," but I replied victoriously, "You've been struck off! Akbariyan and Pourpirali are going!"

During that period, I was constantly calling his father-in-law and asking how Mohsen was. One night, we learnt one of our soldiers from Isfahan had been taken captive a few hours ago. I felt sick to the pit of my stomach and I didn't sleep a wink the whole night. At seven in the morning, I called and asked his father-in-law what had happened. The poor man answered curiously. He asked, "Why are you ringing at this time? Has something happened?" I replied, "No, I'm just calling." Half an hour later, his father-in-law called and yelled worriedly down the phone, "Sayyid, by your grandfather, tell me what's going on!" I could hear the cries and wails of his family on the other end. I told him, "Believe me, I know nothing!" He replied, "They've just put out the photos of Mohsen being taken captive on Telegram!"

Chapter IV

BUILD YOURSELF IN THE DESERT!

Gholamreza Arab

The martyr's co-worker

He put a lot of emphasis on respecting elders. He wouldn't sit in the front no matter how much I insisted. As soon as we said Bismillah to start our journey, he started collecting charity, so we reach our destination safely. We decided to go via the Semnan Highway. He had a clay *tasbih* which he wouldn't let out of his sight and he was constantly reciting *dhikr*.

We ended up in one room in the motel, our beds beside each other's. After class and Dhuhr prayers, we wouldn't see Mohsen again. I asked him, "What do you do in the shrine? You don't eat lunch or dinner. Come, let's go eat something." He replied, "Don't worry, something to eat will turn up." I always woke up to his empty bed. I asked, "Is there someone you know at the shrine?" and he replied satirically, "Yeah, I have so many friends, it's unbelievable!" He continued doing this for one or two nights until I couldn't take it any longer. I swore to him, "I swear to God, what do you do in the shrine for all this time?" He replied, holding back his tears, "One day, we will regret not taking advantage of these times!" He found a corner where he could recite the *ziyarah* during the calm hours of dawn and tears poured from his eyes during the *qunut*[181] of his Salat ul-Layl. I wanted to understand him better, so I asked, "Don't you get tired?" His eyes lit up and he replied, "This is so sweet and enjoyable for me, you couldn't understand."

As we were passing by the bazaar, he saw a woman wearing incorrect hijab. He lowered his gaze and said, "My sister, observe

---

181. A *dua* made during prayers while one is standing and has his/her hands raised towards the skies..

your hijab in front of Imam Rida (a)." I elbowed him in his side and said, "They'll take us and beat us to death!" However, he was loyal to his duty and said, "A person must observe *amr bil ma'ruf* and *nahy anil munkar*[182] in their correct places. Imam Husayn (a) gave his life on this path, we must do what little we can!"

He'd made up his mind and insisted he didn't want to go to the water park. "I came to Mashhad only for Imam Rida (a)!" he told us. He then complained about how these things have ruined the religious image of Mashhad and dissuaded people from going to the shrine.

When we got to know each other a little better, he told me, "I have one request from Allah and Imam Rida (a), and that is to be martyred in the path of Imam Husayn (a)." He paused for a little, his head lowered. I replied, "I'm not willing to let you suffer the way Imam Husayn (a) did!" He said, "I swear to God, I am, you don't know how delightful it is!"

In Mashhad, I overheard he was looking to sell his Peugeot ROA. Once we got back to Najafabad, I followed up on that. He laughed and told me, "This car has become like a money box for me, I've spent so much money on it!" He told me cleanly that the motor needed oil and it didn't have a battery. He mentioned every problem the car had. He then said, "Now go and think about it, and if you want to, come and buy it!" Eventually, we didn't reach an agreement over the car.

One time, I complained to him about my house and told him that every time I walk up the stairs to my flat, I say to Allah out of exhaustion, "I wish I could build my own house!" He told me, "Don't be annoyed, Allah gives opportunities to everyone, good ones too."

---

182. Arabic for 'preventing evil', one of the obligatory acts in Islam where one must deter others from committing sins.

One time, we were together on an operation and from the first day, he insisted they let him stand patrol at midnight. Eventually, I decided to ask him, "What's your secret? Why do you want to go at that hour?!" What hour? 1 am onwards, the time everyone was looking to avoid at any cost. Where? In the middle of the deserts of Ramsheh. The water from his *wudu* dripped into the fire as he replied, "If you want to know, you have to stay with me." I agreed and he told me as he was buttoning his cuffs, "I want to pray Salat ul-Layl." His tears during his prayers had a profound effect on me. He prayed two units and then sat next to me in front of the fire. We chatted for a bit and then he prayed the next two units. Afterwards, he sat next to me and whispered Ziyarah Ashura. When his time to stand guard finished, I got up to wake up the next patrol, but he stopped me and said, "Let them sleep, we're awake, right?" When he left to do *wudu* again to pray Fajr, a few people got out of their tents. We made him stand as the imam. He kept saying he was the youngest and he didn't deserve to lead, but everyone wanted him to lead.

Saeed Hashemi

The martyr's co-worker

Whenever I give my number to anyone, I tell them, "This is Mohsen Hojaji's number!" My SIM card is a souvenir from Mohsen. I told him, "Mohsen, do you think there's a problem with my phone that it doesn't get 3G service?" He replied, "No, it's a problem with your SIM. I have a SIM at home which has 3G. I'll bring it to you." He used the word 'actually' often; actually, I went there, actually I thought and so on. The guys teased him so much over it, he eventually stopped saying it.

He lowered his head so often, one would think he was hunchbacked. I told him it is wrong for a military serviceman to keep his head down. He raised his head a little and asked, "Is this fine?" I told him, "No! Bring your chest out and raise your head further!"

Before he joined the military, they had put a new soldier in my company. When Mohsen enrolled, he caught my eye. I didn't know him neither had I even seen him once in Najafabad before 2014. I thought to myself I needed to bring him into my company at any cost. Eventually, I managed to figure something out and we replaced that young soldier with Mohsen. I was delighted I had managed to get him.

It isn't proper for a commander to like one of his soldiers more than the others and I tried not to, but I liked him specifically. In addition to his military duties, I made him the cultural manager of the battalion, which was one of the less-funded parts of the military. It's difficult to believe that not even one toman had been given by the military to fund the cultural programmes of the battalion. When he realised that running around here and there asking for funds wasn't working, he decided to start fundraising. He set up a competition or a programme and collected the money from the soldiers of the battalion themselves. Despite these harsh conditions, he still managed to distribute gifts.

He brought a series of pocket-sized biographies of the martyrs and said they must be circulated amongst the troops; take them and read them, then put them back so others can read them too. He made two notice boards with cloth, one for the dressing room and one for the company's common room. When we had a lack of money, he always managed to make do. He cut out photos of ten martyred Defenders of the Shrine from a magazine and pinned them to the notice boards in a circle. There was still some space left on which he wrote a quote from the Leader which read, "In those days, martyrdom was an open door and now, a narrow opening. There is still an opportunity for martyrdom. One must purify their heart." He used the same quote on a banner which hung inside the battalion's prayer room.

He framed a photo of Shaheed Musa Kazemi and put it on a stand surrounded by flowers. During our morning assemblies, the first person in line saluted to him in honour of him as the martyr of our battalion. He had a lot of equipment which belonged to this martyr, especially his helmet which had been struck by a bullet.

Eventually, it reached a stage where he was doing three extra-curricular voluntary jobs; military duty, cultural duty, and battalion personnel duty. He repaired any old equipment. He went through the storeroom and brought out a whole bunch of iron and steel and connected it all. He somehow managed to build a shelf. He put all the military equipment in there and the storeroom finally looked decent.

Despite his thin and frail physique, he had quite a toned and tough body. In the physical test of the battalion, only about three or four people could do more than twenty pull-ups, and Mohsen was one of them. He could do twenty-four in one go. He made sure to keep up his stamina. As soon as we left class, he jumped onto the bar and off he went!

One afternoon after work, we were going to the military police department together. I noticed water was dripping from the cooler behind the prayer room. Its pump was broken. The cooler was three metres up and it was difficult for us to get there. We looked around but we couldn't find anyone who worked in the repairs department. I said to Mohsen, "It's such a shame all this water will be wasted until it's fixed tomorrow!" He replied, "Haji, I'll fix it now." He gave me his bag and jumped up. I was amazed; I couldn't believe how he jumped over the wall so easily!

The atmosphere is casual in our company and the soldiers don't generally observe military etiquette. I personally don't ask that of them, but whenever Mohsen entered the room, he stamped his foot. When he saw me outside, he always saluted. He continued to do it even after I told him it wasn't necessary. He gave great importance to the military lifestyle. His badges, uniform and boots were always tidy. When he wanted to go home in the afternoon, he sat in the centre of the room, folded his military uniform, and put them in his cupboard. We always smelt his perfume or cologne before seeing him. He always had a bottle of perfume in his pocket. I asked for his advice whenever I wanted to buy cologne. He wouldn't joke around about his long beard though. Some of our friends wanted to tease him so they said, "Why do you have a den for Satan on your face?" but he didn't get annoyed that easily.

Whenever he took his wife to the doctor in Isfahan, I always knew. He was annoyed and said, "What is this state of affairs?! They're almost coming out naked, why doesn't anyone stop them?" He advised them. They swore and abused him, but he wasn't one to just stand around and act neutral. He had a simple phone, one of those Nokias. He had a sticker on the back which said, "Sinning means [saying] farewell to Husayn (a)!"

When his child was born, he came into work with swollen red eyes. He said in his Najafabadi accent, "Haji, this Ali is killing us. He's always restless, he doesn't sleep at night and I'm forced to take him out in the car until midnight to get him to sleep!"

"Where do you go at that time of night?" I asked.

"I take him to Gulzar-e Shuhada, and we walk around amongst the graves until he feels sleepy," he replied.

He drove me crazy when he wanted me to send him on his first tour. He always said, "Haji, let me go!" but I didn't give in. I said, "It's only been four days since you came, first learn the ropes and then you can go. If you are in the middle of a battle and the guns of the tank get jammed, you must be able to repair it immediately, no?" He twirled his *tasbih* viciously and continued, "Send me, I'll go there and make tea, I'll wash the toilets!" Eventually, his *mustahabb* fasts came to his rescue and his name was written on the list. It was written in his fate. When he returned, he was confused as to why he wasn't martyred.

After his first tour of Syria, he became worse. He drove us up the wall. All he thought and talked about was Syria. It's as if he wasn't even here. He ate while talking about Syria, he walked while talking about Syria, all he talked about was Syria.

Our job entailed going on military camps in the desert. Sometimes, the van's tyre was punctured, or its petrol ran out. They often forgot a company had gone out into the desert to camp and we wouldn't get a drop of water until midday under the relentless sun in our thick uniforms. Not once did I hear him complain over these three and a half years. Even if we thanked him for something he did, he replied, "I didn't do anything, it was my duty." He didn't speak a lot. He wouldn't budge however much we asked him to tell us stories from Syria. It wouldn't hurt him to speak two or three words. I said to him, "I heard you terrified ISIS!" He lowered his head and reply, "Haji, I didn't do anything, the others did all the work!"

On Thursday afternoons, he stamped his foot at attention at my door to take leave. I asked, "Qom again?" I knew he had gone for more than thirty consecutive weeks in the same ruined car with his friends and family, and if there wasn't anyone else to go with, he went alone by bus. I reminded him several times that he had taken too much leave. He texted at midnight. I can't call it a text, it was more of an essay. He swore by Allah, the Prophet and the Ahlulbayt (as) in his four to five-page messages and ask me to let him go. I replied, "No, you've already gone once, and others have priority." When he saw he couldn't get his way, he told me, "No problem, I'll complain about you to Lady Zaynab (a), and you can answer to her." I got angry and replied, "Why are you bringing Lady Zaynab (a) into this? Don't mix everything!" He answered, "Well, don't turn me down ."

I was on a course when they allowed his name onto the list. I wasn't there the day they suggested his name either. I don't know why no one else rejected him. No one said anything. The commander of the battalion only had to say one word to prevent him from going. When he came to bid farewell, he was over the moon. He was jumping for joy. I was certain that as soon as he reaches Syria, he will never come back. I held him by the hand and took him into the battalion's command office. I begged him, "Don't go, you are building a household, your wife is young, your child is young, first experience life a little and then go!" He replied, "Don't worry, Haji! They have Allah!" It was useless. He repeated the same thing no matter how much I insisted, "Haji, I just have to go!" I whispered to him, "Because I love you, I'll pray you aren't martyred!" He laughed and said, "I know you love me, but I have to go and be martyred!"

At nights, I either turn off my phone or put it on silent. My sleep is light, and I can wake up even at the sound of the phone's vibration. Since he went to Syria, I always kept my phone on and on the loudest setting. I was waiting for them to call and give me the news of Mohsen's martyrdom at any time.

Behzad Sadeghi

The martyr's co-worker

Mohsen was the gunner, and I was the driver of the tank. He was adamant to learn how the tank works even though his rank was higher than mine. He said, "It'll be useful one day!" He insisted I open the battery of the tank so he can learn and help. During the month of Ramadan, he came to the hangar with a dry mouth from fasting, even when the others were resting. He was overly sensitive over the machine as it wasn't our property and we needed to tend to it. There are screws on the side and under the tank's tracks. Working with these screws is a pain in the neck because they are so tricky. Their oil must be changed once every three months. The tank commander came and saw the screws were leaking even though it hadn't been three months since they were last examined. He started twisting Mohsen's arm about why Behzad didn't do his work properly, but he covered me and said, "Both his experience and record are greater than mine, I can't complain about him." I argued with the commander, but Mohsen pulled me aside and said, "Don't argue! He's your superior and his rank is higher than yours. Say okay and do your work!"

When we went to the desert, he stopped working as soon as he realised it was time for prayers, rolled up his sleeves and said, "Bismillah, prayers first . Its blessings aside, why delay something we can do now other than later?" During our camps, the nights are mostly spent resting, joking, and laughing, but Mohsen sat in the centre of the tent and started reciting *duas*. He told the others to seek intercession too. In addition to this, he could be seen in the corner reading from a pocket-sized

Quran. He continuously said, "Hold firm to Allah!" He left a small *dua* book in the gunner's section and as soon as we got into the tank, he read a little *dua* and then we got to work.

He signed up to go to Syria twice, but he was rejected both times. One of the times, he bought aash for all of us out of happiness. We joked around and asked what he would do if he didn't get accepted. He told us, "I'll pull it out of each of your throats!" He was informed that his application was rejected, and the others said to him, "Do you want to pull the aash out of each of our throats now?!" He replied, "Damn you! Pay me back!" Whenever he got angry, he said 'damn you'. The commander of the division came and told him he will go whenever his name is drawn, but Mohsen replied, "No! I have to go!"

One Tuesday morning, he hadn't come to the hangar. He told me, "I have something to do, I'll go and come back." A few hours later, he came back in a genuinely nice suit. The battalion headquarters were quite far from the hangar, and the route is very dusty. He had walked all the way to say goodbye. Even though my face, hands and clothes were all black with oil, he hugged me tightly. "I came so you can't say tomorrow that this man left without saying goodbye!" he said, "Forgive me!"

Eiman Ataei

The martyr's co-worker

I had a bad cold. I laid down in a corner of the prayer room and fell asleep. I woke up in a fright and looked at my watch. It was almost noon. I noticed someone had laid a blanket over me. I ran into the room and there he was, sitting behind the desk. I didn't say anything out of embarrassment. "Are you feeling better?" he asked. I replied, "Why didn't you wake me up?" He said, "I felt bad to wake you up from your beauty sleep!" He changed the subject so I wouldn't feel ashamed. He said about his cold, "My mother-in-law won't let me kiss Ali. I've been upset about it for a few days now!" After exercise, we were drenched in sweat. Even though he was sweaty too, once or twice, he put his sports jacket around me so I wouldn't get sick.

From the very first day, he made me feel relaxed. As soon as I went into the office, he said, "I want to work here informally, like two friends. We don't have superiors or soldiers; I don't want you to stand at attention in front of me for twenty-four hours a day. Even if you see me make a mistake, tell me about it!" The atmosphere was very friendly. He sympathised with me. He talked about his personal life and how he acted in his marriage. He had set up his life in such a way that everything was improving constantly. He always advised getting married quickly, "Take the first step and leave the rest to Allah!" We became so close, we called each other by our first names.

One day, he came and said, "A soldier was reciting Ziyarah Ashura in the mosque. He had such a good voice."

"You clearly didn't recognise me!" I laughed.

"Wait, are you a reciter?!" he exclaimed.

He laughed that had he made a greater request from Allah, that would have been fulfilled. From then on, he asked for my help when writing poetry and reciting. I recited *masa'ibs* for him privately once or twice, on Thursday mornings in the base's Husayniyyah when no one was there. He didn't want anyone to find out. He said, "Let it be between us and Allah." When I recited *masa'ib* about Lady Zaynab and Lady Ruqayyah (as)'s captivity, he cried and wailed.

Half an hour before the *adhan* for Dhuhr prayers, he went to the battalion's cultural office in *wudu* and played Hadith ul-Kisa on the loudspeaker, and then he recited a page of Quran.

One or two times, I saw him when the door was slightly ajar. He took Shaheed Musa Kazemi's clothes out the box, put his hand on the part stained with the blood of the martyr and wept. He beseeched Allah to make him a martyr.

When we had nothing to do, he wrote in his notepad. I asked him to read me what it said a few times, but he didn't want to and said it wasn't for reading. Every time, he sent me on a wild goose chase to hide what he was writing.

In the afternoons, we went to the base's Husayniyyah and he taught me many narrations. Two of those narrations stuck in my mind. There is one narration from Imam Ali (a) where he said, "Lucky is the servant who repents after each sin he commits." The other narration was that Imam Sadiq (a) advised reciting the *tasbih* of Lady Zahra (a)[183] as soon as prayers are completed so that one's sins are forgiven. He insisted I put up a different narration on the battalion notice board each day so the forces could read it.

On the days of celebration of the Ahlulbayt (as), he suggested we should give each soldier in the base some chocolate. He insisted we should have celebrations on the birthdays of those drawn close to Allah. We decorated the prayer room to the best of our capability, and we hung up photos of the martyrs all over. There was space for one last martyr, and he said each time, "Eiman! You still haven't put up that photo!"

The day he said goodbye before going to Syria, he told me, "Leave the space for that photo empty for me!" I replied, "Insha'Allah you return safely." He made me promise that if he were martyred, I would remember him during every *masa'ib*. I

---

183. One of the most emphasised post-prayer rites where one recites *Allahu Akbar* (Allah is greater than any description) 34 times, *Alhamdulillah* (all praise is to Allah) 33 times and *Subhanallah* (all glory is to Allah) 33 times. It is mentioned that the prayer is like a flower, and the *tasbih* of Lady Fatimah (a) is the perfume of the flower.

embraced him tightly, laughed and said, "You have to promise that if you come back, you have to bring a souvenir too, but if you reach your goal, remember us!"

Abdorrasoul Ebrahimi

The martyr's co-worker

He went to Syria less than a year after joining the military. When he came back, I was the first co-worker to meet him. He was very reserved and didn't let us know what happened over there at all. I heard different things from the people he went with. I said to him, "I heard on the night operations, you finished the tank's ammunition three or four times! You were firing a lot, huh?" He replied, "Haji, what can we do? We had it at our disposal!" In the battalion, he put a lot of effort into learning how the tanks work. He spent a lot of time with the experienced soldiers so he could learn little things.

He lived with his father-in-law. I thought he was his father because he called him dad. I said to his father-in-law, "In the military world, a person's rank has an effect on who he visits, but I love Agha Mohsen so much, I came to see how he was!" I was at least ten years older than him.

In the last ten days of Ramadan 2016, we set up a course on religious beliefs in Mashhad. I said to Mohsen, "Do you want to come?" He replied, "I wish we could go with our families!" We were both not very well-off, but despite this, we took a leap of faith, knowing Allah will provide for us. The rest had signed up before and they stayed in IRGC hotels, and us two were left not knowing what to do. It was the days leading up to the Layali al-Qadr and everything was pricey. After searching for half a day, we settled for a room at a one-star motel.

After two or three nights, the ladies said the place was intolerably dirty and unhygienic. We went to lessons from morning until afternoon whilst fasting and we came back

exhausted. At *iftar*, we left and stayed in the shrine until midnight. I don't understand how he was so energetic despite only having one or two hours of rest, but he started looking for a room elsewhere. He found a hotel on Tabarsi Street which was offering suitable prices.

I couldn't do *ziyarah* like him. After two or three nights, I couldn't take it anymore. He stayed in the shrine until *suhur*. Sometimes, his wife left their child with him to do *ziyarah*. Even while looking after his child, he didn't put his *dua* book down. As soon as his child made any sound, he put the milk bottle in his mouth. I laughed that he could have at least bought a pacifier! When I started joking a lot, he shut me up with a respectful '*zahr-e mar*'[184]. I don't understand why, but every night, he entered the shrine from a different gate, one night from the Azadi Courtyard, the next from Jami' Razavi Courtyard.

He didn't eat a lot. He said he would eat a cake, a strudel or some food left over from *iftar* for *suhur*. He loved strudels and he talked about them with such an appetite. He prayed Fajr and slept until seven. I had to call him so many times just to wake him up! It was a twenty-minute bus ride to where the course was being held. He made his way to the bus with a pale and sleepy face. I told him, "Mohsen! Don't kill yourself!" He replied between the yawns, "Haji, what else can I do, I have to take advantage of these opportunities!"

After Mashhad, I had an idea to set up a religious organisation in the institute's building and recite Dua Tawassul on Tuesday nights. When I made this suggestion to Mohsen, he said, "I'm down for it, but we have to start with ourselves first." We decided to visit the graves of the martyred Defenders of the Shrine for a few weeks. I kept contacting him to confirm, but

---

184. An expression in Farsi literally meaning 'snake venom' but is used when someone is annoyed

Mohsen was terribly busy with his cultural activities and always said next week. Eventually, the stars aligned, and we visited the grave of Shaheed Kafizadeh, the first martyred Defender of the Shrine of our division who was martyred in 2012. "He is the gatekeeper of this division's martyrs," he said there, "If you want martyrdom, you have to take it from him." We planned to visit the rest of the martyrs in order of their date of martyrdom, but we were never able to do so. One week, he texted me, "Haji, I'm sorry, there's nothing I can do," and the next week, I had something to do.

He came for a few days to help us lay fertiliser around the trees on the farming land. We had to dig holes a certain distance from the tree, pour manure and fertiliser into it and then bury it. I made Mohsen do a good amount of work. At prayer time, I noticed he didn't want to work. My father-in-law said, "We can pray in half an hour when we go to eat lunch. If you go now, your body will cool down." I knew he was bound to his prayers and he was different from us. As soon as my father-in-law left, I winked at him as if to tell him to pray and come back. He went and came back ten minutes later. He said, happy and energetic, "Haji, thank you so much!" After lunch, it started raining heavily. We all crammed into the room to get out the rain. My father-in-law was restless. He put on his raincoat and went to work in the rain. I said to Mohsen, "Wait until it stops raining and then we'll go," but he replied, "No, Haji! We've been waiting for half an hour and it doesn't look like it's going to stop." We wore our raincoats and took our shovels. My father-in-law was incredibly pleased with his work. He pulled me aside and said, "This friend of yours works very well, bring him tomorrow as well!"

One summer night, we went to the park. I said remorsefully, "Can you see how bad the state of the hijab has become?" He started thinking and then said, "It's unfortunate! I wish there was something we could do." I had heard him say this 'I wish there were something we could do' several times in different places and situations.

When his name was chosen for Syria, everyone in the battalion and division was talking about how Hojaji and Akbariyan were leaving. I was on the night shift. I texted him, "Mohsen! You must go, yes, you must go and your head too. Don't let any illegitimate go near the shrine!"[185] He replied quickly, "Haji dear, just pray for me!"

It is still difficult for me to believe Mohsen was taken captive. He was a strong and agile person. When racing, he was always first or second. I told him, "Do you get caught in the moment when you run like that and come first?" One day, he ran so much, his face went pale. I told him, "You're doing this so when the examiner comes, he'll send you to the front immediately!" He suggested we wrestle, but before I could even get ready, he had me on the floor! One of our friends was a bodybuilder. Sometimes when they came from the tank, they started sparring in the company hall. I said to their commander, "Don't you tire them out? Why are they tiring themselves out like this?!"

---

185. Verses from Sayyid Reza Narimani's *nowheh* by the name of *Manam Bayad Beram*

Saeed Kiyani

The martyr's co-worker

I called him 'Jooji dear'. Where did it start? When he was sent for a martial arts and self-defence course, they accidentally wrote his name as Mohsen Jooji. Wherever he saw me, he put his hands on his head. He began his sit-to-stand exercise and joked, "Do you want me to give a test?" It didn't make a difference where we were, in the division headquarters or in front of the prayer room. It was as if I had 'test' written on my forehead. He got good scores in all his tests. He had a strong body. When the IRGC headquarters of the province sent examiners, no one was better than Mohsen! I called him and told him to give a test. Even after the blessed month of Ramadan when their bodies generally become weaker, no one was willing to give a test except Mohsen. He came, happy and energetic. His documents are still in my office with the signature of the IRGC headquarters of the province. Of course, sometimes he asked why I always told him to give a test!

Sometimes, we were on the same shift at night in a small room. He was in his own world. He wrote some things on a small slip of paper. Never did he talk about what he had written, nor did I ever ask. One night, he opened his heart to the four or five of us. He said with regret, "Can you see how they're closing the door to martyrdom? A small passageway had opened up, but we didn't take advantage of it." He said like one of the narrators of the Holy Defence, "Do you remember Dayitaghi? Who could believe it? Did you know he was the commander of the base? Whenever he wanted to solve a problem of one of the soldiers of his base, he told him to meet him before Fajr. He wasn't satisfied with praying Salat ul-Layl himself, no, he wanted to make others pray it too. Which one of us thought he could be like this? We were just stunned that wow... Dayitaghi was martyred?! I am still mournful over Javad Ghorbani. We were in Syria together. He was wounded and they took him to a hospital in Isfahan. He was discharged, went home to his wife and kids and then two or three coughs later, he was martyred! I came from Syria with this hope in my heart that I can be martyred in my own city! Have you ever wondered why Musa Jamshidiyan's troops were so fond of him; why after a year, his troops don't feel like working and say the battalion isn't a battalion without Musa? How did he infiltrate his troops' hearts like that? Didn't we say ourselves that Pooya Izadi was going to be sent home? He was a witty and mischievous youth. In Syria, he told me you're going to get us martyred with your antics! I only pretended to be pious. There were a few loose chickens and sheep around us . Pooya set up a barbecue. He laughed and said whoever wants to be martyred should eat this kebab! Hojaji, don't you want to be martyred? he asked me. I didn't eat. Pooya and I swapped tanks and they hit his tank. I should have been martyred! When they brought his burnt body, I noticed there was a piece of flesh missing on the back of his leg! Allah wanted to show me He knows how to solve it himself!"

Amirhosein Mehrabi

The martyr's co-worker

The charcoal was ready, and the chicken had been marinating in lemon juice, onions and saffron for some time. He turned up as soon as I was going to put the skewers on the fire. I had prayed earlier so I could cook lunch. "What are you doing?" he asked.

"Can't you see?" I replied. "I'm putting *jujeh* on the barbecue for lunch!"

"You've made so much smoke here! What if a child comes by and wants some food? What if a pregnant woman starts craving kebab?" he asked.

He forced us to gather up the barbecue on hungry stomachs and go to a quieter place. We found a forest park and we put down our picnic mats. We asked permission, "Agha Mohsen, do you agree with this place?" and after he gave permission, we lit our barbecue again, far away from anyone else.

From the beginning, he texted, "Ask Amirhosein if he'll be able to come on a journey with us, especially with my *akhlaq*!" When we decided to go to Mashhad for the religious beliefs course, we chose to go in a personal car. That way, we had more fun. He had just joined his battalion and I had never been on a journey with Mohsen before. I had a revolutionary, boring, and dry religious image of him in my mind from before. I still wanted to listen to music in front of him. Amongst the songs, there were a few rhythmic dance songs which I changed quickly. He quickly realised I was only changing them because of him, so he said, "Amir! Don't change it, I'm pretending to sleep as though I can't hear anything, when I fall asleep, I won't be able to hear it. I know if you don't listen to it, we'll run off the road!"

We did *ziyarah* together, but he also visited the shrine at midnight, at two or three in the morning without telling us. After Fajr, he came back to the centre with us by bus. I was surprised how he could wake up after the constant classes from morning until evening!

He never mentioned he was a soldier of the battalion or a tank gunner. He took the responsibility of cultural activities on his shoulders himself. It was Mohsen's idea to wear shirts with a photo of Shaheed Musa Kazemi during exercise. The battalion didn't give him any financial support, but he said, "We have nothing to do with the battalion. Anyone who can donate, please give some money." The money was slowly gathered. He bought the t-shirts quickly and printed photos of the martyr on them.

In the memorial for the martyred Defenders of the Shrine, we made standing cut-outs of the martyrs and placed them along the path. He stood next to them and put his arm around their shoulder. "If we can't be martyred," he joked, "At least we can take photos with the martyrs."

As soon as he got back, he started bothering the commander again. He went all the way from the battalion to the main base in his normal clothes he insisted he puts his name down for Syria again. I whispered to him, "You've just come back, you have a young child, he also has a right, he needs a father. You've done your duty." He said ruefully, "My duty will be completed once I am martyred on this path."

Hosein Farhadi

The martyr's co-worker

We were together for three years, on one tank, in one cabin. We made an agreement that I would teach him about military equipment, and he would teach me *akhlaq*. There's a part at the back on the tank that we call the *gaveh*. I told him, "You have to learn in a way that you can take it apart and put it back together blindfolded!" I took it apart and explained each part and what it does one by one. When my lesson finished, I said, "Bismillah, now it's your turn." He said Bismillah like this, '*Bismi Rabb-ish-Shuhada was-Siddiqin*[186]'. That day, he said, "*Bismi Rabb-ish-Shuhada was-Siddiqin*, don't backbite!" and then he got up to leave.

"Is that all?" I asked.

"What do you mean, 'is that all'?" he retorted, "When you have to give in your report, you'll understand!"

We opened the *gaveh*. I blindfolded him and told him to put it together, but I put a random part in there without letting him know. When he got to that part, he kept pushing, but the part didn't fit. "You didn't learn your lesson properly!" I told him, "Open your eyes!" He realised I had tricked him. "Why are you bothering me?" he asked, but I replied, "You should have known it wasn't a part of the *gaveh* at all!" Now it was time for me to give my report. "Did you backbite?" he asked. I reviewed every interaction I had in the past day and I told him, "Mohsen! I tried a lot, but I couldn't do it!" He replied, "So there won't be another lesson until you fix this!"

---

186. Arabic for 'In the name of the Lord of the Martyrs and the Righteous'.

I messed around with the system inside the cabin to help him learn. I told him, "In combat, you don't have time to think. You have to be experienced enough to solve the problem quickly." He replied, "Haji, don't mess with the systems, over there, Allah will solve our problems."

When you close the cabin hatch, you feel as if you've sat inside a grave. The lack of space and the darkness is frightening, and don't even mention how it feels in the centre of the battlefield! You're worried about where the next mortar will be fired towards you from, which way you must go, the sound of the bullet cartridges hitting the body of the tank, the bullets piercing the tank armour, and of course, the worry of the tank exploding! When you fire a missile from the tank, there is a horrifying sound which throws off your senses and makes you feel stressed. When you fire the first missile, it feels as if someone is hitting you in the head with a sledgehammer. I had heard he fired a lot in Syria. I asked him, "How could you fire so much?" He said with a lump in his throat, "I swear to God, I don't know. It was as if someone had put their hands on my ears. It felt like someone was playing the drum very quietly." Every day before we got out of the cabin after work, Mohsen made a small *dua*. One of his *duas* struck my heart, "O' Allah! Give us a death everyone feels envious of!"

We had gone to Ramsheh for military training. We drove the tank into a trench in stealth mode. The examiner came to look. I told Mohsen and the tank driver, "Normally they ask about the maintenance and safeguarding booklet. Fill in the booklet." I explained to them how to fill in the booklet and I went to the commander's tent. When I got back, they were working on the tank. I asked about the booklet and they told me they had filled it in. When I looked over it, I noticed they hadn't done it like I told them to. I got angry and started shouting at them, "I wouldn't like to be in your shoes if the examiner finds an issue with the booklet!" Half an hour later, the examiner came and asked, "Who is your gunner?" Mohsen introduced himself. He went inside the cabin and called Mohsen to test him. I sat behind the cabin, close to Mohsen. He started answering the questions, but even though he answered them all, the examiner still wasn't pleased. I chimed in, "He only has one year of experience. These are questions even people with twenty years of experience have difficulty answering!" The examiner replied, "Okay, no problem. Bring me the tank's booklet." I was terrified; what was I going to do?! He started pointing out issues, the same issues I had mentioned to them. The examiner left, unconvinced. Mohsen and the tank driver didn't raise their heads out of shame.

Twenty minutes later, I got a text on my phone, "I thought you were just being bossy. Haji, forgive me for thinking about you like that." It was from Mohsen. I switched off my phone. I came back and jumped on top of the tank. I knocked on the hatch and said, "How many times did I tell you to write it properly? Now look what's happened!" They lowered their heads out of shame. I said, annoyed, "You have two hours to go over your lessons before I come back and ask you. I won't let you leave until you've learnt properly." I left and came back, and they answered every question correctly. I asked, "So why did you do so badly in front of the examiner?" They answered, "To tell you the truth, we were nervous!" We could hear the *adhan*, so I said, "Well, come down!"

"Is your phone off?" Mohsen asked from on top of the cabin.

"What do you want with my phone?" I replied harshly.

"Nothing, just asking!" he said.

"Its battery is dead," I explained.

"I have a charger," he said, "Shall I bring it from my tent?"

"There's no need, "I replied, "Just do your studies."

I went behind the tent and took off my socks in front of the water tank to do *wudu*. Someone hugged me from behind and when I turned around, I realised it was Mohsen. He kissed my face and said, "Haji, I won't let you go to the tent unless you forgive me." I wriggled out of his embrace, and he cried, "The guys are going to make me lead prayers now. How can I, a sinner, lead prayers?" I replied, "But what did you do?" He kissed my face again and said, "I sent you a message, but your battery is dead." I replied, "Go, don't worry about it, I read your message."

I needed surgery on my left knee. The day before going into hospital, I wrote down all the tasks of the tank on a slip of paper and gave it to him so he could do them precisely. After my surgery, everyone came to my house to see how I was. I looked around, but I couldn't see Mohsen. I asked our tank driver, "So where's Mohsen?" He replied, "He'd done all the tasks, but cleaning the cabin floor was the only task left." He sent his regards and said he wouldn't visit me until he had done all the tasks.

When I came back from leave, he came to say goodbye. I had no idea he had even put his name down, but now he was off to Syria! He came to the tank in dress clothes. Grease and oil were dripping off my clothes.

"We don't have to hug, I accept it," I told him, "Insha'Allah you will go and come back."

"No, Haji," he replied, "There will be no return."

"You said the same thing last time," I answered.

"No, this time is extremely different," he told me.

He hugged me and I said to him, "Ask Lady Zaynab (a) to break the chains on our legs." He replied, "I will tell her, Haji, but your mother must break the chains on your legs."

Rasoul Fatehi

The martyr's co-worker

While I was working, I felt my phone vibrate in my pocket. I took a glance at it. He sent me a message saying, "Salam, friend! You didn't tell me you were volunteering here!" He was texting me constantly, saying how he wished he could also volunteer there and how lucky I was. I didn't have time to reply, so I called him and asked where he was. He told me he was next to the flower garden. Finding him in a courtyard so wide, a lorry could do a U-turn in was like finding a needle in a haystack. I searched all four corners of the flower garden until I managed to find him. I took him by the hand, and we went to work.

I knew the organisation wasn't accepting new volunteers, they rejected everyone. Every volunteer had been working for them for longer than fifteen years. You could only be accepted if you were introduced by someone well-established. I got to know the director of the organisation, Agha Zahedi while serving the pilgrims at Imam Husayn (a)'s shrine. I was bricklaying with a few other experienced workers. He told me then, "When you come to Isfahan, come and volunteer with the Rezvan Religious Organisation." This religious organisation invites the most famous speakers and reciters in the country, and more than three thousand people attend their programmes.

I pulled him out from the crowd into the kitchen. He said anxiously, "Don't put yourself to trouble for me!" He had heard how coordinated the organisation was. All the volunteers were staring at him, wondering where he had come from. When one or two people asked, "Who is this guy?" I told them, "This is Sayyid Reza's brother!" Everyone believed me; after all, he did look a lot like Sayyid Reza Narimani. I went to find a volunteer's uniform for him, but suddenly, I heard the director of the organisation say to Mohsen harshly, "Agha, what are you doing here? Please leave!" I looked back and saw him looking bewildered. When he saw me, it was as if he had seen his saviour. "He brought me here," he said. Agha Zahedi didn't say anything else. He came to me and I asked him, "Haji, I'm looking for a uniform for Agha Mohsen!" I knew everything would be fine. He whispered in my ear quietly, "Fine, but only because it's you!" He then told me to bring a uniform from the store unit upstairs. Once he left the kitchen, Mohsen said, "I think he's annoyed!" I replied, "Don't you worry, we're best friends." I set the ladder straight and went up. I managed to find one set of uniform amongst all the other things inside. I shrugged the dust off its collar and came down. He was in his own world. He was looking up and reading a *dua* under his breath. When he took the black uniform of the volunteers from my hand, he kissed the 'Assalamu Alayka Ya Aba Abdillah'[187] written on the chest and his eyes glistened. He was over the moon. He hugged me, kissed my forehead, and said with a shaky voice, "My friend, I'll make it up to you!"

He had so much work to do, he couldn't rest for the whole night. Every time he passed by me with a tray of tea in his hands and a sweaty forehead, he winked at me to show how glad he was. At the end of the night, he called me when he was halfway to Najafabad and thanked me. The next morning, he hugged me in the battalion headquarters and asked me how I was.

He came every night, and he even got his wife to help. He cleaned up the tablecloths after dinner and vacuumed the carpets. I caught him staring at the pulpit from one of the

---

187. Arabic for 'Peace be upon you, O Aba Abdillah!'

ladders near the Husayniyyah. Everyone had left, only a few volunteers were cleaning up here and there. I patted him on the back and asked, "What's going on?" He jumped out of his state, gathered himself and replied, "My friend, do you think my photo could be behind the pulpit next year?" Behind the pulpit, there was a room where the lecturers and reciters waited before the programme began. "Would you like to meet Sayyid Reza Narimani?" I asked Mohsen. He told me he always found where Sayyid Reza was reciting and went there. He loved his *nowhehs*. That night, he said in his thick Najafabadi accent, "Haji, who am I to meet Sayyid Reza Narimani?!" He came into the room after me. I knew he had gone to Syria the year before, so I told Sayyid Reza, "This is Agha Hojaji, one of the Defenders of the Shrine." Agha Narimani got up eagerly and they hugged and kissed.

When they switched off the lights, we went to listen to Sayyid Reza Narimani's *masa'ib* and *nowhehs*. Every night, he put his hand on my shoulder whilst crying and said, "My friend, pray I can be martyred like this." He said this when Sayyid Reza recited about how Hazrat Ali Akbar (a)'s body was torn apart, when he recited about Hazrat Ali Asghar (a)'s[188] throat, when he recited about Hazrat Abbas (a)'s[189] severed arms, when he mourned over Imam Husayn (a)'s severed head, and even the captivity of Lady Zaynab (a). One night, I got fed up with him and said, "Are you being serious? Every night, you want to be martyred differently!" He smiled and replied, "Haji, just pray!"

In autumn of 2016, we went to Ramsheh for a week for the Payambar-e A'zam Strength Training Course. Ramsheh is a desert region close to Shahreza. Every battalion and company

---

188. Imam Husayn (a)'s six-month old baby who was martyred on the Day of Ashura in Karbala when the enemy shot an arrow to his throat.

189. The brother of Imam Husayn (a) and his standard-bearer in Karbala, Hazrat Abbas (a) was martyred after his arms were severed.

took part. They'd put up a different tent as well. When I heard Mohsen and I were in one tent, I was overjoyed. From the first night, he wanted to have a programme after Maghrib and Isha. He recited Ziyarah Ashura for one or two nights and then we recited a small *masa'ib* and a few *nowhehs*. The others were tired and said, "Recite for yourself, we want to sleep." He didn't give up so easily though. "Shall we go and recite for the other soldiers?" he asked me. The soldiers there were looking for someone to take initiative. Their tent was two hundred metres away from ours. From then on, we walked to their tent. They welcomed us and listened to Mohsen's *masa'ib* and recitations.

For one or two days, no one knew for certain which direction the Qibla was in their tents. Mohsen made a sign for the direction of Qibla along with photos of the martyred Defenders of the Shrine and sent it to be printed on a banner. At sunset, the banners arrived. There weren't just one or two tents, there were around twenty tents, and they were all hidden and spread out. He came and asked me to come with him to put them up in the tents. He took a communications vehicle and we left. We went into the tents and put up the banners ourselves. We realised that if we continued in this manner, we'd be late. We gave the rest to the managers of the tents so they could put them up themselves. Eventually, it became dark. He put the headlights on and drove around in the desert. Our phones had no signal. After wandering about for a while, we finally saw a tent in the distance. We were doubtful whether we were seeing properly or if it was just a mirage. They were from the Najaf Division. We asked them how to get to our battalion and we eventually got back after reciting *duas* and *salawat*.

After dinner, we took a walk behind the tents. We whispered Dua Ilahi Adhumal Bala'[190] together in the quiet and dark atmosphere. He said, "Build yourself in the desert. Allah hears your voice." He pulled his hat over his eyebrows, zipped up his coat until his chin and asked me to tell him some memories I had from the time I served the pilgrims of Imam Husayn (a)'s shrine. It was freezing and he kept sniffling. We were walking away from the tents, and he signalled that we shouldn't get lost again. When we had this conversation, he still hadn't been to Karbala. I told him, "Do your best, if you don't go to Karbala, your life has gone to waste!" From that night onwards, he fell in love and decided to go and do *ziyarah* of Arbaeen however possible. When we got back, he sat in front of the tent. He wrote with a pen underneath the heels of the soldiers' boots, "Down with the House of Saud, down with Israel, down with America!" He had a bad runny nose. He went inside the tent, got some medicine, burnt it, and inhaled its smoke.

I left the tent before the *adhan* of Fajr. I was shaking from the cold like a leaf. The water inside the tank had frozen. I gathered a few drops of water in my hand to do *wudu*. When he saw me, he laughed, "No way, you pray it too?!" I replied, "Well, as you can see!" Now I was certain that if I stayed asleep in the morning, there was someone to wake me up for Salat ul-Layl.

On the final day, everyone was busy at work gathering all the equipment and tools. Mohsen took my hand and said, "Come, let's go." He took me behind the tents to the desert toilets. "Come," he said, "Let's clean these." I complained, "There is so much we can do, why are you so insistent on doing this?" He replied, "This is ours because no one wants to do this!" We

---

190. A *dua* where one asks Allah to hasten the reappearance of Imam Mahdi (aj), and is incredibly speedy in solving problems and fulfilling requests and needs.

gathered the rocks around the tents. We took down the covers and folded them. We opened the sewage pipe, brought bucket after bucket of water from the tank and cleaned the stones of the toilet. I helped him to this point, but when he said, "Come, let's wash the plastic [waste collection] under the toilet stones," I couldn't do it. I told him, "These have all become *najis*[191], no one will use these!" He replied, "No, it's a waste. If we wash them, they can be reused." He then continued, "All the martyrs of our division have walked here, Dayitaghi, Pooya Izadi, Musa Jamshidiyan, Musa Kazemi." He then got on his all-fours, took a handful of the sand and said, "My friend, this sand is holy!"

Two or three months before he was dispatched [to Syria], they called me and Mohsen to give a physical readiness examination like always. We had to run for three thousand and two hundred metres. While running, he said, "Haji, they're treating us like recruits!" I replied, "Come, let's not run as much this time so they don't pick us next time!" When they blew the whistle to begin, we started jogging. Before we could even warm up, he said, "Leave it, come, let's run." I asked why and he told me, "You know, I went and put my name down for Syria. I'm scared my results will drop and they won't take me."

When he came to say goodbye before leaving, I put my arm around his shoulder and said, "You see, now you're finally going!" He said, his hand on my back, "I beg you, just pray nothing goes wrong!" I told him, "Don't worry, just pray for me when you reach Lady Zaynab (a)'s shrine, bring me back a flag too!" He looked me in the eye and said, "I'm never returning!"

---

191. Arabic for 'ritually impure'.

I was upset and replied, "You have a child, could you do it?" He put his hand on his neck and said, "Can you see this? This must be cut!"

Milad Malekzadeh

The Martyr's Co-Worker

He always said, "My friend! You and I weren't built for the military, but now Allah has blessed us [with this opportunity], be sure that one day, we will make a big impact!" We went to Shiraz Military University together for our first military training. In this course, we were given practical lessons on how to fire a tank. In class, he said, "Learn well, it will help us when we want to go to Syria tomorrow." We were always together for four whole months, from morning to night. Our beds were next to each other, we sat next to each other in class, we wandered around in Shiraz together. I was a heavy sleeper.

He had a notable love for Shaheed Kazemi. He put pictures of Haj Ahmad everywhere, whether it be his wardrobe door or his backpack. He loved the Shaheed Kazemi Institute so much, his wish was to build a house and turn it into an office for the institute.

From the very beginning, he wanted to go to Syria. He was waiting for his training to finish so he could put his name down. As soon as he joined the Najaf Division, he started looking for ways to put his name down and he was getting himself ready. He got what he wanted after thousands of *duas* and oaths. We were supposed to go together, but the dispatch date coincided with my wedding date, and I was left behind. I was waiting for him to call me.

When he got back from Syria, I complained to him, "You just go like that and completely forget you even had friends!" In his own words, as he was a recruit, he couldn't call, "Many of the soldiers wanted to call their families. I didn't have more than one or two minutes to talk!"

A few months before his second trip, we completed a medical aid course in Shaheed Sadouqi Hospital in Isfahan. It was a very memorable course. I still remember him saying, "Come, let's get a Rani[192] and a cookie," all the time. Whenever he fell asleep in class, I took a video of him. One time in the courtyard of the hospital, we took a selfie with our apples, sent it to our wives and wrote underneath, "Us and our spontaneous lunch breaks!" Whenever I wore a lab coat, he constantly called me doctor. The first time he did this, I told him, "A doctor without several female nurses and assistants is useless!" and he became upset. When we got to the nurses' station, we realised they were all men. He laughed and said, "Allah wants you to be a human!"

There was a patient who had been in an accident and his leg was severely injured. We could see the white of his leg bone. The patient was very restless, and the head of the ward insisted one of us go to help the nurse. I suggested to Mohsen that we should go. He was very squeamish, and his face went pale at the sight of blood. He nagged a lot, but I eventually convinced him. As soon as he saw the patient's leg, his face went pale, and he had to lean on the wall. I scolded him, "Do you want to go to Syria in this state?" and he immediately jumped up.

Another time, Mohsen put me to work. There was a ninety-five-year-old man who had bedsores, and no one wanted to help clean him. Mohsen said, "Come, let's go and help him for the sake of Allah." He forced me into the room under the pretext of 'this old man will intercede for us.' He cleaned the old man for almost an hour with shampoo. After, he kissed him on the

---

192. A fruit drink with fruit chunks inside.

forehead. The old man didn't even understand what was going on!

In Ramadan 2017, I was sent to the division's physical training department by our battalion for the athletics championships. On the third or fourth day, one of my classmates snidely remarked, "Your friend is going to Syria as well!"

"Who?" I asked.

"Mohsen," he replied.

"It can't be!" I exclaimed.

"I swear to God, it's true!" he told me.

I was shocked. I was the first name on the dispatch list. Mohsen had been dispatched before and he wasn't even supposed to be on the list. I went straight back to the battalion headquarters and as soon as I saw Mohsen, I asked, "What's this all about?! They're saying you're going to Syria!"

"They're telling the truth," he replied.

"You're such a cheat!" I told him, "You can't go to Syria by taking the rights of others!"

"Well, it's happened now," he replied, "Since the morning, everyone has gone and complained. For my sake, let it slide!"

When he said this, I yelled in front of everyone, "Even though you're my best friend, I won't let you go! I'll destroy the base if I have to, but I need to know what this favouritism is all about!" He laughed and said, "My friend, don't be upset, I'll go, come back and you'll go next time." I replied, "It's clear as day to me that if you go, you will never return!" He said eagerly, "May Allah hear it from your mouth! All I have is from Allah, just don't be angry!" The vice-commander of the battalion summoned me and asked, "Why are you causing problems?"

"According to the list, I should go," I replied, "or Mohsen and I should go together!"

"They've only told me Mohsen Hojaji," he said, "Don't try and negotiate, there's nothing we can do."

When he saw me come out disappointed, he was glad. He laughed, "My friend, don't be annoyed, our friendship is such that we let things like this slide!" I told him, "You've done it now, but I won't let it slide!" Two or three days passed. I went to the commander and said, "It's a shame you chose my best friend, otherwise forget the base, I would have caused an uproar in the whole military!"

My father owned cattle and Mohsen came every night to get milk for his child. He didn't come for a few nights because I acted heavy-handedly with him in the base. I started missing him, so I called him under that pretext and asked, "Why don't you come and get milk for Ali?" He replied, "I don't want to be a burden." I told him, "What are you talking about? Come, I'm waiting for you!" and thus, our relationship returned to normal.

The next day, I went to him. He took me inside the tank and said, "I've been trying to practice more over the last few days so I can use the tanks and APCs[193] more expertly. Teach me whatever you know so perhaps I can use your skills over there." While I was teaching him, he lowered his head and asked, "Are you upset?"

"Shouldn't I be?!" I replied.

"I beg you, don't be upset!" he said.

I hugged and kissed him, and then told him, "I'm upset because I know you'll go, and you won't return!"

---

193. Armoured personnel carriers.

Before he went to the terminal, he came to my house to say goodbye. I said to him, "Well, now you're going, you have to give me something to remember you by."

"I have nothing on me right now," he said.

"You have to give me something, even if it's the clothes you're wearing!" I replied. He realised I was after his *tasbih*.

"No!" he said, "When I came back from Arbaeen last year, I brought thirty of these *tasbihs* back with me, and everyone took them. There's only this one left which I want to use to do *dhikr* in Syria." He then put his hand in his pocket, pulled some perfume out and said, "Here, take this, I just bought it." I said to Mohsen, "May Allah give us all a good end!" He replied, "Why do you say end? Why don't you say now? Tomorrow is late for a good end, ask Allah to be martyred right now!"

I called him at noon the next day. He was still in Iran. He said, "We're leaving in the afternoon." I asked him, "When you go to Lady Zaynab (a)'s shrine, don't forget me." He replied, "Insha'Allah I'll pray for all of you when I get there."

He called a few days later. Whenever he called, he always started by saying, "Salaam. How are you, my friend?"

"Mohsen, where are you?"

"I'm with Imam Husayn (a)."

"Just take care of yourself."

"Nothing is going on here!" The sound was reaching with a delay. I said, "Don't do anything rash and lose your head!"

"Our commander has put his foot down and isn't letting us move a muscle."

"There's no fighting?"

"No, there's nothing, we're all bored here." He asked for someone's number and I told him to hang up so I could find it. He said, "Okay dear brother, I'll call back, forgive me," and that was the last time I heard his voice.

The first time I saw the photo, I thought it was photoshopped. When I zoomed in, I saw the tag 'Jawn, the servant of Mahdi' on his chest. I knew from before that he sewed this on his clothes. The other sign was he was wearing non-matching trousers and a belt. He had a habit of wearing a green belt with camouflage trousers, and a camouflage belt with green trousers. Whenever I asked why, he laughed, "This is my sign!"

Chapter V

LIKE A BOUNCED CHEQUE!

Rasoul Soleimannejad

The martyr's comrade

I was fed up with him. Whenever we met, I thought, "Here we go again." He always mentioned how much fun he had when he went abseiling. He always said 'my son' at the beginning of every sentence, "My son, you weren't there for abseiling!"

During our course in Amir al-Mu'mineen Institute in Isfahan, he won the raffle to go on Umrah[194]. His wife had signed up. He managed to take a loan out to go, but the IRGC didn't allow him to leave the country. He was terribly upset. We went from Najafabad to Isfahan every day in my car. On the way, he explained that he tried everything to go to Makkah, but he couldn't find a way to solve his problem. One time, my wife needed the car, and I was forced to go by bus to Isfahan. He didn't have enough money to go with me, so every morning, he drove forty kilometres with his motorcycle just to reach Isfahan. When the course ended, we were all transferred to the 8th Najaf-e Ashraf Division. Us four, five people who went to Amir al-Mu'mineen Institute decided to go to Shiraz Military Art University for more specialised courses.

From the very first day, we joked that he had studied at an Islamic seminary for two years because of his long beard. Under this same pretext, we made him lead prayers. He always jabbed me in the side and said, "Rasoul, stop it! You're bothering me!" This joke gained traction, and he eventually became the imam of prayers at the mosque.

I would be lying if I said he never missed his Salat ul-Layl. If he could wake up, he prayed it, but he devoutly prayed all

---

194. Pilgrimage to Makkah which can be performed any time of the year.

five prayers a day in congregation in the mosque. After Fajr, he recited *duas* for twenty minutes, but I don't know what kind of *duas* he recited. We decided to exercise after Fajr, but not to keep ourselves and our souls healthy, never! We jogged around in the courtyard together in our slippers, only and only to prepare ourselves for Syria. A few times while jogging together, he said this head must be separated from its body for Lady Zaynab (a)!

He was adamant on learning about tanks. He looked for spare notes in the education centre and library. He was one of the smartest students. Even though he had just joined the IRGC and didn't have much experience, he always said, "If we don't learn anything, we won't have much progress in Syria." We went to the deserts of Shiraz for military training, and I realised he was fasting. I scolded him, "Why today?! You'll pass out!" He laughed, "Don't worry about it!" I was supervising all the soldiers as I was the head of the course. They each had to fill up their water container one by one and get food. I saw him quietly go and fill up the water containers and come back.

He had a special love for Shah Cheragh (a). Whenever he had free time, he asked if we wanted to go and do *ziyarah*. Every Thursday, he tried everything he could to take leave and go back home. One time, we took a taxi from Isfahan to Najafabad. I've never seen someone haggle over a taxi fare before. One of the drivers said to Mohsen, "May I be sacrificed for the black hairs of your beard, leave us alone!" He said, "My dad is a taxi driver himself! I know the rates."

He didn't watch television or football, but he played sports with us . He knew how to play sitting volleyball well. We put a chair on either side of the hall and tied scarves around each other to make a net. When he got up to bring the ball, he walked on one leg and didn't use his hand properly. For a while, the guys had set up a *zourkhaneh*[195]. His friend acted as the trainer and Mohsen was swinging the weights around aimlessly. Everyone had surrounded them and was dying of laughter. We made a volleyball team from the people in our room. When I substituted Mohsen into the game, he wasn't playing very well and kept hitting the ball into the net. I pulled him out quickly. He realised he wouldn't play again that day and he started running around the hall. He didn't want to play badly. On one of his laps, I suddenly realised he had left the hall.

During the course, we wanted to bring our families to Shiraz at least once. He came and asked me to find someplace they could stay. He said, "My son, check for the first of April." I told him, "Why in the holidays? Check after the second so you can use your leave!" After I kept asking him why, he told me. That year, the death anniversary of Lady Umm al-Banin (a)[196] coincided with Sizdah-be Dar and he didn't want to be with his family in case they forced him to go out and have a good time.

Less than a year after the course in Shiraz, we went to Syria. The first day we reached Aleppo, his clothes still hadn't arrived. I gave him a pair of my sweatpants. He went and washed it before wearing it. A few minutes later, he popped his head out from inside and whispered, "Rasoul! Come here, my son!" I couldn't stop myself from laughing. Instead of taking washing powder from the bucket, he'd taken sugar! [If you saw it,] you would have thought he had laid the trousers inside a bucket of honey . We were short on water. He didn't know what to do. The next day, he did another silly thing. I noticed he was

---

195. A *zourkhaneh* (literally, Power House) is a traditional gym where Iranian-style bodybuilding, strength training and weightlifting known as *Varzesh-e Bastani* are practiced.

196. Hazrat Umm al-Banin (a) was the wife of Imam Ali (a) and the mother of Hazrat Abbas (a).

forlorn, so I asked him what happened. He said anxiously, "My son! I was loading the heavy machine gun onto the tank and without looking, I accidentally stepped on the 'fire' button!" He was so worried about where it had gone and what it had hit! I comforted him by saying if something had happened, we would have heard about it.

Two nights later, I was at my post at midnight. Our commander came and told me to go with Mohsen to take the machines to the front line. He didn't want to send Mohsen on his own. I agreed and we put the first tank onto the Titan[197]. Both of us sat next to the Syrian driver, armed. Before leaving, the driver lit his cigarette and started playing music. Mohsen came closer to my ear and whispered, "My son! We're being blessed!" When we left, he was constantly calling different people with a brick phone and talking quickly in Arabic. When we reached the first three-way junction, the Titan switched off. He tried switching it back on a few times, but it didn't start. He pulled out an Android phone from his pocket and got out. There wasn't a creature stirring around us. Mohsen gulped and said, "My son! That simple phone belonged to the IRGC and this Android phone belongs to ISIS!" I turned and whispered to him, "I'm getting out, don't move a muscle from here and take your gun off safety!" I went after the driver. He was checking the Titan with the torch from his Android. He searched for a few minutes until he found the problem. He switched the vehicle on, and we set off. As we were about to get comfortable, a Toyota came out of nowhere and was flashing for us to stop. We took our guns off safety again. They were from the Qods Force. One of them came up and told the driver to drive quickly with the lights off and

---

197. A Titan is an armoured vehicle used to transport heavy machinery.

not to stop anywhere. He advised us to always keep an eye out as well because the road wasn't safe.

Less than ten minutes later, a terrible sound made us jump. The Titan jerked a few times, and we could hear a terrifying scraping sound. When we got out, we saw the metal bridge at the back of the vehicle had fallen and was being dragged across the asphalt. The three of us put it back in place while shaking out of fear and we left. We dropped the tank off at the front line and went back. Suddenly, I realised the road we were driving on wasn't the same one we came from. I told Mohsen, "He's going the wrong way, what if he takes us to our death?!" Neither of us knew Arabic. Mohsen turned around and said to the Syrian driver, "*Sayyidi! Tariq, la tariq!*"[198] The driver kept glancing at him from the corner of his eye. Mohsen paused and thought a little. This time he said, "*Sayyidi! La sirat!*"[199] I couldn't help but laugh. The driver thought we were messing with him and he started frowning. Before we could piece together another sentence to say to him, we noticed he had brought us back to the base from a different route. By the time we loaded the second tank and delivered it to the front line, it was six o'clock in the morning. While loading the third tank, he said to the commander, "This man was at his post last night, let him sleep, I'll go myself and come back." I insisted I wasn't tired, but they didn't let me go. In the end, they sent me inside the base, and he left on his own.

---

198. Arabic for 'Sir! The road, no road!'
199. Arabic for 'Sir! No path!'

Hojjatollah Mehrabi

The martyr's comrade

Mohsen and I got to know each other at Shiraz Military University. One of the guys said, "I saw a Najafabadi today, he's come here to study." He was on another campus. I went there and made friends with him. He seemed well-grounded and passionate. I explained to him there were a few religious organisations there which organise good programmes, but I realised it was like taking coals to Newcastle. He knew Agha Anjavinejad much better than I did, and he was a regular attendee at the programmes of the Rahpouyan-e Vesal Shiraz Religious Organisation. He said they had invited Agha Anjavinejad to the Shaheed Kazemi Institute several times and they had also taken part in his *i'tikaf* with the staff of the institute. We decided to attend the programmes of the religious organisation together. The first time we went to a programme of the Rahpouyan-e Vesal Religious Organisation, he explained to me how terrorists had come before and set bombs there.

As we attended religious gatherings together, I found out there was an Ayatollah giving lessons on Quranic exegesis near the shrine of Shah Cheragh (a). When I told Mohsen, he became irritated and said he is against the government, has conflicting views to the Leader and the misguided people gather around him. I insisted we go and see what he was saying, but he wasn't having any of it.

He mentioned memories from the lives of the martyrs at every chance. Whenever his shelf was full, he took a few books about the martyrs out of his bag and told us to read them.

Our friendship blossomed when we went to Syria. The first night when we reached Ibtin, they took us to a school with two floors. It was in an unbelievably bad condition; no water, no electricity, we couldn't even see. From the very beginning in front of the door, we were faced by the body of an ISIS fighter. The next day, a loader was passing by. I went with Mohsen and asked him to pour some dust over the body so it doesn't start to smell. I would be telling a lie if I said we weren't afraid that night. Everyone was terrified, but Mohsen was so relaxed! He was sitting at the door, his weapon slung over his shoulder and waiting to go to the front line. I couldn't take it. I remarked snidely, "Fear is also a good thing!" He replied, "Honestly, because I've come to protect the shrine of Lady Zaynab (a), I feel as if someone is protecting me!"

The quality of the camouflage clothes they gave to us wasn't great and it tore easily. They brought more clothes, and everyone took a pair except Mohsen. I told him, "It's your right, whether you take it or not." He said, "My clothes still haven't torn. Maybe someone will come to the warfront and won't have clothes, they can use that." I was annoyed and laughed, "I pray your clothes tear soon, so you have to take the new clothes!" By chance, his clothes got caught on a corner a few days later and ripped. We just looked at each other and laughed.

We were on our way to the village of Sabiqiyyah for an operation. I was the tank driver and Mohsen was the gunner. I was reciting Ayat ul-Kursi[200] over the radio. He chuckled, "Hojjat, that's enough. How many times are you going to recite Ayat ul-Kursi?!"

---

200. Ayat ul-Kursi is a reference to verses 255 to 257 of the Quran. These verses are recited to protect oneself from any kind of harm.

"How come?" I asked.

"At least let one bullet, some shrapnel, something come towards us too!" he replied.

"Aha! You thought wrong! If you're with me, nothing will come towards us, don't worry!" I told him.

"Well, don't read it for a bit, let's see what happens!" he laughed.

We liberated the village from ISIS. We took the tank behind a house and took cover. We were waiting for the route to open so we could advance. Every now and then, a bullet, mortar shell or some shrapnel came our way. We couldn't move a muscle from behind the wall. It was time for Dhuhr. Everyone was crouched in a corner so they wouldn't get hit by a bullet or a mortar shell. Mohsen calmly and indifferently stood in a corner to pray. Two soldiers from the Qods Force scolded him, saying it wasn't the time to pray, but he told them in his Najafabadi accent, "Don't worry about what I'm doing, whoever has a problem with it doesn't have to pray!" After he prayed, we went back in the tank. He took out his pocket-sized Quran and started reciting. From the tank's windshield, I saw some dust rise. I asked Mohsen worriedly, "What was it?" He replied, "I didn't see!" We jumped out. A mortar shell had landed without exploding. There was still smoke emitting from its fins. When we went closer, Mohsen looked at the shell and said with a grin, "You're so unfair! You didn't think we were worthy for you to explode!" His words made me laugh. We took a few cobblestones and placed them around the shell just in case a vehicle drove over it.

When the situation calmed down, we went into a road and leaned on a wooden door. While we were talking, I said to him, "I'm fine with any calamity that befalls me, but it will be terrifying if we are taken captive and then martyred." He mentioned a narration from the Holy Prophet (s) very calmly,

"Death for a believer is like a bunch of sweet-smelling flowers." He then added, "Be sure that captivity is the same!" Suddenly, I heard something from behind me, and Mohsen did too. We took our guns off safety and with the signal, we rushed inside. Two or three fat and ready sheep were staring us in the eye. We went back to the soldiers and told them and laughed about how we had been ambushed. The commander said, "The residents of this village won't return right now. Eventually, these animals will be killed by a bullet or some shrapnel. If we run out of food someday, it's fine if you cook one of these animals and let me know. When the city is freed, we will tell the residents." While Mohsen was guarding the gate of the base, one of the soldiers dragged one of the sheep inside. Another sharpened his knife and cut its throat. At midnight, we lit a fire and had a barbecue. We called Mohsen over a few times, but he didn't come. We went to force him to come to the fire, but he said firmly he wouldn't eat.

Hamidreza Jahanbakhsh

The martyr's comrade

I got all the soldiers of the battalion to sit in front of the map in one of the buildings in the village of Tal Azzan and I briefed them under the light of candles and torches. In the first stage, we took the tanks and APCs to the village of Ibtin under the cover of darkness. We were stationed in a school there. In the morning, Commander Iraqi ordered us to start the operation. In that region, our goal was to liberate the village of Shughaydilah. I was part of the first group to enter the village with Hojaji. At around three o'clock in the afternoon, the enemy waged a heavy attack. With the first mortar shell, we gave three martyrs in front of Hojaji's eyes: Ahmadi, Dayitaghi and Qorbani. We were forced to retreat. We held our defensive line behind the village of Ibtin. The soldiers' spirits were low, including Hojaji. This was the first time they had seen their friends martyred in front of their eyes. At night, I gathered everyone inside the school, and we had a session of *sinehzani*. After, I spoke with them to raise their morale.

A few days later, we went to the village of Sabiqiyyah with Hojaji and Pooya Izadi and set up an armoured base. I noticed the fields surrounding the village had ripe and delicious pomegranates. I picked a few and took them for the soldiers. Everyone ate except Hojaji. I offered it to him several times, but he didn't accept. I told him, "These lands have been occupied by the terrorists for a few years now and no one has watered them, they've grown themselves. Now if we don't eat, it will fall off the tree and go bad. We're not picking them to take them back to Najafabad!" The nights were cold, and the soldiers slept inside the houses. When I left the room at midnight, I saw Hojaji praying in the middle of the road. I asked him once, "Why here in the cold? Go inside!" He replied, "I'm more comfortable here." I told him many times these lands had been freed and the houses weren't usurped, but he didn't accept.

There was a shop that had been damaged by bullets. Pooya Izadi came and said it would be a shame if these sunflower seeds inside the shop went to waste. I understood what he was trying to say. I told him, "Go and bring them so the soldiers can eat them together." I understood Hojaji's behaviour by then, so I radioed him, "We've bought some seeds from the shop at the top of the road, come and eat!" He laughed, "I'm not coming!" I told him, "If you are martyred with this behaviour, you'll make it difficult for us! Come and eat some food so you don't get martyred as well!"

The tank personnel stayed at the infantry base for two nights. After two days, they went back to rest, take a shower, call their families, and come back energetic. I had to fight with Hojaji over going back every time. He said, "I want to stay on the front line!" One night, he really got on my nerves. I hurled his bag in the trunk of the car and yelled at him, "Go and tend to your business! You're tired, you'll fall asleep at midnight and cause more trouble for us!" On the morning of Tasu'a[201], Hojaji's team came to participate in Operation al-Humrah. After the *adhan* of Fajr, they started moving and reached the infantry. I was fifty metres away from the tank. I saw a light travel above my head and when I looked back, I noticed a mortar shell had struck the tank. Another shell came, but it missed the tank. I went back quickly. There was nothing left of Pooya Izadi's clothes. We recovered his body with Hojaji and took it back.

---

201. The 9th of Muharram.

Under these circumstances, Hojaji was raising my morale. I understood he was in a worse state than myself, but he was saying, "Haji, don't be upset! Insha'Allah Allah will give us this fate too!" I went and laid out the path to return. We could get lost under the darkness of night. We had to return secretly at night through the towering hills. One of the APCs had been hit by a shell. We decided to tow it with a tank and bring it back. We laid the body of the martyr inside it and we set off. I was walking in front of the tank. Hojaji jumped out of the cabin and said, "Haji, go inside the tank." I replied, "Go, don't worry about what I'm doing!" A few feet forward, he came again, saying I was tired and should go in. I had no more energy left. I had been on the front line since morning and the martyrdom of Pooya Izadi had really affected me, but I had to find the trees and bushes I had marked so we wouldn't go astray. The next time he came, I shouted, "Just leave me alone! Let me pay attention to the path so we don't get lost!" He couldn't bear to leave me alone in that state, so he accompanied me on foot for the whole seven-kilometre journey.

The day he was returning to Iran, he said, "Do you know why I wasn't martyred on this trip?" I said no, and he explained, "I have discovered several issues in myself that I have to go and resolve." In Najafabad, he was constantly trying to flatter me so I would take him to Syria. One night, he invited me and my family to his house. He let us know indirectly that if I were to go to Syria, I should watch over him. He wanted to make a secret arrangement. That night, I said to his father-in-law, "If I let go of Hojaji, he'll be martyred quickly!" One time, he was passing by my house with his wife and mother-in-law. When he saw me, he got out and asked me how I was. His mother-in-law asked, "Aren't you going to Syria?"

"Why do you ask?" I said.

"I want to give Agha Mohsen to you so you can take him," she replied.

"Where do you want to send him?" I asked, "If he reaches Syria, only his body will come back!"

Khodadad Ahmadi

The martyr's comrade

I said to Mohsen while doing pull-ups, "You're going up and down so easily, you're built like a piece of straw!" He stretched his neck and said, "Allah gives each person strength according to their body."

We were dispatched to Syria in September 2015. We went to Aleppo from Damascus in a cargo plane, and they took us straight to the village of Bahuth. We had to take forty tanks close to the front line. We got to work, six or seven of us, and it took us from the *adhan* of Maghrib to the *adhan* of Fajr to complete the job. When we got back to the base in the morning, I said, "Scoundrels! No one even came to say thank you!" Mohsen replied, "Don't nag so much. We've come to work for Allah!"

In Bahuth, we didn't have the most basic of facilities. Pooya Izadi decided he wanted to shave the heads of the soldiers, but Mohsen didn't do it. Pooya insisted if not that, to at least let him trim Mohsen's beard a little. A few days later, Pooya Izadi was martyred. I can still remember how Mohsen cried. He was sitting in a corner of a school courtyard, his arms wrapped around his knees. We didn't even have enough time to mourn because of the amount of work. They assigned a duty to Mohsen which meant he would have to go to Latakia. We didn't see Mohsen again until we went back to Iran.

A year later, we took another journey together: the walk of Arbaeen. We went to my cousin's house in Izeh[202] with the group. We all sat at the dinner spread, but Mohsen was sitting against the wall. My cousin asked, "So why isn't this Shaykh

---
202. Izeh is a city in the Khuzestan Province in the south-west of Iran.

coming forward?" He replied, "I don't think it's correct that all of us come and bother you." We went from the Chazabe Border to Najaf in an open-top lorry. He said, "Insha'Allah next year, we'll pay some money and go with a bus like a normal human being!"

On the path from Najaf to Karbala, he said one morning, "Guys, come, let's recite Dua Ahd." I objected, "Leave it! We've read so many *duas* and prayers, my back's about to break! Let's eat something instead." He replied, "Don't starve yourself! Go and eat well then come and read the *dua*."

We were supposed to meet at pole 735[203], but we lost each other. I was standing there doing nothing for almost fifty minutes and I didn't have signal on my mobile phone either. We managed to find each other via text. When he got there, I said, "Where did you go? Did you sit in another *majlis*? Did you think you could correct yourself so easily?" He loved *masa'ib* and *sinehzani* so much, I thought he had found a *majlis* and had stayed there. He apologised, saying, "No, I had lost you too!" We then sat down and ate some pomegranates. The pomegranate seeds were as red as blood. He laid his scarf on the floor and said, "There is a seed from heaven in every pomegranate. Be careful you don't waste it!"

At night in Karbala, we slept in the *mawkib* packed together like sardines in a tin. There was no space. We let Mohsen sleep in the space above us. Any hour of the night we arranged to go to the shrine together, we woke up and saw he had already gone.

We didn't get a chance to go to Syria together a second time. His dispatch date was everchanging. One day, I joked with him, "You're like a bounced cheque, you go and come back. At least go and be martyred so we can eat some good food [at your

---

203. On the path from Najaf to Karbala, there are 1,400 poles which are used as markers, and each pole is fifty metres away from the other.

funeral]!" He laughed, "Pray I'm martyred so you can get your wish sooner!"

Majeed Forouzandeh

The martyr's comrade

He set up a 'Quit Drinking Tea' campaign with one of the others. They made herbal tea in their flasks. I went and said to them, "Give me some of your herbal tea!" Mohsen said, "Don't give him any! He hasn't paid for it yet." He took a thousand tomans from me and said, "Welcome to the campaign!" Every day I paid for the tea, he told me I was richer than the others. We made a rumour against them that we saw a worm amongst the plants they gave us to drink. We called it 'The Worm Campaign'. He announced to everyone, "I will drink one cup for everyone who doesn't drink!"

In Syria, he drank everything except soda, which he gave to the others. Due to our constant activities, our blood sugar dropped. Instead of soda, Mohsen drank fruit juice, but he insisted on respectfully pouring it into a cup and drinking it. When the news spread amongst the battalion that we were being dispatched to Syria in 2015, he became terribly upset. He always came into our room with his head down. I asked him, "What is it? Why do you keep coming here?" He replied ruefully, "It would be so nice if I could come too!" Our co-worker Agha Qaderi told him, "You've only been in the military for two days, where are you planning to go? You have to struggle first, go and dry your sweat, then maybe!" He called everyone 'Haji'. He replied, "No, Haji! There are all these recruits coming, what harm would it be if I came too?" I had heard one of the soldiers had some issue and was looking for a replacement. Qaderi replied, "If you say it yourself, you know it! How can we take an inexperienced soldier with us?!" When I saw how forlorn he was, I couldn't hide it from him. I pulled him aside and told him to go to the commander of the 3rd Battalion and tell him he had come as a replacement for so-and-so. He ran faster than a bullet. Close to the *adhan* of Dhuhr, someone jumped on my shoulders. I looked back to see who it was. He started kissing me out of excitement and told me he was going too! Qaderi couldn't believe it and said, "So you finally did it!" He then laughed, "Wait until we get there, I'll hand you over to ISIS myself!"

We went to Tehran. Only a few passports had been stamped out of the hundred and twenty that had been sent off, and Mohsen's was one of those. He kept parading in front of us and showing off. Qaderi and I got him back in the prayer room though. We started slapping him around and he was crying out, "Haji, forgive me!"

We joined them two days late. He kept us awake under the pretext of standing guard and patrol so we could finish the day with Salat ul-Layl. He joked, "Eventually, it will be some spiritual savings for you and also, when you're martyred, people will say it is because of the blessings of Salat ul-Layl." In this manner, I slowly started praying Salat ul-Layl, but I never managed to wake up before him. One night, I left the room, and I didn't see Mohsen. I thought to myself, "Yes! I got up faster than Mohsen tonight!" I prayed and went to sleep. I asked the others, "There's no sign of Mohsen!" They replied, "He's in the hangar, in the ruined room!" He had finished praying and was reciting *dhikr* on his *tasbih*. I went closer to give him a jump scare, but his face was drenched in tears, and I didn't dare to go closer.

Naseeri and I decided to put on a play for him. When he came in, we pretended as if we were grieving and deep in thought. He asked worriedly, "What happened?" We replied, "We had an intuition we will be martyred in the next operation! We feel upset for you because you'll be all alone here!" When

Mohsen heard this, he started crying and he wouldn't calm down! He started begging us that if we were martyred, to take his hand too. Naseeri and I started laughing, but he wouldn't believe it was all an act. He always talked about the great sins which repel the blessing of martyrdom.

He loved Shaheed Musa Kazemi even though he had never met him and was martyred before Mohsen had even joined the division. On Thursday nights, he gathered the soldiers in the warzone, and we recited the Quran in memory of the martyr.

I called my mother. She didn't know I was in Syria and I had told her I was going for training. As soon as my mother picked up the phone and said salaam, the artillery guns started firing! Mohsen was next to me and laughing his head off. I elbowed him in the side to quieten him. My mother asked, "What's that noise?" and I told her, "It's very cold here, you can hear the wind!" Mohsen said loudly, "Haji, tell your mother we will have your back if a bullet or shrapnel comes our way!" I glared at him from the corner of my eye to tell him to calm down because she was listening.

Mohsen, Naseeri and I were sent to Latakia to learn how to use T-90 tanks. The rest of the soldiers completed their service and were ready to leave. In Latakia, we went to the seaside. A few people took off their clothes and went swimming. Mohsen pulled his trousers up and laughed, "What nice water! Come, let's go and swim with the dolphins." I wouldn't enter the water no matter how much he insisted. He teased me, "City kids have to have their towel with them to go swimming!"

We joked with each other like this. Before we went to Syria, me, Mohsen, Behzad Sadeghi and Abdorrasoul Ibrahimi went for cupping. Behzad and I were fat while Mohsen and Abdorrasoul were thin. Mohsen was minus twenty-five kilos and Abdorrasoul was minus four kilos! On the way, Behzad and I joked, "You two don't have more than four drops of blood in your body, I think we need to give you a blood transplant instead!" However, mine and Behzad's blood sugar dropped and those two were completely fine and energetic. Mohsen and Abdorrasoul laughed at us so much that night. However, one time, I beat Mohsen. We were neighbours and our apartment blocks were facing each other. One afternoon when I was walking into the compound, I saw him hanging up clothes on his balcony. I shouted at him, "Hey, zanzaleel[204]!" He replied while hanging up the clothes, "Haji! Say khodahafez and go home now." I teased him so much about this in the battalion's base after that.

We found out about Javad Qorbani's martyrdom while we were in Latakia. This news hurt Mohsen very much. They were exceptionally good friends. Qorbani always said to Mohsen, "Prepare yourself, it's time for martyrdom!" He cried to me, "Did you see how he always told me I would be martyred? He himself left and I've been left behind!" From that day onwards, I never saw Mohsen happy again. He was always deep in thought and sitting in a corner, mourning with his arms wrapped around his knees.

After training, we immediately went to Aleppo and we were stationed on the front line. On our way to al-Ays Mountain, which was the front line of combat, the tank's escape hatch opened. We tried everything, but we couldn't get it to close. Naseeri's leg was hurting and couldn't exert much physical force. Mohsen said, "Let me go and close it from the bottom!" I replied, "How are you going to do it with your skinny body?" He radioed Commander Amini and requested assistance. I said to him, "Have some shame, man! It's wrong to ask a commander for this!" He justified himself, saying, "Come on, this is jihad,

---

204. In Farsi, this word literally means 'humiliated by his wife', and it's used for a man whose wife gets him to do everything around the house

and we are all brothers, we shouldn't be stuck on the warfront!" Eventually, he went himself and closed the hatch with some rope.

We completed a difficult operation. Mohsen and his group fought like lions that night and most of their missiles hit their target. Haj Qasem [Soleimani] dubbed that night *Laylatul Futuh*[205]. When we got back from the front line, the brigade from Nishapur started congratulating us. Amongst all the celebrations and happiness, Mohsen was standing in the corner and doing *dhikr* on his *tasbih*. I called him over and said, "Hey! Everyone's having a good time here, why do you have such a blank expression!?" He replied indifferently, "I didn't do anything to be happy about! This was all Allah's work, I'm showing my gratitude that He saw us capable to do His work!" The next day, Commander Iraqi sent us some money as a gift, but Mohsen didn't accept it. He said he hadn't come here for the money. I told him, "Firstly, this is a gift and secondly, it's not even that much!" I suggested he put some of it inside the *zareeh* of Lady Zaynab (a) and use the rest to buy some souvenirs for his wife. I was at peace as I thought I had convinced him. When we got back, he didn't buy much from the bazaar after doing *ziyarah* at the shrine of Lady Zaynab (a). I asked, "Weren't you supposed to buy souvenirs with that gift?"

"It went where it was supposed to go!" he replied.

"You mean you put it all in the *zareeh*?!" I exclaimed.

---

205. Arabic for 'The Night of Victories'.

Ebrahim Naseeri

The martyr's comrade

They pulled me aside and asked, "Are you willing to go to Latakia for T-90 training?" I was waiting for such an opportunity to arise, so there was no way I could reject it. They emphasised, "This isn't a joke, from now on, you work as if you are completely fresh. Imagine that you just reached the area today and you will be staying for sixty more days. If you're ready, go ahead!" I put their minds at rest that I wouldn't fail them. They said this to Mohsen too and he also stood by his word firmly. We set off for Latakia together. They appointed me as the commander due to my superior experience and Mohsen was appointed as the gunner.

Latakia is known for its lack of hijab and widespread corruption. In the morning when we left for the training location, he sat at the back of the minibus immediately, closed the curtains and started reciting Ayat ul-Kursi loudly so the others could read along too. He constantly lowered his gaze so he wouldn't look at the women without hijab walking by on the street. One of the guys jokingly shouted at him, saying, "It's a shame you aren't using these divine blessings!" He then ran and forced Mohsen's face towards the window. Mohsen didn't fall for it and closed his eyes quickly.

The Russians taught us with three T-90 tanks. This was the first time we had seen this kind of tank ready and armed. Mohsen went and learnt how to use the tank eagerly. We had to learn about the tanks within three to four days; the other soldiers were waiting on the front line impatiently. After training, we went to take the tanks. There were two or three minor defects in the tanks that had to be resolved. The translator said, "The Russian mechanic says they will repair the tanks completely and deliver them to you. After that, your mechanic can do whatever he knows how to do."

It was almost noon and we had been on our feet since the morning. It was hot and sticky in Latakia, and I couldn't be bothered to work anymore. I said to Mohsen, "Come, let's wash our faces and grab a cup of tea." He replied, "Haji, you go, I'll stay. I want to learn everything from their mechanics, it'll be useful for us later."

He kept asking when we were leaving. He kept making excuses that the soldiers are on their own and we needed to leave soon. I joked, "Don't you feel bad to leave these beautiful trees and scenery to go and be bombed by the enemy?" He remarked snidely, "Did we come here to have a good time?" I replied angrily, "Stop acting all holy. Go and do your work, you don't need to say anything!" When the commanders came to hear our reports, he ran and told them our tank was ready to go, even though it still needed repairs. I told him, "This tank still hasn't passed its examinations! If we go there, we'll need to repair it!" He replied ruefully, "Haji, just let us go to the front line!" His enthusiasm bore fruit and we set off in the first tank to Aleppo. I told him, "You see, you finally got what you wanted!" Our tank driver said, "We're not going to a wedding, okay, we're going to war!" He laughed, "Well, that's what we came for!" We loaded the tank onto the Titan. I told him, "Mohsen, go in the Toyota and I will sit in the Titan with Majid Forouzandeh." He replied, "No, Haji! You go." On the way, we stopped somewhere. I noticed his eyes were bloodshot from fatigue, so I told him, "Go and rest on the back seat of the Toyota!" but he didn't go. He was insistent that I was the commander and must rest.

As soon as we reached Aleppo, they told us Commander Amini wanted to see us. We went to the second floor of a concrete building and the commander said, "Load the tank with ammunitions so we can go on an operation." We got to work immediately. Once again, Mohsen came and said he would load the ammunitions himself and all I had to do was hand him the missiles from the top. Passing the rocket shells down one by one was a difficult job. You had to take the cone-shaped missiles, each one weighing more than twenty kilos, out from the cabin, take it to the end and load it into the gun of the tank.

The Syrian driver we had come with brought some herbal tea which they call maté. It looked like dried mint. He offered it to us many times, but we refused. He asked, "Why don't you people ever drink anything?!" Mohsen managed to piece together a sentence with his broken Arabic and say, "They are no good, you drink it, don't worry about us." I told him, "Mohsen! Thank God he doesn't speak Farsi, you had us all in stitches!" He laughed, "No, Haji! It's no problem, let's continue."

We loaded the tank onto the Titan by sunset. We were fifty kilometres away from the front line. There were no Toyotas there. Mohsen ran onto the tank and jumped into the cabin. I told him, "Come and sit in the front," but he didn't. I sat in the front with the Syrian driver and his assistant. The Titan has one seat for the driver and one seat for a security officer, but we managed to cram three people inside. I only just realised what they had to go through on the journey from Latakia to Aleppo, but the Titan was still much safer and more comfortable than the cabin of the tank.

We unloaded the tank and took it to the foot of the al-Ays Mountain. There were two mountains, and we took cover by the left one. Taking the tank over the mountain wasn't a simple job. The commander on the front line was Karim Nami, who we realised was from Kerman by his accent. Karim came and said, "I'll take the driver of the tank up so he can see the route, then he can go back and bring the tank up." Mohsen and I waited for Majid Forouzandeh to go and identify the route. Our destination was a mine close to the highway, a strategic position which we had to liberate from the Takfiris. Karim came back on a motorcycle and asked, "Who's the gunner of the tank?" I replied, "Agha Mohsen." He said to Mohsen, "Get on the bike!" Mohsen asked, "Where do you want to go?" Karim replied, "The operation intelligence headquarters." Mohsen's face changed and said, "I won't move a muscle unless my commander comes." The operation intelligence headquarters was at the foot of the mountain on the right. I whispered, "Mohsen! This is a motorcycle, it isn't a Toyota. Go yourself." He replied, "No! I won't go anywhere without you!" Karim moved onto the fuel tank of the motorcycle and said, "Come, you and your commander!" All three of us sat on the bike and we left. The vice-commander of the infantry was Commander Iraqi, one of the intelligence officers. They identified the targets with thermal night-vision binoculars. Commander Iraqi asked, "Who is the gunner? He should come here now!" Mohsen said, "Commander! Tell my commander, I will do whatever he says." He had become a gunner for the first time with everything he had learnt over those three or four days in Latakia. I thought to myself, "Mohsen, what should I do with you?!" I sat next to Commander Iraqi, and he showed me the targets one by one. He then slapped me on the leg and asked, "Did you see them all?" Mohsen was standing behind me. I asked, "What happened?" Mohsen replied, "Ask them to show the targets one more time." He saw the targets on the screen once more.

In ordinary times when there's no combat, sitting inside a tank is suffocating, let alone in the heat of battle! There is such little space that if you want to move, your clothes will get caught on something, but under those circumstances, we were holding AK-47s too. Mohsen, Forouzandeh and I went to the top of the mountain. Despite my sixteen, seventeen years of experience as a gunner, Mohsen put me to shame. When we were going to shoot, he activated the radio and asked, "Are you ready?" The gunner must inform the driver and commander for every missile as the tank jerks heavily. He then turned on the outer microphone so everyone could hear. He yelled "Ya Zaynab!" and fire. That night, we fired twenty-two missiles and we fought until 1 am. We went to the base, two hundred metres below the mountain. It was the days of Muharram. Contrary to Latakia, the weather was very cold. I was looking for flat ground so we could readjust the tank. They directed us into a small room. We walked quietly in the darkness to not wake the others up. There was a fuel heater in the corner of the room. A few people were sleeping side by side. We sat in a corner and one of the soldiers brought blankets so we could lay down. Under these poor circumstances, Mohsen asked pleasantly, "Haji, put our names down for patrol!" Under these conditions where we had arrived in Aleppo from Latakia during the day, then we were immediately sent to the front line at night in addition to the stress and exhaustion of the operation, he was now asking me to put our names down for patrol! The man said they had closed the list for patrol, but he gave us patrol duty for the entire next day, but Mohsen didn't go down without a fight. He said, "No, Haji! If you don't give permission, I'll go right now and stand outside until morning!" I thought to myself, "O' God, do I have to be with him for sixty days?! Why is he doing this to us?!" Eventually, he forced that soldier to let us be on patrol duty. In the morning, one of the soldiers from the operation came and said, "Last night, you brewed up a storm!" I asked how, and he laughed, "The only person who didn't get up to congratulate and applaud us was Commander Iraqi, he was too embarrassed!" They were watching everything on the screens inside the operation room. They showed us the videos. Not even one missile missed the target. There was a sniper inside one of the buildings who was bothering us very much. Mohsen fired a missile. I told him, "Fire another!" He replied, "There's too much dust in front of me, what shall I do?" I asked, "Have you moved the gun?" When he said no, I replied, "Then don't delay it, fire!" We saw on the video that when he fired the second missile, it demolished the entire building.

We were stationed in that base for three or four days. Our bodies and clothes were caked in dust. I told Mohsen many times, "Come, let's go back, take a shower and return!" but he didn't want to. He raised his eyebrows and said, "No, Haji! We have to stay on the front line!" Every night, we had to deal with the cramped conditions of our room; a three by four-metre room, including our rucksacks, weapons, and the gas heater. I slept stuck to Mohsen. I don't understand how he woke up in the middle of the night and left without waking me up. Whenever I left the room for Fajr, he was either standing and praying Salat ul-Layl or reciting the Quran in the corner with a flashlight.

One night after praying Isha, they came quickly and told us to take our tank to the front line. We got ready without eating dinner and they took us inside the same operations building to show us the targets. While we were getting ready to go and shoot, someone came on a motorcycle. He was sent on Commander Iraqi's behalf and he carried a message that the targets had changed. He then asked, "Who is the commander of the tank?" I went and stood beside him.

"Come, let me show you the targets from the tank," he said.

"I'm not going to leave it in the enemy's view and range for fifteen to twenty minutes!" I exclaimed.

"The commander said so," he replied.

"Go and tell him the tank commander doesn't permit this!" I told him.

He left angrily. Another person came back with thermal night-vision binoculars. We were laying down behind the cover. When he spotted the target, he gave me the binoculars and asked, "Can you see that wall with the olive tree next to it? Go up and hit it!" I went inside the tank and found the target on the monitor beside me. I told Mohsen, "Can you see the target on the screen? Hit it directly!" He always hit the target accurately. We were on top of a hill and there was a bunker in front of us. The infantry advanced from beneath the bunkers. We couldn't stay in them for long. They made a few gaps so our position couldn't be identified, otherwise, they fired mortars towards us. We went and shot from one gap and come back, then we fired from another gap. I got out, climbed the bunker, and identified the targets with the binoculars, then I went back inside the tank. I warned Forouzandeh every time, "Move quickly, if you take long, they'll hit us!" Mohsen said, "Haji, don't worry, even if they hit us, we'll be martyred!" I replied, "How about we put you in front like a sacrifice, so a bullet hits you right in your forehead?!" We didn't sleep a wink until morning. We reloaded the tank four, five times, and each time we loaded twenty-two rockets. When we went back, Mohsen didn't let me reload the tank and said, "Haji, you go up and hand down the rockets to me, I'll reload it myself."

The next day, we went back to the school. Peace had returned to the area and it looked like there would be no operation for a few nights. We were stationed inside the school. We showered and took some rest. It turns out Karim had come and taken Mohsen quietly to the front line. At midnight, I laid down after my patrol. Suddenly, Forouzandeh burst into the room and started shouting, "Mohsen! Mohsen!" I said, "Shh! What's wrong with you? The others will wake up! Mohsen's gone to the front line!" He asked, "Ibrahim, is that you?" I replied calmly despite my irritation, "What are you going on about at this hour of the night?" He begged me to come outside. As soon as I stepped through the gate, I realised his tank had been hit by a missile. I was devastated. A missile had struck the wings of the hatch. He was lucky the missile had ricocheted, but the shockwave had obliterated the inner periscopes. I ran down the steps and a Toyota entered the school compound. It was Mujtaba, Karim's apprentice. I ran, opened the passenger door, and yelled, "Where's Mohsen?!" He was terrified and blurted out, "He's right here!" I shouted at the top of my voice, "I asked, where is Mohsen!?" Mujtaba was clasping to the window and said, "I told you, he's here!" It turns out he was sitting in the back, but I couldn't see him under the darkness of the night. Mohsen opened the door and held my hand. He said, "Haji, I'm here! Why are you shouting?" I hugged him and pressed him to my chest. He sat inside the Toyota and took a deep breath. He said extremely calmly, "Look at my luck! Amongst all these missiles and shrapnel, all I got was four burnt hairs on my hand!" He didn't stay though; he forced his way to the base on the front line once again.

I went upstairs and laid down, thanking Allah for his safety. I couldn't sleep. I tossed and turned and eventually, I got up and went to the school courtyard. I saw Mujtaba had dropped Mohsen off and come back. I went and told him, "I want to go to Mohsen." He replied, "You have to stay here, you have to stand patrol." I told him, "Even if this place is demolished, I have to go!" Whilst Mujtaba and I were talking, Commanders

Amini and Mokhtari arrived. They were informed via radio that a T-90 tank had been hit by a missile and they came as soon as possible. They thought the three of us had been martyred. When they heard my voice, the commander asked, "Naseeri?! You're alive?!" I said yes and he asked, "What about the other two?" I said, "They're alive too!" He raised his hands and said, "Thank God." Mokhtari asked, "Where's Mohsen?" I told him he had gone to the base. He replied, "Come, let's go and visit him." We went to the base. Before Mokhtari could even switch off the vehicle and get out, I jumped out and ran towards the room we slept in together. I saw him leaning on the wall, reciting the Quran with a flashlight. I called him and asked him to come outside. I pulled him into the hall by his hand. He was a bit nauseous, so I picked him up from his underarms and carried him outside. When he saw Mokhtari, he tensed up. He was worried he would send him back. I whispered to Mokhtari that he was feeling nauseous. He wasn't willing to go to the medical clinic so the medic could examine him. He was repeating one sentence, "I have to stay here tonight." I told him, "We are here. If needed, we'll go onto the front line, you go." We forced him into the vehicle and sent him to the medical clinic. Less than an hour later, he came back, excited and smiling. They hadn't found anything during the examination, and he said, "I'm just a little shell-shocked, that's it!"

Out of nowhere, they came and told us we had to return to Iran. Only fifteen days had passed of those sixty days we had been promised. We begged Mokhtari to let us stay, but he didn't budge. We went and begged Commander Amini. He said, "One of you can stay." Mokhtari said, "No, all of them have to go back." Mohsen started crying in the middle of the hall and said, "There's not that long left until Arbaeen, I beg you, Haji! I've made an oath to stay here until Arbaeen!" They sent us all to Damascus against our own will. On the way, Mohsen didn't stop crying. He said woefully, "Our friends were martyred here, but we are leaving them alone and going back, and it isn't even certain whether we'll be able to come back or not! Memories will remain in their place, but Iran isn't like the warzones where we can go and renew our memories!" At Damascus Airport, he came and told me he bought an *abaya* for his wife. He didn't know if it would fit her because she was pregnant. I turned to him with surprise and asked, "Your wife is pregnant?"

"Yeah, why?" he replied.

"You mean for all this time you've been here, your wife has been pregnant?" I asked again.

"Yes," he said.

"Did anyone else know?" I asked him.

"No," he replied, "You are the first person to know."

He knew himself that if anyone knew on the day of dispatch, there would be no way he would be able to go to Syria.

Chapter VI

IT WAS HIS OWN FAULT!

Seifollah Rashidzadeh

Commander of the 8th Najaf Ashraf Division

I went and held his coffin from the back in Isfahan Airport. When we went towards the people, I thought to myself, "You are a commander who is following his soldiers!" I felt lowly. I kept whispering to him, "What you did truly deserves commendation!"

I had witnessed heartrending scenes when my friends had been martyred in the Iran-Iraq War, by bullets, shrapnel, shells, some were martyred by shockwaves and others were hit directly by a tank missile. Some were burnt inside the tank and we had to go and pull their bodies out. On the other hand, I have seen what happens to criminals on death row; they can't talk, their legs go weak to the extent that they can't walk and sometimes, they even soil themselves. These were people who terrified every rival into submission.

I witnessed Hojaji's martyrdom from afar. I saw the videos and photos of how they took him captive and beheaded him. Whenever I witnessed his bravery, I thought to myself, "What you did truly deserves commendation!"

One night at eleven o'clock, someone rang our doorbell. I looked at the doorbell camera and I saw him standing there. It was Mohsen Hojaji. I went to the door in my informal clothes. I thought maybe he wanted a loan or a transfer. After saying salaam and asking how he was, I asked, "Why have you come at this time of night?" He lowered his head and said, "I've come to ask you to give me permission to go." I asked, "Where?"

"On a mission," he replied.

"You couldn't find a better time than midnight, Muslim?!" I exclaimed. "Wasn't I at the base where you could have asked me?"

"I came here to beg you," he said.

"You've already gone once," I told him. "Now it's the others' turn who haven't gone."

"I beseech you [by Allah]!" he shouted.

"You can't do that for no reason, go, go now!" I replied.

He started crying, so I looked into his teary eyes and said, "If it's written in your destiny, it will happen." He wiped away his tears with his hand and left. I leaned on the front door and watched him walk away until he disappeared into the darkness. A while after this, Agha Akbariyan called me to say *khodahafez* from Imam Khomeini Airport while I was in Mashhad. I told him, "Have a safe flight. By the way, what happened to the second person?" He replied, "Hojaji came." I sat on the couch and exclaimed, "Who?!" Akbariyan and Pourpirali had signed up already, they had given their passports in and even arranged to leave the country. I asked, "So what happened to Pourpirali?"

"Something came up at the last minute and he dropped out," he replied.

"You trickster!" I exclaimed. "Where is he now?"

"He's outside," he said.

"When he comes inside, tell him to call me," I told him.

Twenty minutes later, he called me on his own phone. I told him, "You see how it was written in your destiny? You're so smart!" He said, "Haj Agha, forgive me for being a burden!" I laughed, "Forgiveness isn't handed out so freely, I'll only give you mine on one condition!" He asked what it was, and I said, "Pray a two-unit prayer in the shrine of Lady Zaynab (a) on my behalf. Of course, I'll pray for you in the shrine of Imam Rida (a)." He accepted the condition eagerly.

While sitting in the command office at eleven o'clock in the morning, my phone rang. I realised it was from Syria from the number that appeared on the screen. My heart sunk and I thought to myself, "Ya Hazrat Abbas! It isn't protocol to call from there!" The system in Syria is separate and the forces we send there run on that system. By principle, they only call to give news of martyrdom or injury. Before picking up, I told the soldier in my office to go outside. It was Akbariyan. As soon as I answered his salaam, he started crying. He couldn't talk through his tears. I had no doubt he wanted to tell me about one of the soldiers' martyrdom. Between his tears, he said clearly, "Hojaji has been martyred!" I asked, "What? Hojaji?!" His tears were obstructing his words. My eyes had welled up with tears, but I collected myself and scolded him, "Gather yourself! Tell me properly what happened!" With great difficulty, he explained to me that Hojaji's base had been attacked in the early morning.

Sayyid Majid Iyafat

The martyr's comrade

We went on intelligence operations with Hosein Qummi. The base where Jaber[206] was working was the final point of our territory. We went there in the afternoon so we could go towards enemy lines as soon as it became dark, whether by drone, motorcycle, or foot. The Americans had established a no-fly zone on the border of Jordan in an area by the name of Tanf where they trained and armed ISIS fighters. ISIS was stationed in the town of Qa'im in Iraq and invaded Syrian soil. The soldiers of the resistance axis were stationed in Palmyra and Deir Ez-Zor. The base where Jaber was stationed was almost where all three countries bordered each other, an extremely sensitive and perilous region. During those days, ISIS had attacked the bases of the Syrian Armed Forces several times and inflicted losses upon them. They were so dominant in the area that they had laid mines on the roads to prevent passing of vehicles. Under these circumstances, we were constantly searching for intelligence forces, soldiers who were strong in terms of quantity and quality. A few people suggested Jaber for this job and thus, whenever we went on intelligence operations, I watched him when we reached their base. I decided to ask the soldiers of the Fatemiyoun[207] and the Heydariyoun[208] about his personality. They all agreed, "He never misses his Salat ul-Layl!

---

206. All soldiers have a codename, also known as a jihad name. Shaheed Hojaji's jihad name was Jaber.
207. An Afghani brigade fighting against terrorism as part of the resistance axis in Syria and Iraq.
208. An Arab brigade fighting against terrorism as part of the resistance axis in Syria and Iraq.

After every prayer, he also recites Ziyarah Ashura!"

On our way back from our intelligence operations, we were more afraid of our soldiers shooting us than the ISIS fighters. Slowly, we took a liking to Jaber. When we left, we asked him to watch our back, and he replied in his thick Najafabadi accent, "Haji, don't worry!" Even when I didn't go a few times, I told the intelligence forces to watch out on their way back and they replied assuredly, "Jaber is there." He always waited for us at the forefront of the trenches. As soon as we radioed, "Jaber, we're on our way back," he replied, "Haji, don't worry!" One night when we were in the base, Hosein Qummi told me over the radio that they were going to attack that night. I asked, "How are you so sure?" He replied, "Drones are spying on us overhead." One or two hours later, I heard a lot of noise over the radio. I told him, "You're riling the troops up, huh?" He replied firmly, "No, no! We shot down one of their drones, I have it here with me now," and it happened. In that attack, they took Jaber captive.

Sayyid Reza Mirfendereski

The martyr's comrade

He was putting elastic in the hem of his gaiters so he could wear them over his boots. I asked him, "Do you have any spare?" He replied, "Let me cut off enough for my trousers and I'll give you the rest." He wrapped the elastic around his hand and said, "I need something from you." I turned my ear towards him as if to say, 'go on'. He whispered, "Don't send Agha Akbariyan in my place." I shook my head as if to ask why. He explained to me in detail that Agha Akbariyan is the commander of the battalion in the Najaf-e Ashraf Division, that he has a family, and he is older. We arranged that during those two months they were working in Palmyra, Akbariyan would stay in the region for a month and Jaber would also stay for a month. However much I drummed it into his head that he will burn in the fifty-degree heat even when he's in the shade from the sun, that there is no shower in the desert, that the region is insecure, he didn't let up. When I realised he was too persistent, I told him, "For now, stay for the first month and we'll see afterwards."

We went to the region together and I introduced him to the commander of the Qasemabad Base. Qasemabad is a border region which is three hundred kilometres away from the Iraq-Syria border. Every day, we went to the region and inspected his tanks. I noticed all the T-72 tanks were ready for operation and up to date. The tanks' fuel tank and DShK and Goryunov ammunition were all prepared. Before Jaber arrived, the commander of the Fatemiyoun was unable to brief the forces on how to prepare the armoured units within a day, but when Jaber explained it to the soldiers of the Fatemiyoun, he told them that

Sayyid Reza had asked for the tanks to be ready by the next day, and at sunset, they radioed and asked for someone to come and examine the tanks. I wanted to take him to another region, but when the Qasemabad commander found out, he begged me not to take Jaber. Why? He was good with everyone, the Iranians, the Fatemiyoun and the Heydariyoun. He went and sat in their trenches, ate with them, slept in their tents at night and made sure they didn't ever need anything.

I appointed Jaber as the armoured commander of the Abbasabad region, a few kilometres further forward than Qasemabad, on the front line. There were four bases he had to visit every day and assess the condition of the armoured units. Apart from this, his responsibilities extended to supplying the tank personnel with food and necessities. An operation took place in that region and almost the whole border was liberated. With binoculars, we could see the flags of the Popular Mobilisation Forces[209], the Iraqi forces, to our right, but there was a small chance there were still some ISIS forces between us and the Iraqis. At every moment, we were ready in case they hit our vehicle with a missile. Under those circumstances, Jaber visited the bases on foot without a vehicle. After a few days, I managed to find a vehicle for him. With great difficulty, I had them bring a Toyota for him from Palmyra. I put some canned food, mineral water and fruit juice in the back and left in another vehicle. At around one o'clock in the afternoon, we reached the fourth base where Jaber was stationed. The soldiers of the Fatemiyoun all held on to the rope. Jaber cut it with a knife and officially took the keys to the Toyota. As soon as he sat in the driver's seat, everyone started reciting *Salawat*. We then prayed,

---

209. The Popular Mobilisation Forces, or the Hashd al-Sha'bi, are an umbrella organisation consisting of more than forty militias, and is an integral part of the resistance axis fighting in Iraq.

ate lunch, and sat to discuss the conditions of the region. At six o'clock, I was called over the radio and told to go to Qasemabad immediately. Whilst saying *khodahafez*, I pulled Jaber aside. I don't know why I couldn't help feeling restless at that moment. The ground of that area didn't allow us to build trenches. The digger of the loader kept hitting stones. After digging twenty centimetres into the ground, we hit a stone which weighed half a tonne. They had built trenches in the first, second and third bases with great difficulty, but the fourth base where Jaber was stationed didn't have proper trenches. I advised him, "It's true you aren't in charge of the base, but you are in charge of your own life. Even if the soldiers of the Heydariyoun fall asleep, stay alert!"

After saying goodbye, I called Jaber every half an hour. At half-past twelve, one o'clock, I told him, "I'm going to sleep now." He said goodbye and insisted I come to them by eight o'clock to eat breakfast together. The soldiers of the Heydariyoun had prepared some *kellehpacheh*[210]. I promised him I would come if I didn't have any work. Right there behind the steering wheel, I pushed the chair back and closed my eyes. At Fajr time, I noticed there was a lot of noise coming from the radio. I jumped out of the vehicle and went to the commander of the base. My sixth sense told me that the fourth base had been attacked!

---

210. A traditional dish of stewed sheep parts such as head, stomach and feet which is usually eaten for breakfast.

Mohammad Abedi Toughi

The martyr's comrade

It was so hot, we were all laying down inside the tent. Jaber came and asked me for a vehicle so he could drive around the region and come back. Abu Muhammad, one of the veterans of the IRGC from Khuzestan, joked, "You have a vehicle, and you want another?!" He laughed and explained that his vehicle hadn't been working for a while now. His burnt face showed he had been doing a lot of walking. I offered him to sit and drink some tea with us, but he was in a rush. He wanted to visit the bases before sunset to examine the tanks. Abu Muhammad went and brought him a vehicle while he waited for his tea to cool down. He said, "Go and return quickly." He went and came back. He gave the key to Abu Muhammad and thanked us greatly for helping him with his work. It was prayer time, so he sat on the floor of the tent and took off his socks. I was shocked; I had never seen such large blisters. There was nothing left of his sole. I felt bad for him and I started radioing here and there to find a car for Jaber.

At around three or four in the morning, we noticed the ISIS fighters from the operations room. Three groups entered from three points on the border of Iraq, and they attacked three bases simultaneously. Before the operation, they sent a suicide vehicle which exploded next to the trenches of the base. The explosion was so great, it blinded the drones. We were around sixty kilometres away from the conflict. We reached the base at nine o'clock in the morning because the route was unsafe, and we couldn't go via the main road. Whichever soldier of the Fatemiyoun I asked, they told me Jaber had been martyred and they had sent him to Palmyra. They showed me where he had been wounded. They said he had been shot in his flank behind this wall and he was martyred.

'Ayyub'

The martyr's comrade

At ten or eleven o'clock at night, the armoured commander of the region entered the base with a smile playing on his lips. I asked, "What is it? You look overjoyed!" He replied, "My replacement has finally arrived." I asked who it was, and he replied, "Someone called Jaber, he's one of the soldiers of the Najaf-e Ashraf Division." He had a right to be so happy. He had stayed in the region for three months, and what a region it was! It made the Lut Desert[211] look like a beach! A barren and arid two hundred and fifty square kilometre desert, surrounded by overlooking mountains. Many people have gone missing in this desert and fallen into the hands of ISIS. Any kind of signpost you planted into the ground was gone within two hours. Storms arose and you couldn't see anything. Sometimes, it would get hotter than sixty degrees centigrade. Under these conditions, we had to live in the white tents of Red Crescent without any fan or air conditioning.

Two days later, he called me over the radio in his Isfahani accent. Instead of using my jihad name, he called me Haj Agha. He said, "I need you for something." I told him my coordinates and he came quickly. He wanted platforms for the Qasemabad bases so they could climb the tank bunkers and shoot, then come down and hide inside the bunker. I told him, "No problem, show me the areas and I'll tell you whether they're fine or not." He insisted, "No Haji, you have to come yourself." He had great respect for me as I was a veteran of the Iran-Iraq War. I told him, "I have things to do here!" but he insisted, "I'll wait

---

211. Located in Iran, the Lut Desert is the world's twenty-fifth largest desert.

for you to finish your work." We went and identified the areas. Whatever I said, he lowered his head and say, "Whatever you say!" We delivered the platforms, and I went back. We had to go to Palmyra and set up some armoured units. It took me a week until I got back to the region. As I got back onto the road, I heard Jaber calling the regional commander over the radio. I understood from what he was saying that his vehicle had broken down in the desert. What did this mean? It meant goodbye our soldiers, hello ISIS! I realised where he was from the description he gave. I quickly called the regional commander on my mobile to tell him I was entering the region and was going after Jaber. The commander was overjoyed. I found him at around two o'clock in the afternoon. He was standing there perplexed with a soldier from the Fatemiyoun. I looked at his vehicle; it was a terrible vehicle, it wouldn't be worth more than two riyals. It was one of those dying Mitsubishis. According to the rules, they should have given this man a proper vehicle so he could navigate this region quickly. From morning until evening, his job was to visit areas and the bases in that region, but he didn't say anything, nor did he complain. I towed his vehicle and took it to Qasemabad.

From then on, he listened to the radio to see who was going to the place he needed to go. He called and asked if they could take him too. He became that person who always asked for rides. He could have just sat in Qasemabad and waited until they brought him a vehicle. Sometimes he even walked through those mountains. For hours, he walked around in the middle of the desert all alone. The soldiers who had gone back on leave were coughing for months. They said, "Our lungs are full of the dust of Qasemabad!"

In the early morning, ISIS entered the region from Iraq and started advancing. We were ten kilometres away from Jaber's base. We noticed the presence of the enemy through our thermal binoculars. I radioed the soldiers and informed them. They told us, "Yeah, we have them!" Suddenly, a suicide vehicle came and hit the second trench of the base. We got to the base as quickly as possible. They had only come to do a hit-and-run, they didn't want a battle. Jaber's radio had fallen in the hands of ISIS. Our radio had been occupied. We could only communicate between those two areas where we were close to the ISIS fighters. We couldn't get a message to Qasemabad. They were reading a war poem constantly on the radio, "We have come to war with you by the permission of Allah and His Messenger, we have come to kill you!" I quickly replied to them, "We are the children of Ali ibn Abi Talib, by the permission of Allah and His Messenger and with the help of Ali ibn Abi Talib, we will crush you into the earth!"

I reached the base as the fires were settling. I asked one of the soldiers of the Fatemiyoun where Jaber was, and he told me he had been martyred. He explained himself how a bullet had hit Jaber in the flank. He said, "I noticed he was unconscious, but he was breathing. I went to switch on the vehicle and take him back, but it didn't switch on. When I went back, he had been martyred." He took me to a body with a blanket spread over it. He told me, "This is Jaber!" I pulled the blanket aside and saw half his face. I quickly covered his face with the blanket and said *Salawat*. The Iranians boosted the morale of the Heydariyoun and the Fatemiyoun. If they saw the Iranian martyrs, they would lose their morale. I told one of the Iranian soldiers, "Put the Iranian martyrs in the back of the vehicle quickly and take them away." After that, whenever someone asked where Jaber was, I told them we had sent him to Me'raj. When we contacted Me'raj, they told us all the Iranian martyrs and martyrs of the Heydariyoun had been sent to Iraq. A few people were sent to

Iraq to identify Jaber's body. They went and they didn't find him. The next day, the video of Jaber being taken captive was released. I then realised they mistakenly identified that martyr as Jaber.

Ahmad Akbariyan

The martyr's commander

They called me in the morning to leave for Tehran at night and choose someone to go with me. I immediately called the soldiers of the battalion and asked if they would like to volunteer for an operation, and twenty people lined up outside my office. The rest of the battalion found out by word of mouth and the number of volunteers increased. I ruled out a few at first by saying, "Whoever has gone before mustn't wait at all, he mustn't take my time nor his own!" The next criterion I set was if their mother and wife were pleased with this. I said, "Call them right now and give me the phone so I can speak to your mother and wife." I don't know where Hojaji came from amongst all this. Who had told him?! He turned up outside my office in his informal clothes. I had just signed his leave of absence two hours ago and he had left the base. I told him, "You've gone before, go do your business, don't waste your leave of absence for no reason." Every time I called the wives and mothers of the soldiers, they were jumping up and down restlessly. Some were chosen but either their wife or mother wasn't answering, and some others said they would convince them by the morning. I didn't have more than an hour to announce my volunteer. Hojaji started begging me again, saying, "Haji, don't destroy my dreams!" To appease him, I asked, "Are your mother and wife pleased with this?" He quickly took his phone out of his pocket and made a phone call. He told his wife that the manager wanted to know if her heart is pleased with him going or not. He then gave me the mobile. I spoke with his wife and I saw there was no issue. He then immediately rang his mother. I was standing next to him. I could hear his mother say on the other end, "I am pleased with this!" As soon as I heard this, I said to Hojaji, "You don't need to give me the phone, send my salaam to your mother, I've accepted it." I still didn't let him go though. I waited to see if any of those who hadn't gone before had met all the criteria to go. I waited until the last moment, but the only person who ticked all the boxes was Hojaji. Contrary to my desires, I sent his name to Tehran before noon. Now, he started worrying about buying a ticket. I stopped him and told him not to hurry and that it will be sorted.

At three o'clock in the afternoon, they called from Tehran to tell me our trip had been delayed and to wait for the next call. As soon as I told Hojaji, he went off on one. He was crying, "What if they don't take us? What if they're looking for someone else?" From the next morning, he kept knocking on my door. Every hour, he came and asked, "Haji, is there any news? Have they called? Don't you want to follow up?" My patience ran out and I snapped at him, "If you come here one more time, I'll cross out your name!" He didn't manage to last for more than one or two days. He went and begged the operations officer to call Akbariyan and ask him when he was leaving. He also sent some of the soldiers of the battalion to ask me. I called him into my office and threatened him, "I don't want to see you going to the operations officer or the foot soldiers. If this happens again, I assure you, you won't see Syria!" I told the operations commander that I wanted to replace my accompanying forces. While I was looking for replacement soldiers, they contacted me from the Ground Forces and said, "We've found three people for you." I didn't cross out Hojaji, but I added one of the soldiers by the name of Agha Pourpirali.

This running back and forth in restlessness of Hojaji continued for another twenty days. On the 18th of July 2017, they called and told us to be in the Tehran office the next morning. I sent Hojaji home at eleven o'clock to gather his things. At noon, he called to tell me he had booked three bus tickets for eleven o'clock at night. I scolded him, "Why did you go and buy tickets by yourself? It's Monday today, buses leave every half an hour!" At quarter past three in the afternoon, the Ground Forces called to make sure we were ready. I realised from the way they were talking that they thought we were only two people. I reminded them that we were allowed three people. They put me on hold for a few minutes and eventually said, "No! The Najaf Division is only allowed two people!" I exclaimed, "You added one person yourself! Now I've bought tickets for three people!" During this time, Mohsen was constantly calling. They eventually told me they would inform me who had been crossed out. I put the phone down and answered Hojaji's call. He was overly eager and kept asking what time he should be at the terminal. I told him I had been informed I was only allowed to have one companion and he might be crossed off. A few minutes later, he called to ask if they had called. Two or three times, I didn't even pick up his calls. One time, I answered the phone and snapped, "Leave me alone! Why are you calling so much?! Let me see what I can do!" At 4:20 pm, they called and said I was going with Agha Hojaji. When I told Hojaji, he was so glad, he didn't want to return Pourpirali's ticket.

When we reached the terminal at night, he had brought a whole group of people with him. I asked him who they were, and he told me they were his family who had come to see him off. His father-in-law came and said, "This Agha Mohsen has a love for martyrdom, pull his brakes!" I reassured him that I would look after him. When the bus left, he pulled out his classic Najafabadi bag and started eating kashk and nuts. He kept offering me some. One after the other, he was calling people and asking them for forgiveness. I asked, "What are you doing at this time of night? Go to sleep!" He chewed the kashk in his mouth and replied, "I won't have another chance! They'll take our mobiles there!"

We prayed Fajr in the southern terminal [of Tehran] and went to the Ground Forces Office. We were sorting out our paperwork until noon. In the afternoon, I saw him sitting and writing a will. We had to hand in our phones before leaving for the airport. He came to me and said, "Sir, bear witness that I want to make my will." He put his phone to his mouth and started talking. He recorded his wills to his wife and son separately. He said to his wife, "I don't know if I'll be martyred this time or not, but I want to return with my head held high, whether it's through martyrdom or the opportunity of servitude, but I want to make a difference. Pray I'm not embarrassed in front of Lady Zaynab (a). Pray I can be of use there, that I can do a service to Islam and be of some benefit, lest I become fearful or sad over my attachments… Raise my son in whichever way that he will become righteous and a soldier of the Imam of our time (aj). I really want him to join the IRGC or to become a scholar, but it is his choice and whatever he wants to do. Just bring him up in a way that he can be a soldier of the Imam of our time (aj) in this society." His heart-to-heart with his son struck the chords of my heart when he said, "Forgive me, my dear, for leaving you during your childhood! If we don't go, the shrine of Lady Zaynab (a) will be abused or, may Allah never allow it, Lady Ruqayyah (a) may be forced to reside in the ruins once again," when he said, "I want to be martyred on this path, once before the reappearance [of the Imam (aj)] and once after His reappearance!" when he said, "I named you Ali so your role model will be your master and leader, Ali," and when he said with a lump in his throat, "Sometimes, cutting off attachments from certain things means you will get some better things, I have cut my attachment from you and your mother so I can attain the blessing of serving Lady Zaynab (a)." He had two phones. The last person gave his phone in and we left for the airport. Before boarding the flight, he handed out headbands and the ziyarah of Lady Fatimah (a) from his bag to everyone as a gift.

We reached Damascus at night. We did *ziyarah* at midnight and returned to our place of residence. Hojaji quickly went to the officer in charge of distributing the troops. He learnt everything about the area such as where the fighting was taking place and which regions required reinforcements. They mentioned that Palmyra was in a critical condition and there was fighting there 24/7. He made his decision and insisted we had to go to Palmyra. He managed to convince the officer in charge of distributing the troops after much insistence. They called us before noon to tell us the vehicle was ready to take us to Palmyra. He was in such a hurry, he didn't get to eat lunch. We were sent to the armoured division of the Heydariyoun Brigade, under the supervision of the Nasr Base. I told him, "You see? You finally got what you wanted!"

The recently liberated ground route between Aleppo and Palmyra was extremely dangerous. There was even conflict on one section between ISIS and the Al-Nusra Front over a cement factory. If you stretched your neck out the window of the vehicle, you could see the forces of the Al-Nusra Front on the mountains. We travelled for five stressful hours until we reached Siwanah. We were forty-five kilometres away from Palmyra. The armoured support of the Heydariyoun was stationed there. We spent the night there. All night, we slept with one eye open in case they carry out a suicide bombing on us.

In the morning, we went to the operational region, a base called Qasemabad, close to the Iraq-Syria border. We had to travel through a meandering route to reach the base. The U.S. had set up a base close to Qasemabad on the border of Jordan and were watching everything within a sixty-kilometre radius. One of the soldiers of the Fatemiyoun said they accidentally went towards them once, and their planes immediately flew out and let out a red smoke as if to say this is the red line. Hojaji and I went and collected the tanks from that region. Over there, we chose our jihad names; I became Ahmad and Hojaji became Jaber. Jaber stayed in a tent in that base as a permanent soldier. There was also a building which no one could stay in because of the heat. They told us it was used as a stable for sheep before us. For that reason, they put up a few white Red Crescent tents outside the building on top of the sheep wool without any kind of cooling device, no fan nor air conditioning!

At nights, we went to the roof of that building. We stayed awake until three or four, sometimes even until morning. No one dared to sleep because ISIS were passing by and there was possibility of an attack or suicide bombing. If we took a nap after Fajr, the noise woke us up. I went back and forth from Palmyra with the armoured support. Many times, I saw ISIS fighters transporting oil tankers through our ranks. The soldiers of the Heydariyoun had set up six bases around Qasemabad which Jaber visited daily and assess their armoured units. The soldiers of the Fatemiyoun used these units. Every night, these tanks shot five or six times. Some nights, I went and slept next to him in the tent. After a few days, I noticed he had put a few photos of martyrs from the Najaf Division on a scarf and placed it in a corner of the tent. He had left one spot empty. When the soldiers of the Heydariyoun came in, he told them in broken Arabic to recite a Fatihah for them. He then pointed at the empty spot and ask them to pray that this spot is also filled soon, and then he pointed at himself.

He became close with the soldiers of the Heydariyoun quickly. One of them whose hair reached his shoulders came and signalled to Jaber as if to ask him to plait his hair. I watched him plait that Iraqi's hair with such patience while laughing. It was because of this *akhlaq* that when he went to the surrounding bases, they forced him to stay the night. In the afternoons when the sun was beating down on everyone, he got the Iraqi soldiers to sit in the back of the Toyota and took them to the well. They took off their clothes and washed themselves. One time when I went with him, I had an undershirt from the base with me. I told him, "Go wash yourself and wear this undershirt," but he wasn't willing to use anything that belonged to the public. I realised he had bought his military uniform with his own money from Isfahan.

When Jaber's vehicle broke down, their visits to the well also came to an end. Two of his tyres became flat on the way between two bases. We couldn't move it. I took him to the base so we could look at it the next morning. The ISIS fighters had broken the windows of the vehicle overnight. When I saw the vehicle from afar, I told Jaber not to go closer as they may have placed a bomb. We approached carefully and we saw there was nothing wrong.

For a while, he walked around until I managed to get him a motorcycle. He took it for a ride and when he came back, we could smell burning from inside. I told him, "You know it better than I do! Fix it." He opened the engine and said, "Its wires are burnt." We took the motorcycle back, they sorted it out and gave it back to him.

A few days later while I was lubricating some machinery, he came with wounds all over. I was shocked. I asked him, "Did you fall off your motorcycle?" On the way, a few sheepdogs started chasing him. He said he recited a verse of the Qur'an until they left him alone, but a bit further forward, he got stuck in the sand and fell on the ground.

The driver of the Titan came to take one of the tanks to one of the bases, but he didn't know the way. If he didn't have a guide with him, he may have gotten lost or driven right into ISIS territory. I asked Jaber, "Can you go and show him the way?" He was sceptical at first and he said, "Can I not go? I don't know it well." I had to go to the other base. While we were looking for a solution, he took a leap of faith and said he would do it. He left but came back five minutes later. I asked him what happened, and he said while dusting himself off, "My motorcycle got a puncture!" I asked him what happened to the Titan and he said, "I flashed my headlights amongst the dust, but he didn't see me and left." He finally gave up on the glimmer of hope he saw in his motorcycle.

He went to assess the units at one of the recently established bases, and I went to pick him up at sunset. We had to get back to Qasemabad before it became dark. We weren't allowed to travel under the darkness of night. In a way, it was like playing with death. ISIS may have laid mines on our route. We delivered dinner and ammunitions to the bases before dark as well. The soldiers of the Fatemiyoun insisted Jaber had to stay with them that night. I told Jaber, "I'm alone over there, come, let's go." He took me into a quiet corner and explained, "These forces have just entered the region and this desert might be frightening for them. Me being here will give them the strength of heart." I agreed and went back on my own.

The next day, I called him to tell him I was waiting for him. He kept delaying leaving until it became dark. I shouted at him over the radio, asking why he didn't come. He replied, "The driver of the loader came late, and my work was delayed." Once again, he stayed there that night.

In the morning, I went to him. I searched for him at the first base, but he wasn't there. I found him in the second base. We prayed Dhuhr together and like normal, he recited one page of Quran immediately after prayers and then Ziyarah Ashura. We managed the armoured units in that base until sunset. That night, he didn't come back with me, and he continued doing this for a few nights.

At half-past one in the morning, I was laying down on the roof with a gun in my hand and grenades to my side. The operation officers of the Heydariyoun were busy assessing the region. Jaber radioed to say that Hasan didn't have bread. Hasan was one of the soldiers of the Fatemiyoun who five hundred metres away from me. He heard mine and Jaber's communications and he immediately radioed, "Don't come, two vehicles are passing by who might hit you." At around four o'clock, I heard a lot of gunfire. We could hear it from Qasemabad. For a second, I fell asleep but woke up to the sound of two or three terrifying explosions. I realised they must have attacked one of the bases. The soldiers of the Fatemiyoun also mentioned their communications had been jammed. The U.S. had given ISIS a gadget called a jammer which they used to prevent our communications. I called Jaber several times, but there was no answer. I saw a lot of vehicles with my binoculars moving around with their headlights on and beaming.

At around five in the morning, we went to the bases. Nothing had happened at the first base. We went inside the second base, and it looked like the desert of the Day of Judgement. Vehicles were moving around speedily, and we didn't know whether they were ours or the enemy's. A few of the soldiers of the Fatemiyoun had fled. They told us they had attacked the fourth base. As soon as I reached the fourth base, I only asked about Jaber. The soldiers of the Fatemiyoun told me, "He was martyred, and we sent his body back." I pulled one of them aside and told him to clearly explain to me what had happened. He explained that amongst the tumult, they saw three vehicles speeding towards the base. He shouted and let everyone know. They went behind the bunker with Jaber and started shooting. The first suicide bomber exploded three hundred metres away from the base, the second exploded outside the first bunker and the third continued inside the base. Amongst those explosions, Jaber was wounded in his flank. He said, "I went and took the key to the vehicle from his pocket which he signalled to me to go with. I then saw him calmly close his eyes and he was martyred." I hit the bonnet of the vehicle we had just given him and said to it, "You traitor! What use are you then?!" Its entire body was riddled with holes.

I repaired the punctures and returned to Qasemabad. I asked where the bodies of the Iranian martyrs were, and they showed me three bodies. I recognised Hosein Qummi and Mahdi Azeemi. I removed the third blanket in the hope of seeing Jaber. I turned around and yelled, "So where's Jaber?!" They told me that was him. I screamed at them, "This is not Jaber!" I called to tell them that Jaber wasn't one of these martyrs and they should search for him. They said there were no other martyrs there, they had sent them all back. Apart from one or two remaining units, the whole base had been cleared. I didn't believe it. We searched every inch of the region until night, we even looked with the surrounding drones. It was as if he had turned into water and been absorbed by the ground. They said, "They may have taken his body to Baghdad with the Iraqi martyrs." I got ready and left. At one o'clock in the morning, the soldiers of the Heydariyoun showed me a photo. A Chechen had his knife behind Jaber's head. I couldn't believe it. I said the photo was fake. On the border of Iraq, the ISIS television channel was constantly announcing they had taken an Iranian commander captive. I still didn't believe they had taken Jaber captive. Despite all this, we went to identify the bodies the next morning. I checked the bodies of the Iraqi martyrs one by one. They didn't resemble Jaber at all, some of them even had tattoos. There was just one body left which was headless. While I was looking at him, an Iraqi woman came. I told my companions that this wasn't Jaber. When that woman saw him, she said, "That is my son!" She then started complaining while shouting, "Why did you bring his body here? I had offered him to Sayyid ash-Shuhada[212], take him to the desert with his head." She then left.

In the hotel, I saw ISIS showing a special programme on their channel. That night, I watched the programme. After the battle and burning the base, ISIS held a great celebration. When they got into their vehicles to leave, Jaber got up from behind the bunker. The ISIS fighters went to him immediately. He was unconscious when they found him. They untied the laces of his boots and tied his hands from behind. He was bleeding from his flank. On the way to the town of al-Qa'im, they were constantly hitting his face in the vehicle. They took him into a room and interviewed him. He said firmly and with great dignity, "I am Mohsen Hojaji, a soldier from Isfahan, the town of Najafabad. I am a tank commander and have one child." In the programme, they showed how they beheaded him and then they tied his legs to a truck and drove it around the city. I couldn't watch the rest of the programme, as I fell unconscious...

---

212. Meaning 'the master of martyrs', a title of Imam Husayn (a)

Mahdi Neysari

The martyr's comrade

I asked him to tell me the number on his dog tag over the radio several times, but he told me he didn't have it. When I went to the base, he told me it was in the tent and when I reached the tent, he complained that he didn't know where he had put it and he would find it now. Eventually, he was martyred. We had to write down his dog tag number to file a report on his condition. I went to the base and searched his backpack. I found seven or eight notepads. I flicked through the pages in case he'd put them inside a notebook, but it wasn't there. I looked at his writing. It was either *nowhehs* or memories and messages to his family and child. When I unzipped the small pocket at the front of his backpack, I found a crumpled green cloth. When I pulled it out, I heard the jingling of dog tags. I breathed a sigh of relief and looked at them. I wasn't sure whether these were new dog tags or if they were from his previous tour. I compared them with Agha Akbariyan's dog tags. When I found him on the list, I noticed they only differed by one number.

We searched for kilometres surrounding the base in the hope of possibly finding his body. We even sent drones to search a few times, but there was no sign of him. We gave a one percent chance that after filming his captivity, ISIS had martyred him and buried him nearby in the desert. I was gathering my things to go back to Iran. I had caught a bad flu and was on a drip for two to three days. One of my friends came and mentioned we were going to swap Hojaji's body. They said I had to stay to identify him. I was overjoyed and they told me to rest until further notice.

They called me at around half-past ten, eleven o'clock at night and said we had to go. At first, I thought they were going to bring the body into the base in Palmyra, we would identify it and that's it, but I found out later we had to go to the Hezbollah base in Lebanon. ISIS had stationed ten thousand of their best soldiers and commandos on the border of Lebanon. From these people, only six hundred had remained in western Qalamoun, half of them women and children. They had surrendered, saying they didn't have the will to fight and wanted to leave the area. Hezbollah killed two birds with one stone; they established complete security on their border with Syria by letting ISIS leave and under this pretext, they swapped the bodies of Shaheed Hojaji, two other martyrs and one of their captives. Hezbollah transported all the wounded soldiers and captives of ISIS out of Qalamoun in fifteen buses and eleven ambulances. The schedule was such that they would go to Palmyra and from there, they would go to one of the regions on the outskirts of Deir Ez-Zor by the name of Bukamal. At around eleven o'clock at night, they reached the Palmyra-Hamimah Highway.

They told me to get ready quickly to leave. By the time they completed the necessary arrangements, it was midnight. We travelled eighty kilometres until morning. The region wasn't secure, and we had to drive carefully to not alert the enemy. In some regions, the U.S. had set up bases and we had to drive around them. We performed *tayammum*[213] and prayed Fajr inside the vehicle. When we reached the area where the swap was supposed to take place, the sun had risen fully. They told us to bring six people, three people to identify the body of Shaheed Hojaji, two people from the Hezbollah and one person from

---

213. *Tayammum* is a ritual ablution performed with dust in times where there is a shortage of water or using water would cause great difficulty instead of *wudu* and/or *ghusl*

the Red Crescent. We were waiting for them until noon in the middle of a desert without any facilities, and they were saying they would update us. They told us over the radio that ISIS was saying the U.S. was planning to attack them. They sent their fighter jets two or three times and broke the sonic barrier. The Americans were insistent on keeping the ISIS fighters in Qalamoun. Their presence in Lebanon was comforting for Israel.

We spent the night in the cold. My bones were shivering until the morning despite wearing a jacket, adding a runny nose, a fever, and chills to the mix as well. We didn't know what we were doing until noon the next day. Hezbollah had set up some sort of camp for the ISIS captives with food and hygienic facilities. In the end, they told us the swap zone had changed. We came back two or three kilometres. While we were on the Hamimah Highway, they told us to drive thirty kilometres inside. Now, their new game was that no more than three people could enter the zone. When we told them it was not an issue, they told us the swap wouldn't take place there again and they would tell us the new zone. When we went back a few kilometres, they told us to drive ten kilometres inside towards Sakhnah. Now, they created more problems and said only one Iranian could come for identification. We slowly became suspicious that they were planning something.

Haj Abbas, one of the Hezbollah officers, came and asked, "Are you willing to go on your own?" I accepted fearlessly. They called and introduced me, and it was decided: I would be the only one to go. I realised that if I needed to talk there, I didn't know Arabic. I mentioned this and after some negotiations, they decided to send one of the Syrian soldiers by the name of Haj Saeed as my interpreter and someone from the Red Crescent. When I was leaving, they each came and hugged me as if to bid farewell. There was no hope for my return under those conditions. They were saying that when the ISIS fighters see we are exchanging this many living soldiers for one of our martyrs, it would be natural for them to want one of our living soldiers. I told them that whatever was to happen will happen. Hezbollah told me not to worry about their martyrs and captive and just to identify the body of Shaheed Hojaji. They gave me the location of one of their military bases. We drove twelve kilometres into the heart of ISIS territory in a Syrian Red Crescent ambulance. They were constantly telling us to turn *yamin* and *yasar*[214]. Finally, the last sign they gave us was the fire from an oil well. We were driving in complete darkness at ten o'clock at night in the middle of a desert on paths which weren't proper roads. We drove over a few hills until we saw the headlights of a vehicle. We got out ten or fifteen metres away from them. The agent of the Red Crescent signalled for me to take gloves and a mask. I didn't believe in this equipment. I wanted to bless my entire existence by touching the body of the martyr. When I went closer, I noticed there was a pickup truck parked nearby.

The ISIS representative was wearing a long white dishdasha[215], a scarf tied around his waist and had covered his face with a red scarf. I introduced myself as one of the family members of the martyr. For this reason, I wore a long shirt which covered my camouflage trousers. When I went towards him, he jumped two steps back. He was afraid I was going to attack him. I stopped and Haj Saeed said salaam. In reply, he shouted, "Iranian, up!" The back of the vehicle was suspended eighty centimetres from the ground. They had opened its side doors. The ISIS representative signalled that the body of the Iranian was inside the body bag in the vehicle. I asked, "So where is the

---

214. Arabic for 'right and left'
215. A dishdasha is a long robe worn normally by men in the Middle East

Hezbollah captive?" He told me he was four kilometres behind. I had seen all the videos of Hojaji's captivity and martyrdom several times and checked the areas he had been shot and his boots and trousers that could help me identify him. When I went to the body, the Red Crescent agent started filming. The ISIS fighter told him to film from an angle, so he doesn't come into the shot. In the silence of the night, I unzipped the body bag. I saw a blanket inside. I moved the blanket aside and was taken aback: there was nothing inside! I turned around and looked at the ISIS fighter. I noticed he had his gun pointing towards me and wasn't looking away. I turned back to the body bag. I thought maybe they had put the body in upside down. I unzipped the bag completely. When I held the bottom of the blanket, I felt it was heavy. When I pulled it aside, I was met by body parts, a mutilated and headless body! I didn't expect to witness such a heartrending sight at all. His modest face and thin body were constantly running through my mind. I had forgotten all my illnesses and pain in my bones. I didn't even feel a trace of my fever and chills. That mutilated body wasn't fit to be identified. They had looted his shirt. I gave a fifty, sixty percent chance it was him from his torn trousers and tattered boots. In the photo where they had put his head on his body and hung his legs, he only had one boot. I saw in the video of his captivity that he was only wearing one boot. They had tied his hands with the laces of one of his boots. I found a leg inside the body bag which was inside the boot. The bootlaces were proof that this was Hojaji. He always tied his laces to the top and said, "We must always be ready for combat in this region," but this wasn't enough proof for me.

I turned back to Haj Saeed and exclaimed, "How am I supposed to identify this torn-apart body?!" I was in an awfully bad state. I went towards that ISIS fighter. He retreated a metre back and withdrew his gun. I yelled at him, "Are you not Muslim?!" I pointed at the body bag and asked, "Was he not Muslim? So where is his head? Why did you do this to him?!" Haj Saeed was quickly interpreting my words. That ISIS fighter cleared his name, saying, "We didn't do this, you have to ask those who took him to al-Qa'im." I realised he wanted to save himself from this calamity. I shouted at him again, "Where does it say in Islam to torture your prisoners like this?!" The ISIS representative replied, "It was his own fault!" I asked, "For what crime?!" He was speaking bit by bit and Haj Saeed was interpreting, "Because he exhausted us, he didn't give us any information, he wasn't regretful, he didn't beg! It was his own fault with those looks and smiles!" You could see the fear and horror in the eyes of that ISIS fighter. He explained with a shaky voice that they took all their anger out on him and scattered his body parts across the desert. After a few days, they realised this person was particularly important for Iran and their commander ordered them to collect what remained of his body and bury it in one place. It was clear from what he was saying that they had predicted this body may come into use for them someday.

I couldn't understand it at all. I told Haj Saeed, "If we approve this body, we do the swap and tomorrow, we realise ISIS had tricked us and show off the real body of the martyr, what will we do?" Haj Saeed asked the ISIS fighter if we could take a part of the body for more accurate identification. He yelled, "No parts!" I went to the body bag again and I asked Haj Saeed to tell the Red Crescent agent to shine his camera on the boot. I shook the dust off the boot to see the size and then I would ask his acquaintances what his boot size was. His boots were size forty-two. The Red Crescent agent was recording everything and there was nothing more I could do. I moved my head closer and sought intercession from Lady Zahra (a), "During the Holy Defence, I benefited from your intercession greatly, now I am looking to you with hope again!" My eyes fell upon a piece of bone. A thought popped into my mind to take it, but I knew it wasn't possible in front of this ISIS fighter and the lens of the Red Crescent agent's camera. Also, I was sure we were being watched by their security team and they would see us. I took a leap of faith and decided this was an inspiration from Lady Zahra (a). I pulled Haj Saeed to the side and told him to make conversation with the ISIS fighter. He asked why and I explained quietly, "I want to take a piece of bone." He was surprised. He remained calm and asked if I could do it. I replied, "Insha'Allah it will happen." The three people were standing on my left, first Haj Saeed, the ISIS representative was standing a metre away from him and the Red Crescent agent was standing behind him. I bent my whole body over the body bag. Haj Saeed had a great idea and stood between me and the ISIS representative. He was constantly talking, and he didn't sound angry. I started searching with my left hand. I shouted inside myself, 'Ya Zahra (a)!' and within a split second, I took the bone with my right hand and tried to put it in my trouser pocket. I realised the bone didn't fit in my pocket. It was too wide. I think the bone was from the pelvis. I tried a lot, but it didn't fit in my pocket. I lost all hope. I could hear Haj Saeed talking Arabic next to me. I closed my eyes and asked Lady Zahra (a) for her help again. This time, I managed to jam the bone into my right pocket. It made a sound and went in. I thought the bottom of my pocket had torn. My long shirt stretched over my trousers, and the bone couldn't be seen from outside. I let out a sigh of relief and got up. I took the ammunition belt to look natural and asked Haj Saeed, "Ask him if we can take this with us for a closer examination?" The ISIS representative didn't agree, however. He was insistent on his words of '*Suwar faqat!*'[216] I put the ammunitions belt back inside the body bag and said to Haj Saeed, "Let's go!" He asked, "Is it done?" I nodded and we walked away from the pickup truck. I was calling out to Allah in case someone saw us from the surroundings. I wanted to leave the area as soon as possible. We told the ISIS representative that we would be in touch soon.

When we got to the car, I told Haj Saeed to tell the Red Crescent agent to get us out of that hell as soon as possible, and Haj Saeed passed on the message. The ambulance switched on, we hit the gas, the tires screeched, and we sped to the Hezbollah base . I quietly took the bone out of my pocket and put it in one of the masks I had on me. After travelling for two or three kilometres, we saw the silhouette of a man. I was devastated. I thought their security forces had seen us. We prepared ourselves for battle. We quickly took our guns out from underneath the seats. When we got closer, we saw it was Haj Abbas. He stopped the ambulance and we got out. He ran eagerly and hugged us one by one. He was worried about why it took us so long to identify the body. He started walking in the desert all on his own in the hope of finding us.

We got in and went to the Hezbollah base where the ISIS captives were being held. The Red Crescent agent sent the video of the body identification to Haj Abbas's phone via Bluetooth and left. My blood pressure had dropped. I was insistent on returning to Palmyra as soon as possible so I could rest in the armoured unit's base. They told me to wait so they could send me with security. One vehicle was driving ahead of us and one behind us. We reached the last point under Hezbollah supervision, and those two vehicles returned. A guard stopped us and asked where we were coming from. We explained we

---

216. Arabic for 'photos only!'

were coming from Haj Abbas. They stopped us and told us we had to be escorted. We said, "We know the way and there's no danger," but they insisted it was an order. Once again, we went to Palmyra with one vehicle ahead of us and one behind us. When we reached the two-way junction to turn towards the armoured unit's base, they said we had to go to the Hezbollah base. Haj Saeed explained to them that my blood pressure had dropped, and I needed to be on a drip, but they replied firmly, "No one has the right to leave."

When we reached the Hezbollah base, their commander Malik came to welcome us. He hugged us tightly and said *ahlan wa sahlan*[217] pleasantly. It was clear he wasn't expecting us to return either. We sat down and explained the whole story to him, about the condition we saw the body in which it couldn't be identified. He quickly picked up the phone and called someone. He told them exactly what we had told him word-for-word. He was talking to the person on the other end in Arabic like a soldier under their command. While he was speaking, I heard him say the phrase '*Sayyid, ala ayni*[218]' several times. I signalled to Haj Saeed to ask who he was talking to and he said, "Sayyid Hasan Nasrallah!" Malik called Haj Saeed over and told him to talk on the phone. Haj Saeed started talking in Farsi and mouthed to me that he was talking to Haj Qasem [Soleimani]. I just realised Haj Qasem and Sayyid Hasan Nasrallah were overseeing this operation from Beirut. I told Haj Saeed to tell him about the bone. When he mentioned this, I heard Haj Qasem exclaim over the phone, "Are you serious?!" He said he would call back and then he put the phone down. Less than two minutes later, the phone rang and Malik answered it. He spoke

---

217. Arabic for 'welcome'
218. Arabic for 'on my eyes, Sayyid", a respectful manner in which to tell the other person they will definitely obey his command

quickly and said goodbye. He told me, "Bring the bone quickly!" I went and brought the bone from inside the vehicle. Malik used that time to tell one of his soldiers to put petrol in the vehicle and go to Tripoli. They wanted to take the bone for a DNA test. As far as I understood, the conditions weren't right to send it to Iran. When we were saying *khodahafez*, Malik hugged us and relayed Sayyid Hasan Nasrallah's message to us, "Thank them a lot, tell them they are the champions of the resistance and they carried out the greatest religiously lawful theft."

That night, we went back to the armoured unit's base. I had no spirit left in me, not in my body nor my soul. In the morning, I was informed the DNA test had come back positive and the swap had taken place. I went to take a shower with peace of mind to get ready to go to Iran. I went and washed the trousers I had slept in. When I put my hand in my pocket, I froze. A small piece of bone had remained in my pocket. Only then did I realise that the noise I heard when I put the bone in my pocket was the bone breaking. I told the Iranian soldiers quickly and they told me not to mention it for now and to keep it with me. I asked Mohsen's co-workers what his foot size was and they said it was forty-two. I covered it in a piece of cloth from the shrine of Lady Zaynab (a) and put it in the pocket over my heart.

I went to Damascus and before the flight, they took me to do *ziyarah* of Lady Zaynab (a). When I entered the shrine, one of my friends came and told me Shaheed Hojaji's father and wife were also there. He took me by the hand and told me the martyr's father wanted to see me. I wasn't prepared to meet him whatsoever, but it was too late by then. When the martyr's father saw me, he hugged me and said, "You smell like my Mohsen." He asked me, "What have you brought from Mohsen?" I didn't know what to say. I calmed myself down and told him to visit the base and see over there. He swore to me by

Lady Zaynab (a) to tell him. I said to him, "Please don't ask me this!" He put his hands on the grills of the *zareeh* and said, "I gave the whole of my Mohsen to this lady, if you tell me you've brought a nail or a piece of his hair, that will be enough for me!" I took a deep breath, lowered my head and said, "Not only does he not have a head, but they tore his body apart like Ali Akbar (a) as well!" The martyr's father turned to the *zareeh* and said, "My dear lady, accept this gift from us!"

I went back to Iran and wasn't willing to part from that piece of bone. It was sitting over my heart all that time until they returned the body of the martyr to Iran. They informed me to take it to Najafabad when the funeral took place. Parting from that piece of bone was extremely difficult for me. I wrapped it in a yellow headband which said '*Kulluna Abbasuki Ya Zaynab*'[219] and gave it to the martyr's family as he was being buried.

---

219. Arabic for 'We are all your Abbas, O Zaynab'.

www.ingramcontent.com/pod-product-compliance
Lightning Source LLC
Chambersburg PA
CBHW051557010526
44118CB00023B/2733